North Routt Revolution

GRIT. GRIEF. GOLD.

NOLAN FARWELL

BUGTOWN PUBLISHING

ISBN: 979-8-9999051-0-9 (paperback)
ISBN: 979-8-9999051-1-6 (hardcover)
ISBN: 979-8-9999051-2-3 (e-book)

Library of Congress Control Number: 2025922694

Cover Design by Katie Farwell

To the Zehners, steadfast rocks of Hahns Peak Village, whose unwavering support and wisdom launched us on this remarkable research adventure. Your guidance and friendship were the heart of our journey.

Thank you.

To Kenton, an incredible son, brother, grandson, nephew, cousin, and friend. We love you, miss you, and cherish our memories of you. Your spirit will always be with us.

When peace, like a river, attendeth my way,
When sorrows like sea billows roll;
Whatever my lot, Thou hast taught me to say,
It is well, it is well with my soul.

Though Satan should buffet, though trials should come,
Let this blest assurance control,
That Christ hath regarded my helpless estate,
And hath shed His own blood for my soul.

"It was my pleasure to sleep one night under a blanket on the Rocky Mountains - 15,000 feet above the sea. Waking early in the morning in that clear sky and dry atmosphere, it seemed that the stars were so near together that there was room for no more. As day began to dawn they vanished gradually, until only 'the bright and morning star' was visible, and soon that was gone as the glorious sun captured the whole horizon.

Christ says of himself, 'I am the bright and morning star.' As I saw the unnumbered millions of stars fade away, leaving only that one to introduce the light of day, I had a most vivid lesson, that the flowers could not give me, of what it means to worship Him instead of the multitudes of earthly influences and facts which must fade away like these stars when the last day comes for earthly light - 'There will be no night then.'"[1]

-John V. Farwell

---

[1] Farwell, John V. (1906). *Corner Stones of Character: Some Ways of Making Them*, Page 165. https://nrrbook.com/CornerStonesofCharacter

TABLE OF CONTENTS

ACKNOWLEDGEMENTS

It has been a true privilege and joy to discover, research, preserve, protect, and promote the history of the Farwell Ditch, International Camp, and many other facets of northwestern Colorado's early history that tie back to my family's history. What started as a random discovery on a family vacation in 2014 has evolved into a lifelong passion, and we have met many new friends and acquaintances who have supported our endeavors. A special thank you goes out to the following, in no particular order:

Marge Eardley: For taking my phone call at the Hahns Peak Area Historical Society in 2019 and becoming like family over the years. Your sharp wit and hospitality always put a smile on my face. Also, a huge thank you for allowing us to stay at your cabin while we researched and worked on this project.

Doug and Vicki Slaight: For your friendship and support, and for allowing us to park trailers and machines on your property.

Hahns Peak Area Historical Society: For your steadfast pursuit of preserving the history of the Farwell Ditch, even before we were involved.

Katie Adams, Curator of the Tread of Pioneers Museum: For allowing us to dig through old records at the museum and present our knowledge of the Farwell Ditch as part of your summer Brown Bag series in August 2022.

Emily Katzman, Arianthé Stettner, and Kristen Rockford of Historic Routt County: For the countless hours you put into preserving this history on the Routt County Register of Historic Properties and National Register of Historic Places.

James Clouse: For your support and willingness to always lend a ride.

Jay Fetcher: For donating a section of pipe from the Farwell Ditch to help preserve history.

Michael Woodbridge and Jason Strahl of the United States Forest Service: For your support in pursuing historic designation of the Farwell Ditch.

Damion Pechota of History Colorado: For your leadership and counsel during the National Register of Historic Places nomination process.

Jill Riddell and Raghav Rao of the Office of Modern Composition: For your guidance and expertise in helping mold this book into its final form.

Lynn and Carol Doolittle: For allowing us to use your acreage as a meeting point on our journeys to Colorado. It was always a treat to pull in and chat with you as we moved machines, equipment, and coolers from vehicle to vehicle. Also, thanks for the popcorn!

Brother and fellow "ditchman" Rodney Farwell: What an adventure it has been to discover, research, learn, share, and preserve this fascinating piece of history. It truly was a 50/50 effort to make all of this happen.

My beautiful wife, Katie, and children, Blake, Brenna, Adrian, and Jace: For supporting me and being flexible with me as I took time each year to pursue this project! You willingly sacrificed during busy seasons of life while I was "gone ditchin.'" Also, a special thanks to Katie for designing the cover of the book!

David Joe and Judith Zehner: Words cannot express how much your knowledge and support for this project have meant. None of the progress made in preserving this history would have been possible without you. On top of that, I am most thankful for your friendship and will always treasure memories of our time together at your cabin in Hahns Peak.

FOREWORD

Every family carries with it a tapestry of history. For the Farwell family, it is woven with faith, enterprise, and endurance. Our threads stretch from the streets of Chicago to the mountains of Colorado and the plains of Texas. And every now and then, someone picks up one of those threads and traces it back in time until the pattern becomes alive again.

This book exists because my cousins, Nolan and Rodney Farwell, did exactly that. What began with a hunch in the Colorado high country turned into years of exploration and discovery. They walked the ridges of Routt County, dug through archives, spoke with experts, and gave a voice to history that was nearly lost. What they've done here isn't just research, but an act of stewardship.

At the center stands John V. Farwell, a man whose ambition matched his faith. He built big but believed even bigger. He gave his land and his name for Farwell Hall, the first YMCA building in Chicago. Later, he and other business leaders helped rebuild the city after the Great Chicago Fire; in Texas, he built the State Capitol and helped shape one of the largest ranches on earth; and in Colorado, he built a seventeen-mile ditch to carry water to a new frontier. His vision carried a sense of purpose that was founded in his faith in God. John V. believed in the strength of people and the growth of a young America. That spirit still lives today, rebuilt, rediscovered, and carried forward by the youngest generation.

This book is not just a story about where we have been, but a reminder of what still matters: faith, vision, and the will to see things through. Nolan and Rodney did not just uncover history; they brought it back to life and have brought family back together. In their work, the same spirit that drove John V. finds its way forward. My hope is that as you read this book, you will feel a part of the journey too. May it stir something in

3

you to build, restore, and leave your own mark on the world around you.

Drew F. Knowles, XIT Ranch

INTRODUCTION

Colorado joined the Union when it became our nation's 38th state on August 1, 1876, but this was hardly its beginning. Within its borders, a cultural and industrial revolution was already well underway. Perhaps this was no more evident than in the northwest corner of the state on land that would become Routt County. The men and women of this time truly experienced it all. Cultural tension, a construction boom, economic and infrastructure development, politics, fraudsters, fire, harsh weather, lawsuits, a religious uprising, and, of course, countless prospectors and gold miners looking to strike it rich are just a handful of the factors that drove this transformation.

This book has two Parts, which can be read in either order.

Part One provides a written, factual record of the broad events described above, with a heavy emphasis on the impact of John V. Farwell, a highly successful Chicago businessman of deep faith, integrity, and high moral regard, and the lasting legacy he left in the region. With his substantial investment in gold mining claims, a mining camp, wagon roads, and the mind-boggling engineering feat that was the seventeen-mile-long Farwell Ditch, Farwell established what is considered to be the first wage-paying enterprise on Colorado's western slope, and his impact would be felt for decades. John V. aimed to transform gold mining in the region from basic placer mining, consisting of shovels, pickaxes, and gold pans, to an advanced, industrial operation, utilizing hydraulic water pressure to feed vast amounts of pay dirt into sluice boxes, hoping to reap a profit from the shiny yellow metal that had captured the hearts and minds of thousands of men and women before him.

The Hahns Peak Mining District was expected to become a gold-mining epicenter, perhaps even destined to surpass the legendary Black Hills of South Dakota in production. Despite Farwell's best efforts to reshape and develop the mining district to help it reach its potential, the unpredictability of the Wild West intervened, and a cultural battle that spiraled into chaos, rather than being avoided, forced Farwell and his men to rethink their plans. Even so, John V. was not deterred, for his true hope and satisfaction were not found in economic success, money, or influence, but rather in his deep Christian faith and belief in Jesus as the One who bestows true contentment. In his own words:

"What are we if we are not God's children? And if we cannot have faith in our Father in Heaven, where can we put our trust for the work of life? It seems as though men generally trusted in everything else first, instead of the promise, power and purpose of God to fill all the wants of that complicated physical, mental and spiritual machinery called human nature; and that, too, in the teeth of all past experience against it. Trusting yourself and leaving God out of the problems of life, constitutes the basis of most men's architectural work, in the mental and moral character building which makes up our life. The foundation is sand until the Rock of Ages is set under it in a man's faith. Why? Because if the structure is to get above the clouds into the clear, eternal sunshine, sand will not sustain it. It may do temporarily for the man who says, 'Death ends all,' but when he at last sees the sands of time slipping from beneath his structure, in the last earthly storm, which death really is, and he has to leave all that he has made on earth, where he found it, in bitterness of soul he can only exclaim, 'Surely, life is not worth living.'

...

He was a beggar to begin life with, and with countless millions hoarded he leaves it and life, only as he began - a beggar - because he has missed in his accumulations to take God into company with him, to direct his investments of time, money and influence, so that results to him might live forever. All life that wishes to live forever, and enjoy it, must 'have such faith in God'

6

as will keep it within the law and the Gospel, which God, as a Father, has revealed to us for that very purpose."[2]

In subsequent years in the Hahns Peak Mining District, there were booms, busts, and legal battles as other men came and went, all of whom built upon the legacy Farwell left behind. Much of this incredible history was nearly lost. To the best of my ability, this book aims to provide a detailed and accurate account of these historic, intertwining events that contributed to Routt County's rich past.

Part Two tells the fascinating, yet unlikely, story of how the Farwell Ditch was randomly stumbled upon by distant family members of John V. Farwell, nearly 150 years after it was constructed. A moment of discovery sparked curiosity, speculation, and a years-long adventure of two brothers exploring, learning, and researching the history of the land we would come to love, and the fingerprints left there by family years ago. Escaping to the mountains and forests of northwest Colorado became not only recreation but also a passion, and time spent off the grid, exploring the rugged beauty of this land, was good for our souls, perhaps even therapeutic in a way. Piecing together not only a significant part of Colorado's history but also an unknown part of our own family's history has been tremendously fulfilling. We will forever be grateful to the people we have met who have helped in these efforts, and many of them have become close friends.

Throughout the book, references will be made to various locations, landmarks, historic sites, GPS tracks, mountains, creeks, Ute reservation boundaries, and features of the Farwell Ditch and its surrounding terrain (among many others). To help visualize this and put it all in perspective, I encourage you to explore a map detailing all of this information at the following link:

---

[2] Farwell, John V. (1906). *Corner Stones of Character: Some Ways of Making Them*, Pages 61-62. https://nrrbook.com/CornerStonesofCharacter

https://nrrbook.com/map

Here, you can view all of these points of interest on various maps. CalTopo is a fantastic tool to document and visualize this history, as it gives users the ability to change not only what specific features and/or landmarks you want to see, but also which base map (layer) is being viewed, including Forest Service maps, satellite imagery, topographic maps, and even the historic map from 1911 that is shown on the back cover of this book. Please dive into this tool as you follow along in the book!

Most of the historic sites discussed in this book are located on land within the Routt National Forest today. This gives you the ability to explore much of this history for yourself. I encourage you to do this, but please be aware that you will be hiking through a rugged, natural forest, not maintained hiking trails. Traversing through many areas of the forest requires especially challenging "combat hiking," where thousands of beetle-killed pines lie on the forest floor and make progress very difficult. Waterproof boots, a tough pair of jeans or pants, a hatchet, ax, or machete, multiple layers, a backpack, and plenty of food and water are all must-haves, along with your standard safety equipment. Explore at your own risk, and <u>always, always respect the history and private property!</u>

Please email me at <u>nolan@nrrbook.com</u> with any questions or comments you may have. I'd love to hear your feedback!

Enjoy the book!

HANN'S PARK, JULY 29, 1875

"The time has been when it was the popular belief that nature's richest gems were hid in roughest places, but a day's ride through the different mining camps in this region will almost prepare one to look for a little Eden in future searches for gold. True, the peaks surrounding are rough, but they encircle as pretty a park system as can be found in the Rocky Mountain country. Every park is a meadow and every meadow contains its clear spring water. The heaviest timber comes down to the very edge of the tall grass, and all through the magnificent forest we find huckleberries almost ripe, Juneberries nearly mature, strawberries and wild currents thoroughly ripened, and the most luscious fruit to be found in the country. Today I have ridden through patches of all these fruits and just across the brook from where I am writing the miners have started quite a garden. Onions, potatoes, radishes, peas, and other vegetables are flourishing."[3]

---

[3] The Snake River Mines. (August 19, 1875). *The Laramie Daily Sentinel*, Page 3. https://nrrbook.com/LDS-1875-08-19

PART ONE

METTLE & METAL

CHAPTER 1: HAHNS PEAK MINING DISTRICT

"Some men are so led by the false glitter of gold, that they put small value on a soul made in God's image."[4]

-John V. Farwell

Long ago, gold meant nothing to the native inhabitants of the idyllic mountain setting that would become Routt County, Colorado. Instead, its richness came in the form of other resources: stunning beauty, prominent peaks, hot springs, crystal-clear creeks and rivers, and, perhaps most notably, bountiful wild game and fish. Due to the abundance of natural resources, several Native American tribes frequented the region. *"The Routt country was a meeting grounds for the mountain tribes such as the Arapahoes and Gros Ventres, and the Sioux and Cheyenne Indians of the Great Plains, and the Utes of the Colorado and Great Basins. The hunting and fishing facilities that center in this area plus the fact that it is accessible from the Laramie Plains, the Red Desert, the Arkansas River and the Colorado River, all natural wilderness highways, probably were responsible for this intermingling of different tribes."*[5]

It is well established that the Utes, in particular, considered this area part of their homeland, having inhabited the region for hundreds of years. Being a nomadic tribe that moved with the seasons, hundreds of Utes would gather in the summer in

---

[4] Farwell, John V. (1906). *Corner Stones of Character: Some Ways of Making Them*, Page 120. https://nrrbook.com/CornerStonesofCharacter

[5] *History of Routt National Forest 1905-1972.* (May 4, 2020). Page 1. National Forest Service Library. https://nrrbook.com/HistoryofRNF

present-day Routt County to hunt, fish, and visit the natural hot springs.

In the 1800s, European settlers became more prevalent, with trapping and fur trading as the primary industries. *"The Routt country saw such famous mountain men as William Ashley, Pegleg Smith, William and Milton Sublette, Thomas Fitzgerald, Jean Gervais, Jim Bridger, Jim Baker and Kit Carson during the fur trapping period from 1825 to 1845. Routt streams were rich in beaver, the most sought for fur of that era."*[6]

Pegleg Smith had quite a story. Born Thomas Smith in Kentucky, he had a confrontation with a teacher in high school, and as a result, decided to venture west. By 1824, he had moved to Colorado. In 1827, Smith was traveling through the North Park area with a group of trappers when Native Americans suddenly attacked. Smith was struck in his left leg with an arrow just above the ankle, leaving him with a compound fracture. He attempted to grab his rifle to defend himself, but the exposed bone stuck into the ground and stopped him in his tracks. Smith's fellow trappers were unable to amputate his leg, so he did it himself with a butcher knife. Smith's stump was then seared with a hot iron by party member Milton Sublette. Nearly dying, Smith was carried by the group westward to their final destination at the Green River. The stump eventually healed with help from some friendly Utes, who chewed up roots and spit on the wound. A wooden leg was then fashioned, and Thomas was thereafter known as Pegleg Smith.[7]

The Rocky Mountain Fur Company, established in 1830 by Henry Fraeb, Jim Bridger, Thomas Fitzpatrick, Milton Sublette, and Jean Baptiste Gervais, worked the present-day Routt County lands. This company ceased operations in 1834.

---

[6] *History of Routt National Forest 1905-1972.* (May 4, 2020). Page 1. National Forest Service Library. https://nrrbook.com/HistoryofRNF

[7] *History of Routt National Forest 1905-1972.* (May 4, 2020). Page 2. National Forest Service Library. https://nrrbook.com/HistoryofRNF

In a separate partnership known as the American Fur Company, Fraeb and Bridger would later build a trading post in southwest Wyoming. On August 21, 1841, Fraeb and a band of trappers were out while Bridger remained at the post. As the story goes, they encountered a band of Sioux, Cheyenne, and Arapaho who were angry that Fraeb had previously traded them whiskey for meat, and then went on to kill more buffalo for even more meat. The band of natives sought revenge and launched an attack. *"Jim Baker, who was in the battle says that there were about 500 of the Indians who were armed with some rifles and also with bows and arrows."*[8]

Baker had been sent by Jim Bridger, his employer, to warn Fraeb about increased hostilities, but it was too late. Baker arrived just as the battle was beginning.

"The trappers and their Snake allies sent their squaws to a mountain south of the battlefield where they could be safe. The Indians made about forty charges during each of which the outnumbered trappers held their fire until the Indians were within ten or fifteen paces of the breastworks that the trappers had hastily erected."[9]

Unfortunately, Fraeb was killed early on in the battle. Baker took charge, facing incredible odds. On his side were approximately twenty trappers, hunkered down behind trees and dead horses, while their foe had hundreds of fighters. That was not their only problem, though. They had a limited supply of ammo, so every shot had to count. Baker's strategy was to fire only half of the guns at a time, while the other half were being reloaded. This approach allowed them to be ready to fire at all times while also reducing the rate of ammunition consumption. The battle lasted into the night, when the band of Natives, also weary from battle, ultimately decided to give up, gather their dead and wounded, and leave.

---

[8] *History of Routt National Forest 1905-1972.* (May 4, 2020). Page 3. National Forest Service Library. https://nrrbook.com/HistoryofRNF

[9] *History of Routt National Forest 1905-1972.* (May 4, 2020). Page 3. National Forest Service Library. https://nrrbook.com/HistoryofRNF

Baker and the survivors could not believe they survived through the night. The Natives would later claim that they were fighting some kind of supernatural force, as they could not comprehend how their army of hundreds could have been defeated by so few on the other side.[10]

"Baker says that about a hundred Indians were killed in the 12 hour battle. Of the twenty three trappers, ten were killed including Fraeb. The trappers also lost 110 horses in the battle and came through with only 45 live ones."[11]

As a result of this battle, Battle Mountain, Battle Creek, and Squaw Mountain were all named. Squaw Mountain was renamed Petite Tetons in 2022.

Baker was an absolute legend, evidenced by a tale of him killing two bears with nothing but a knife.[12] He was born on a farm in Illinois in 1819, but was not destined to remain there. Around age twenty, Baker traveled to St. Louis, where his parents had arranged for him to apprentice as a shoemaker. Instead, he met Jim Bridger of the American Fur Company. Bridger convinced Baker to sign up for an 18-month trapping expedition, and in May of 1839, they departed for the Platte River area in Colorado and Wyoming.

Baker would grow very close to the Shoshone tribe, learning their language, living among them for some time, and even receiving a Shoshone name that translated to "red-headed Shoshone." He would go on to marry several Shoshone women, though the timing and details of those marriages are unclear.

---

[10] Daily, C. S. (September 23, 2023). True Wyoming Mountain man Jim Baker beat impossible odds on Battle Mountain. *Cowboy State Daily.* https://nrrbook.com/BakerBattle

[11] *History of Routt National Forest 1905-1972.* (May 4, 2020). Page 3. National Forest Service Library. https://nrrbook.com/HistoryofRNF

[12] *An Inventory of the Papers of JIM BAKER.* (1994). Page 4. Colorado Historical Society. https://nrrbook.com/BakerPapers

In 1859, Baker and his wife settled in North Denver, but by 1869, they had moved into a teepee in Middle Park. In 1873, they relocated to a hand-built cabin situated between Slater, Colorado, and Savery, Wyoming. This cabin was essentially a small fort with a watchtower and turret, as he always wanted to be prepared for an attack. This cabin still stands today, having been moved to the Little Snake River Museum in Savery, Wyoming. Baker's Peak is named after Jim Baker.

In June 1844, the famous explorer John C. Fremont, along with Kit Carson, traveled through the region during his second expedition. They traveled along the Little Snake River, went up Savery Creek,[13] crossed a mountain divide, down to present-day Encampment, and followed the Encampment River to the Platte River. *"They turned up the Platte entering North Park, which Fremont called New Park. On June 15 Fremont estimated the elevation of the park at 7,720 feet from the temperature of boiling water and gave its latitude as 40° 52' 44."* *He was pretty close to right on both counts. He says 'It is from this elevated cove and from the gorges of the surrounding mountains and some lakes within their bosoms that the Great Platte River collects its first waters and assumes its first form and certainly no river could ask a more beautiful origin.'"*[14]

Numerous other trappers, traders, and mountain men are known to have frequented the area.

Nearly two decades later, in 1861, Joseph Henn arrived on a gold prospecting trip. Originally born in Germany in 1824, Henn served in the German army and fled to Switzerland after

---

[13] There are conflicting records on whether Fremont and Carson traveled up Battle Creek or Savery Creek. In Fremont's own words, on pages 708 and 709 from *The Expeditions of John Charles Fremont, Volume I*, "we encamped a little below a branch of the river, called St. Vrain's fork…Leaving St. Vrain's fork, we took our way directly towards the summit of the dividing ridge." It is likely that St. Vrain and Savery are referring to the same creek, with different spellings developing over time due to different pronunciations (Fremont is of French descent). Fremont's map of this expedition marks St. Vrain's fork, and the line generally matches today's Savery Creek. https://nrrbook.com/FremontMap

[14] *History of Routt National Forest 1905-1972.* (May 4, 2020). Page 7. National Forest Service Library. https://nrrbook.com/HistoryofRNF

his army was defeated, as he did not want to become a prisoner of war. Henn later emigrated to the United States in 1852. He first worked in Michigan and then ventured west to Georgetown, Colorado, and on to present-day Routt County, where he began panning for gold.

While born Henn, Joseph pronounced his last name with an "ah" sound. From historian Thelma Stevenson: *"Hahn is said to have spelled his name 'Henne' or 'Henn,' although he himself used the guttural, German utterance of 'Hahn.' As a rule this is the commonest pronunciation. Local early-timers, however, to this day pronounce Hahn as 'Han' with a short 'a' as in hand."*[15] Henn, Henne, Han, and Hahn will be used interchangeably in this book.

Using basic tools, including a shovel, pickaxe, and pan, Henn prospected for gold in the most basic form of placer mining, extracting gold from the sediment and gravel along Willow Creek. Initial results were promising. Four years later, in 1865 (delayed by the Civil War), Henn would return with William Doyle and Captain George Way. In Doyle's own words: *"I had been working in the various diggings for some time, and in 1863 met Joe Henn in California Gulch. He told me of his prospecting trip, and said that he found gold in a canyon two miles below the peak in 1861. This is in a basin, from which the waters run out, but it was never named by us. No arrangements were made until the spring of 1865, when Henn, Way and myself started out from Empire on a general prospecting trip, with the peak as our objective point. We scouted all over the country, and were on the lookout for Indians, for there were said to be over 4,000 warriors in Middle Park...On August 27, 1865, we struck camp about two miles from the peak, and on Monday, the 28th, I climbed to the top and in boyish glee named it Henn's Peak in honor of the first discoverer."*[16]

---

[15] Stevenson, Thelma. (2005, 4th Printing). *Historic Hahns Peak*, Page 3.

[16] The Naming of Hahn's Peak. (August 31, 1895). *The Georgetown Courier, Volume XIX, Number 18*, Page 3. https://nrrbook.com/GC-1895-08-31

Doyle left a piece of paper declaring, *"This is named Henn's Peak by his friend and comrade, William D. Doyle, August 27, 1865,"*[17] inside a waterproof, screw-top Preston and Merrill baking powder tin anchored among the stones on the summit, and one of the most prominent mountains in Northwest Colorado received its name. Initially, the spelling varied due to the numerous forms Henn's last name took on (Henn, Henne, Han, Hann, Hawn, Hahn), but over time, Hahns Peak has become the accepted name. Per Doyle: *"In the first place that name is spelled wrong. Joe always spelled it Henn, and not Hahn, but I suppose the Hahn way will always go down in history."*[18]

Henn's Peak it was, and Hahns Peak it is. Notably, there is no apostrophe in Hahns Peak, likely due to the frequency and regularity of locals simply leaving out the apostrophe when spelling the name in its early days.

In addition to naming the famous peak, Doyle and crew were responsible for naming six of the gulches they mined. *"We named six of the gulches after ourselves and our place of nativity. The gulches were called Henn's, German, Way's, Virginia, Doyle's and Nova Scotia."*[19] Of these gulches, only the locations of Ways Gulch and Nova Scotia Gulch are known today. Doyle's Gulch was likely at the eastern foot of Anderson Mountain, as that peak used to be known as Doyle Mountain. Henn's, German, and Virginia Gulch locations remain a mystery. The only clue we have to their location is that they were west of Ways Gulch and Nova Scotia Gulch. *"The greater amount of gold was found on the east side in Way and Nova Scotia gulches."*[20]

---

[17] Burroughs, John. (1962). *Where the Old West Stayed Young*, Page 91.

[18] The Naming of Hahn's Peak. (August 31, 1895). *The Georgetown Courier, Volume XIX, Number 18*, Page 3. https://nrrbook.com/GC-1895-08-31

[19] The Naming of Hahn's Peak. (August 31, 1895). *The Georgetown Courier, Volume XIX, Number 18*, Page 3. https://nrrbook.com/GC-1895-08-31

[20] The Naming of Hahn's Peak. (August 31, 1895). *The Georgetown Courier, Volume XIX, Number 18*, Page 3. https://nrrbook.com/GC-1895-08-31

Henn, Way, and Doyle would stay in the area until late fall that year and made plans to return in 1866. *"We prospected around Henn's Peak that fall and remained so long that we were afraid we couldn't get across the range. We buried our tools, took a whipsaw with us and started out for Empire, intending to return the following spring and bring a few selected friends with us, for we knew that we had $10 a day diggings. We made the trip all right and that winter Henn went to Atchison, Kansas, Way went over to John S. Jones' ranch with 29 head of cattle, which he let freeze to death, and I stayed around Georgetown, Empire and the diggings around Central City. As we were partners we made arrangements for taking 14 men with us. To a few I told the truth, but for the general stories we didn't care what we did tell, only they were not favorable to the diggings. It was reported that we had brought out 200 pounds of gold in the fall of 1865; although it was hardly that much, I do not care to tell the amount."*[21]

Whatever the actual amount was, it was large enough to draw them back, and the group began their return trip out of Central City on May 31, 1866. Despite initially planning to take only fourteen men with them, the number swelled to fifty-one when votes were counted to form the Hahns Peak Mining District in 1866. Among the others was Charlie Utter. Henn was elected as the surveyor, Way the judge, Doyle the recorder, and a man with the appropriate last name of Reason, who was a friend of Henn and a fellow German, the sheriff. *"It was agreed that Henn, Way and myself (Doyle) were to have 500 feet of ground in each gulch and the others were to draw lots for claims."*[22] Utter was a proponent of including Steamboat Springs in the new mining district, but he was unable to be present for the vote after being accidentally injured by a man named James Cooper

---

[21] The Naming of Hahn's Peak. (August 31, 1895). *The Georgetown Courier, Volume XIX, Number 18*, Page 3. https://nrrbook.com/GC-1895-08-31

[22] The Naming of Hahn's Peak. (August 31, 1895). *The Georgetown Courier, Volume XIX, Number 18*, Page 3. https://nrrbook.com/GC-1895-08-31

while hunting a bear. He nearly died, but did recover from his wounds.[23]

The prospecting that Henn, Way, and Doyle did in 1865 paid off in 1866. *"We didn't prospect in 1866, for we were in some good diggings...The ground was tolerably rich in places. One peculiarity in a large section was that by shaking the grass roots one could get colors and it was no better at bedrock. The gold was everywhere and not alone in the gulches."*[24]

Their luck soon ran out.

"The three of us started that spring with plenty of grub, but during the summer we loaned several sacks of flour and some bacon, so as to get men to dig ditches for us. Grub commenced to become scarce. With winter coming on the miners began to leave camp for the winter. In fact there were only seven of us left in Middle Park that winter. It was decided between us that Way should go out for grub and on Oct. 1, 1866, he, together with several others, pulled out, intending to get back by the 14th, but he never came back. Our supply of gold was very heavy and he carried this on his pack animals. It was more than double that of the previous year, when it was reported we had cleaned up 200 pounds of gold."[25]

Way never returned. Henn and Doyle initially assumed he had gotten lost, but in later years, they would hear rumors that he was alive and well in Georgetown, New Mexico.[26] Did Way take the gold and run? Author John Burroughs had this to say: *"For many years Captain George Way lived in various mining camps*

---

[23] "In the Days of Old." (June 29, 1904). *The Steamboat Pilot,* Page 2. https://nrrbook.com/SP-1904-07-06

[24] The Naming of Hahn's Peak. (August 31, 1895). *The Georgetown Courier, Volume XIX, Number 18*, Page 3. https://nrrbook.com/GC-1895-08-31

[25] The Naming of Hahn's Peak. (August 31, 1895). *The Georgetown Courier, Volume XIX, Number 18*, Page 3. https://nrrbook.com/GC-1895-08-31

[26] The Naming of Hahn's Peak. (August 31, 1895). *The Georgetown Courier, Volume XIX, Number 18*, Page 3. https://nrrbook.com/GC-1895-08-31

on Colorado's eastern slope and in New Mexico, where he died in 1883. No further comment concerning him seems necessary. The record speaks for itself."[27]

Meanwhile, conditions were deteriorating rapidly for Henn and Doyle. Determined to ride out the winter in their mining camp in Ways Gulch, they survived primarily on rabbits and even hunted a mountain lion at one point when the rabbit population started to dwindle. When the weather allowed, Henn and Doyle spent their time whipsawing over 4,000 feet of lumber to be used the following year.[28] Despite their efforts to make it work, their circumstances proved unsustainable.

"The storms setting in and the water freezing we didn't do much work after Way left, and only cleaned up a few hundred dollars. There was one snow storm which lasted for 38 days, and everything was covered, it being at least twelve feet deep on a level. Grub was getting scarcer and it was decided that Henn and I (Doyle) should start out for Empire. On April 22, 1867, we started out...we decided upon heading for Jones' ranch, although neither one of us had been there before. Joe thought it was at the junction of Muddy Creek and the Grand, and I thought it about two miles below the junction."[29]

This would not be an easy journey, especially when food and, therefore, energy, were scarce. *"Being expert woodsmen, they were careful in selecting their route to conserve energy by not losing altitude. Hence they worked eastward from Hahn's Peak to the North Fork of Elk River by way of what is known as 'Scott's Run.' Heading upstream, they crossed the Continental Divide, dropped into North Park - probably by way of the Frying Pan Basin - and turned south."[30]*

---

[27] Burroughs, John. (1962). *Where the Old West Stayed Young*, Page 93.

[28] Burroughs, John. (1962). *Where the Old West Stayed Young*, Page 92.

[29] The Naming of Hahn's Peak. (August 31, 1895). *The Georgetown Courier, Volume XIX, Number 18*, Page 3. https://nrrbook.com/GC-1895-08-31

[30] Burroughs, John. (1962). *Where the Old West Stayed Young*, Page 92.

"He was not very adept on snowshoes and I could have traveled three miles to his one. Our grub played out on Saturday and on Tuesday the 29th of April, it snowed hard and we traveled fifteen miles in this new snow. Although it let up at sundown, we continued on until 9 or 10 o'clock that night when we sat down on the banks of the Grand to rest."[31]

While this account references the Grand River (present-day Colorado River), Doyle almost certainly meant Muddy Creek. A separate account published in the July 6, 1904, edition of the *Steamboat Pilot* says *"that night they reached the Muddy and rested until 9 o'clock."*[32]

Doyle continued: *"When we got up to resume our journey he staggered like a drunken man and finally fell down. I helped him up and he said that we had better stay there that night. We put down our blankets and turned in. During the night he woke me up by rolling and tumbling and talking in a rambling sort of way, and I couldn't get run of the conversation. When the sun was a half hour high, I wrapped him up and then started for Jones' ranch but couldn't find it in either place, we had supposed it to be. Taking off my coat and placing my revolver in my mouth I swam the creek and concluded to get to Hot Springs. I knew I had been close to it, but didn't know where. After rambling all day, I returned to Henn and found him dead, death having been brought on by hunger and fatigue. I wrapped his body in the cavalry coat and his blankets and then started out on my search for food and shelter at the springs."*[33]

At forty-three years old, Henn was dead. Unless his luck changed soon, Doyle was next.

---

[31] The Naming of Hahn's Peak. (August 31, 1895). *The Georgetown Courier, Volume XIX, Number 18*, Page 3. https://nrrbook.com/GC-1895-08-31

[32] "In the Days of Old." (July 6, 1904). *The Steamboat Pilot*, Page 2. https://nrrbook.com/SP-1904-07-06

[33] The Naming of Hahn's Peak. (August 31, 1895). *The Georgetown Courier, Volume XIX, Number 18*, Page 3. https://nrrbook.com/GC-1895-08-31

"Expecting to meet the same fate as Henn, I wrote a farewell in my notebook and gave the address of my relatives. I built a fire, but couldn't sleep. My eyes began hurting. I knew that there were a couple of men stopping at the Hot Springs that winter. When daylight came I could hardly see and when wild geese came flying overhead I could not see to shoot. When I reached Muddy creek I was afraid to cross as I had done the day before. I got a pole and commenced to search for a shallow place. Just then I heard a gun crack.

John C. Summers heard my cry and together with Gus Lankin and Ashley Franklin came to me. This was on the third day of May, and I had been without a morsel to eat for six days. On the fifth we reached the (Mammoth) Hot Springs. After remaining here some time I was taken to Empire, reaching there on the second day of June, and my bones are not lying on the mountain side bleached by the passing years."[34]

The near-death experience had lifelong implications for Doyle.

"I was blind for six months and my right eye has never recovered from the hardships experienced on the trip of almost thirty years ago. I never returned to the diggings, for I heard that the claims had all been gobbled up. Since that time I have virtually spent all of my time in Clear Creek county, near Idaho Springs, and though I have never kept the fact of my existence secret, yet some of the old-timers around Hahn's Peak have given me an interesting obituary notice. If I had known about the renewed excitement in that county early this year (1895) I would surely have returned to the scenes of my early exploits. I think that country will develop into something good and I will go there myself early next spring."[35]

---

[34] The Naming of Hahn's Peak. (August 31, 1895). *The Georgetown Courier, Volume XIX, Number 18*, Page 3. https://nrrbook.com/GC-1895-08-31

[35] The Naming of Hahn's Peak. (August 31, 1895). *The Georgetown Courier, Volume XIX, Number 18*, Page 3. https://nrrbook.com/GC-1895-08-31

As stated in the July 6, 1904, edition of the Steamboat Pilot: *"Although he fought in many hard battles during the Civil War, his hardest was that winter's siege, blockaded by twelve feet of snow and the heroic effort to run the blockade."*[36]

Henn's body remained along the Muddy Creek bank until November 1868. Paul Lindstrom of Empire, a friend of Henn, sent a man to bury his remains.

"This man fell in company with W.N. Byers while going into the park. They went to Hot Sulphur Springs where they found one Capt. Horn. This man, while fishing in the Muddy the previous October, had found the remains.

Byers and his comrade interviewed Horn and then, being guided by him, found the skeleton and clothing, with other evidences which unmistakably identified them as those of Hahn. These were collected and buried and one of his snowshoes was planted at the head of his grave.

Hahn's grave is about a quarter or a half mile from where the Muddy empties into the Grand (Colorado) river, near the present town of Kremmling."[37]

With Henn dead, Way long gone, and Doyle not returning due to his own traumatic near-death experience, mining activity around Hahns Peak fell into new hands. In the summer of 1867 or the spring of 1868, John Brockmeyer (nicknamed Bibleback Brown for his propensity to read the Bible in his rucksack on a regular basis) discovered shovels and other mining tools along Willow Creek. After a night of drinking, he revealed his findings to a Union Pacific colleague named Bill Slater. Brown and Slater would return to the area in 1870 and begin mining. George Howe and David Miller joined them later that year. The following year, two new prospectors from Rawlins, Wyoming,

---

[36] "In the Days of Old." (July 6, 1904). *The Steamboat Pilot,* Page 2.
https://nrrbook.com/SP-1904-07-06

[37] "In the Days of Old." (July 6, 1904). *The Steamboat Pilot,* Page 2.
https://nrrbook.com/SP-1904-07-06

named W.R. Cogswell and J.C. Miller, arrived and claimed the ground that would later become Poverty Bar.[38]

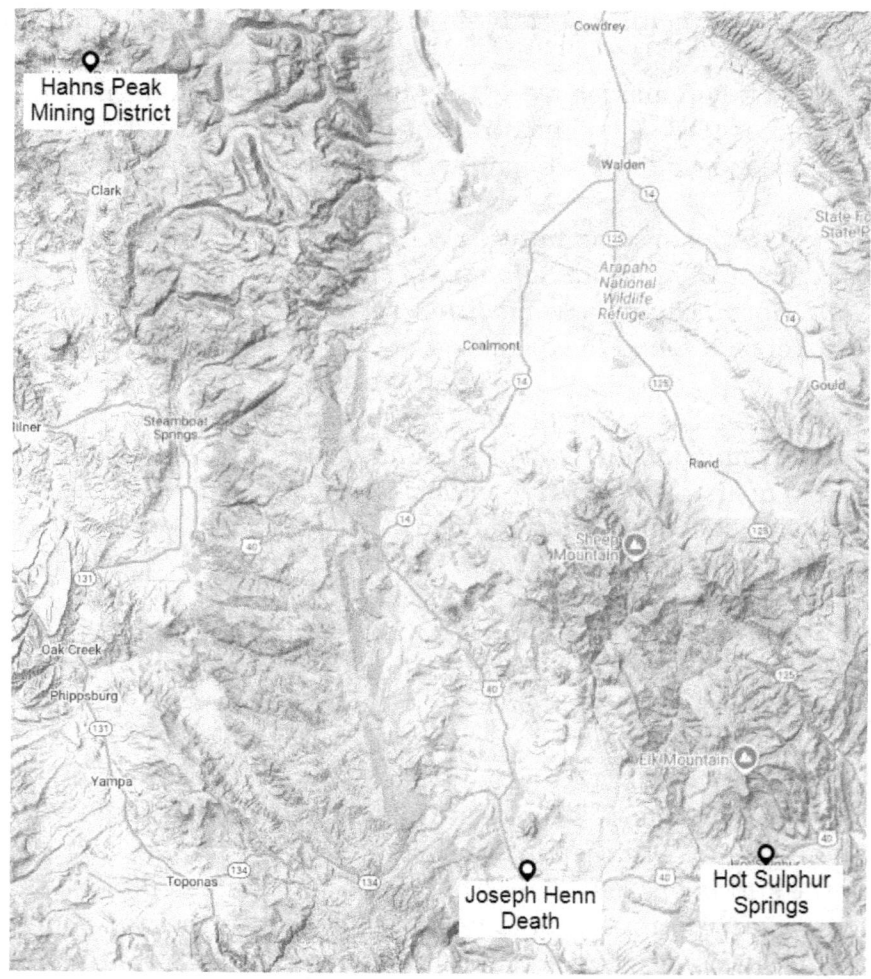

Above: Present-day map showing the locations of the Hahns Peak Mining District, the approximate location of Joseph Henn's death, and the town of Hot Sulphur Springs.

Additional prospectors arrived as gold-rich gravel bars were discovered around Hahns Peak. On November 9th, 1874, a new

---

[38] Burroughs, John. (1962). *Where the Old West Stayed Young*, Page 94.

"Hans Peak Mining District" was formed in what was then Grand County. Officers were A.S. Hutchison (Recorder), A.S. Moulton (Secretary), and S. Montgomery (President). This district *"extended down the waters of Bear River five miles in a southerly direction from Han's Peak, also down the waters of the Snake River five miles in northerly direction from Han's Peak and five miles East and five miles West of said Peak."*[39] The new district covered 100 square miles, with Hahns Peak situated at its center.

Two companies were prominent in the new district. First was the Hans Peak Gold & Silver Mining Company, which had a claim to "Poverty Hill" that was considered *"one of the most extensive deposits of placer gold ever discovered. Mining experts from San Francisco, Arizona, and our own territory pronounce its wealth at nothing less than millions, their estimates being made from careful prospects at different points and various depths throughout the grand deposit."*[40] At the time, S.D.N. Bennett was Superintendent of this company. Thomas Brooks, who would later be named Superintendent in 1876, prospected Poverty Hill extensively. He claimed the pay gravel was twenty to thirty feet deep, with good pay from the surface down to bedrock, and estimated that Poverty Hill contained $15 million in gold. *"The company has 100 acres on 'Poverty Hill,' which has been thoroughly prospected by Mr. Brooks, an old California miner, and by him calculated to contain at least $15,000,000."*[41]

The Purdy Silver Mining Company was active from 1872 to 1875, aiming to establish a larger-scale operation. *"...the Purdy Mining Company, Hopkins, Harris, Dunbar & Co., Lambert & Bell, and others, began operations there in earnest, and have been rewarded with good returns for their energy and outlay.*

---

[39] Burroughs, John. (1962). *Where the Old West Stayed Young*, Page 97.

[40] "Poverty Hill" (August 19, 1875). *The Laramie Daily Sentinel*, Page 3. https://nrrbook.com/LDS-1875-08-19

[41] "Snake River Mines, Some Rich Diggings" (July 1, 1875). *The Laramie Weekly Sun*, Page 1. https://nrrbook.com/LWS-1875-07-01

Lambert & Bell own altogether about eighty acres of good gold bearing grounds, besides extensive and valuable water privileges, embracing the Middle and South Forks of Willow Creek, which cover several hundred acres of placer claims, the dirt of which yields all the way from $3 to $6 per day to the hand...The slopes, as well as the bed, of the gulch are rich in gold, and good 'color' has been obtained in the timber, high up on the mountain. Several quartz veins, both gold and silver, have been located in the vicinity, and a party of prospectors from Montana, who arrived some time in the summer, claim to have found very rich placer diggings within a mile or two of the mountain, and are preparing to work them on a big scale next year. Mr. Bell informed a News reporter that about one hundred and fifty men spent the past season at the mines. Although operations commenced late, and most of the above number spent their time in prospecting, the crop of gold already harvested may safely be put down at $10,000 or $12,000. Two men, named Brown and Slater, sluiced out in five weeks, nearly $2,000."[42]

Both companies showed promise, but they shared a problem. An increased supply of water was necessary to sustain and grow their operations. Without it, their mining season typically lasted only about six to eight weeks and concluded by July. Working independently, both companies began to build out a *"splendid system of reservoirs and ditches."*[43] Included in this system was a three-mile ditch constructed from the north fork of Willow Creek to Poverty Hill by the Hans Peak Gold & Silver Mining Company. Having filed a ditch claim in Grand County on July 13, 1874, this ditch was constructed in 1875.

Purdy had bigger plans. The bulk of its mining claims were located one to two miles east of Poverty Hill near String Ridge and along Beaver Creek. Plans to tap Beaver Creek with a ditch

[42] "Hahn's Peak Gold Fields" (October 7, 1874). *Weekly Rocky Mountain News,* Page 3. https://nrrbook.com/WRMN-1874-10-07

[43] "Poverty Hill" (August 19, 1875). *The Laramie Daily Sentinel*, Page 3. https://nrrbook.com/LDS-1875-08-19

to carry water three to four miles to String Ridge were considered, but ultimately scrapped. The challenge with Beaver Creek was that it had insufficient water in the late summer months, which would grind mining to a halt. To solve this dilemma, Purdy planned and surveyed a ditch, estimated to be fifteen to twenty miles in length, from the Elk River.[44] These were bold plans, but the estimated cost of $50,000 to finish their project was more than they could afford.

For the merchant prince of Chicago, opportunity was knocking. In 1876, John V. Farwell, along with partner Benjamin F. Jacobs (a Chicago real estate mogul), was lured to the Hahns Peak Mining District by a close friend named Jerome Stillson. Stillson, who was acquainted with S.D.N. Bennett, the Superintendent of the Hans Peak Gold & Silver Mining Company, recognized that Farwell had the business expertise and deep pockets to help the Hahns Peak Mining District pursue its full potential. Acquisitions began soon after.

On May 11, 1876, Farwell and Jacobs signed an agreement to acquire land and water rights from Thomas Brooks, who owned approximately four hundred acres of mining claims in the area (separate from the Hans Peak Gold & Silver Mining Company, for which he was Superintendent), in a deal valued at $100,000.[45] Brooks had personally traveled to Chicago to discuss the potential deal and also brought samples of ore to be assayed by a local chemist named Gilbert Wheeler. After several conversations, the agreement[46] was signed with the following terms:

- $20,000 cash investment by Farwell and Jacobs
  - $1,500 initial deposit upon signing the deal

---

[44] "Snake River Mines, Some Rich Diggings" (July 1, 1875). *The Laramie Weekly Sun*, Page 1. https://nrrbook.com/LWS-1875-07-01

[45] Using a rough inflation factor of 30:1 from 1875 to 2025, the deal would be worth $3 million today.

[46] J.V. Farwell & B.F. Jacobs agreement with T.W. Brooks. (May 11, 1876). Grand County Clerk and Recorder's Office. https://nrrbook.com/FarwellBrooks

- $3,500 payment upon inspection of the land and approval of the deal by Andrew J. Bell (Farwell & Jacob's Power of Attorney)
  - $6,500 payment 30 days after the 2nd payment
  - $5,000 payment 30 days after the 3rd payment
  - $3,500 final payment to cover surveying, platting, & recording costs

- $80,000 from the mines' production
  - The first $25,000 of production to Brooks
  - The next $40,000 of production to Farwell & Jacobs
  - The next $25,000 of production to Brooks
  - The next $50,000 of production to Farwell & Jacobs
  - 50% of the next $60,000 of production to Brooks

In addition, multiple contracts were signed with Purdy Mining Company, including one for $50,000 on our nation's first centennial, July 4, 1876.[47] These deals encompassed hundreds of acres, including Ways Gulch, Nova Scotia Gulch, String Ridge, and claims along Beaver Creek. Also included was a water claim in Ways Gulch.

While the deals with Purdy went through as planned, business with Brooks turned ugly. As stated in the contract, Farwell & Jacobs paid an initial deposit of $1,500, with the full investment expected to total $100,000. The land covered in the contract consisted of several hundred acres located near the southern end of Hinman Canyon, as well as one claim on Hahns Peak known as the Widow Lode. Andrew J. Bell, having been named Power of Attorney[48] for Farwell & Jacobs on June 10, 1876, immediately departed Chicago for Colorado to inspect the properties as stipulated by the contract. He was shocked by what he found.

---

[47] Purdy Mining Co. agreement with J.V. Farwell & B.F. Jacobs. (July 4 1876). Grand County Clerk and Recorder's Office. https://nrrbook.com/FarwellPurdy

[48] A.J. Bell Power of Attorney for John V. Farwell & B.F. Jacobs. (June 10, 1876). Grand County Clerk and Recorder's Office. https://nrrbook.com/AJBellPOA

"Brooks showed me what he had sold to J.V. Farwell & B.F. Jacobs as the Widow Lode. No work had apparently been done on the so-called lode except during the last 24 hours preceding the examination. The fresh tracks in the snow surrounding showed this fact conclusively. There was not over three feet of the excavation at any point shown me by Brooks on the Widow Lode or its extensions or by any other person."[49]

At first glance, the placer ground near Hinman Canyon wasn't much better. *"The placer property was of little value. Some was too low to work by hydraulic process, others was deep but nearly barren. I found traces of gold in most of the claims as I could get in almost any part of the neighborhood for miles around. There was very little water, where plaintiff represented was sufficient for six pipes. There was not enough in sight for two pipes. In regard to the lodes none existed nor no indications that has been of sufficient importance to cause any prospector though many have been on the mountains to make further examination."*[50]

After inspecting the land for two weeks, Bell returned to Chicago. While the Widow Lode had proven to be a bust, he wanted more time to examine the placer ground near Hinman Canyon. A few weeks later, he returned to the mining district with "apparatus and testing supplies" to see if a greater source of water could be located. It was a lost cause, however, and he deemed the land worthless due to the insufficient water and trace amounts of gold found. Brooks, meanwhile, tried a new tactic: intimidation.

"The plaintiff (Brooks) repeatedly promised to make me rich if I (Bell) would make a favorable report, and I knew of his making similar propositions to other parties in the mines if they could bring about a favorable report on his property, or so called

[49] Thomas W Brooks vs John V. Farwell & B.F. Jacobs, Denver, CO District Case Number 4026. (1879). Pages 83-84. https://nrrbook.com/FarwellBrooksCase

[50] Thomas W Brooks vs John V. Farwell & B.F. Jacobs, Denver, CO District Case Number 4026. (1879). Page 89. https://nrrbook.com/FarwellBrooksCase

property, or could induce me to do so...Threats came to me through others and at this time, Brooks brought into camp & slept at his house a Pioche Saint,[51] which among miners is recognized as a character who will murder any man for money. And this man it was publicly known was there for business in his line if need be. In my surveys & examinations I was assisted by J.B. Stillson, and my assistant Mr. Stillson while making examinations of property of plaintiff described in contract or deed was driven in by threats of violence by Brooks and this Pioche Saint and others."[52]

Poor results in hand, Bell traveled back to Chicago. Roughly one month later, he returned to the mining district with John V. Farwell, who brought his brother, Charles B. Farwell,[53] a lawyer, along. While in Hahns Peak, Brooks presented the deeds to the contracted properties to Bell and the Farwell brothers.

According to Charles, *"When at Hahns Peak, Mr. Bell handed to me a bundle of deeds about 20 to 30 in number, which purported to be the title papers or deeds and which I examined and found that same were executed by different persons in different states of the Union, and that all of said deeds were written and*

---

[51] The nicknamed "Pioche Saint" most likely hailed from Pioche, Nevada. Known for its high levels of lawlessness and violence during a silver mining boom in the 1860s and 1870s, Pioche was considered "the bloodiest town in the West during the Wild West Era." An 1873 report to the Nevada State Legislature said "Peaceful! Sure, if you stayed out of the way of the bullets." The "saint" portion of the nickname was clearly used in jest.

[52] Thomas W Brooks vs John V. Farwell & B.F. Jacobs, Denver, CO District Case Number 4026. (1879). Pages 91-92. https://nrrbook.com/FarwellBrooksCase

[53] Charles B. Farwell, in addition to being a lawyer, served as a U.S. Representative in the 42nd, 43rd, & 44th Congresses as a Republican. His election to the 44th Congress was contested by his opponent, John V. Le Moyne, and the Democratically controlled Congress removed Farwell on May 6, 1876. Farwell would serve again in the 47th Congress. In 1887, he was appointed to fill the Senate seat vacated by the death of John Logan. In this role, Charles was a supporter of a Constitutional Amendment granting women's suffrage (the right to vote). The 19th Amendment, which granted this right, would not pass until 1920, seventeen years after Charles's death.

executed about the same date and were all written by the same handwriting, including the body of the deed the signatures and the acknowledgement of same, except some two or three of said deeds. And I at once saw that the title papers or deeds were all fictitious."[54]

The Farwell brothers and A.J. Bell had seen enough. Brooks, who ridiculously claimed his properties contained enough gold to pay the national debt (over $2 billion in 1876), was a fraudster. The deal was off. Farwell & Jacobs wanted their $1,500 deposit refunded, while Brooks demanded the balance of the $100,000 investment. Although all parties had verbally agreed to a refund clause, it was not written into the contract. *"The verbal agreement before it was reduced to writing was that this money should be refunded if Mr. Bell's report was unfavorable."*[55] Both parties sued each other, but the cases were eventually dropped. No additional money changed hands beyond the original $1,500 deposit.

Charles, being interrogated as part of the lawsuit, stated, *"I know of nothing more to add unless it be that when I saw Mr. Bell at Hahns Peak in the summer of 1876, he congratulated himself on the fact that he had prevented my brother J.V. Farwell from being swindled by promptly reporting against the property."*[56]

Perhaps the most damaging testimony against Brooks in the lawsuit came from chemist Gilbert Wheeler. When describing the ore samples he assayed, he stated, *"I understood that the specimens came from the Widow Lode in the State of Colorado. Both of the specimens were unusually peculiar in their appearance more so than any I remember to have ever assayed.*

---

[54] Thomas W Brooks vs John V. Farwell & B.F. Jacobs, Denver, CO District Case Number 4026. (1879). Page 68. https://nrrbook.com/FarwellBrooksCase

[55] Thomas W Brooks vs John V. Farwell & B.F. Jacobs, Denver, CO District Case Number 4026. (1879). Page 150. https://nrrbook.com/FarwellBrooksCase

[56] Thomas W Brooks vs John V. Farwell & B.F. Jacobs, Denver, CO District Case Number 4026. (1879). Page 69. https://nrrbook.com/FarwellBrooksCase

The rock was nearly pure white, exceedingly porous, resembling somewhat masses of dried plaster, except that they were heavier and harder. The naked eye could discover several of the pores or cavities on the exterior of the specimens small particles or scales of gold. These particles did not appear to conform in shape to the surfaces upon which they rested, or in the least to be imbedded in the surrounding rock. On breaking open the specimens of rock they presented on the interior surfaces precisely the same structure, with this difference: that no particles of gold whatever were visible to the naked eye or by the aid of a lens...In my judgement the particles of gold did not come naturally into the cavities in which they were observed, but were probably artificially introduced."[57]

Jerome Stillson's testimony summarized it very simply: *"...the plaintiff has no property of any value worth anything and thus a fraud was being attempted upon the defendants..."*[58]

Farwell's men involved in the lawsuit were hardly the only ones who had a poor opinion of Brooks. The July 4, 1900, edition of the Steamboat Pilot, looking back to 1876, had this to say: *"...T.W. Brooks was made superintendent. He appears to have been entirely unfitted for the place and soon had the finances of the company in a terrible shape. He was a fine looking, imperious man, a convincing talker who carried everything before him by the sheer force of his nerve. Many of the Denver members of his company were his strong partisans and were not satisfied until they had placed him in as manager. He spent money very recklessly, had a fine cabin built for himself and employed men at the company's expense to prospect and work claims for himself."*[59]

---

[57] Thomas W Brooks vs John V. Farwell & B.F. Jacobs, Denver, CO District Case Number 4026. (1879). Pages 155-157. https://nrrbook.com/FarwellBrooksCase

[58] Thomas W Brooks vs John V. Farwell & B.F. Jacobs, Denver, CO District Case Number 4026. (1879). Page 109. https://nrrbook.com/FarwellBrooksCase

[59] "Map of Hahns Peak District, 1876" (July 4, 1900). *The Steamboat Pilot*, Page 4. https://nrrbook.com/SP-1900-07-04

We can only assume that Farwell and Jacobs agreed to the deal with Brooks after Wheeler's assessment due to the refund clause that had been verbally agreed upon. In their minds, they had an escape clause. On paper, they did not.

Despite the trouble with Brooks, business went on.

Building on the water claims acquired from Purdy Mining Company, Farwell and Jacobs filed a water claim on July 17, 1876, with the Grand County Clerk and Recorder's Office for the Main Fork of the Elk River (known as Trail Creek today) for *"the waters of this entire stream for the purpose of Placer Mining and Hydraulic Purposes."*[60] Having been surveyed by Purdy in 1875, construction of the seventeen-mile Farwell Ditch to carry this water began that very day and would not be completed until August 1878. The Farwell Ditch, as it would come to be known, will be discussed in detail in Chapter 5.

John V. filed a claim for twenty additional acres on July 23, 1877: *"Notice!! I hereby give public notice that I claim twenty acres placer ground - commencing on the Purdy corner on the Beaver Creek and running up the eastern side of same stream to corner of A.J. Bell and with his line westerly twenty rods to stakes. Thence down said stream about one hundred and sixty rods to Purdy corner, and with his line to the beginning twenty acres more or less. This claim was claimed to be taken in 1876, but forfeited under ditch laws for non-representation and is now re-located as an abandoned claim."*[61]

A separate 160-acre claim[62] in the Ways Gulch area was filed by a group of eight people that included John V.'s wife, Emeret

---

[60] Main Elk River Water Claim. (July 17, 1876). Grand County Clerk and Recorder's Office. https://nrrbook.com/FarwellDitchClaim

[61] John V. Farwell Mining Claim. (July 23, 1877). Book B, Page 6. Routt County Clerk & Recorder's Office. https://nrrbook.com/JVFClaim-1877-07-23

[62] Charles & Emeret Farwell Mining Claim. (July 1, 1877). Book B, Page 15. Routt County Clerk & Recorder's Office. https://nrrbook.com/WaysGulchClaim-1877-07-01

Cooley Farwell, and brother Charles. Interestingly, John V. himself was not listed on this claim.

Farwell, with vast financial resources available, planned to build a gold-mining empire. The opportunity for millions of dollars in gold was now his, and he had the resources to finish what Purdy started. Fifteen years after Joseph Henn found gold while prospecting with basic tools in Willow Creek, John V. sought to revolutionize the region's placer mining industry.

The International Mining Company,[63] considered to be the first wage-paying industrial enterprise on the western slope of Colorado, was now in operation.

---

[63] There are multiple erroneous reports that refer to Farwell's operation as the Continental Placer Mining Company.

CHAPTER 2: GOLD STANDARD

"Every young man who is desirous of making his life bud, blossom, and become fruitful in all that is good and sublime, should remember these two things - that goodness is the foundation upon which sublimity rests, and that he must dedicate every power of body and mind to achieve such a result so glorious. In other words, he must make a business of it."[64]

-John V. Farwell

John V. Farwell, who became the namesake of Farwell Mountain, was a prominent Chicago businessman in the mid-to-late 1800s. At his peak, he owned one of the largest wholesale dry goods companies in the country, which was appropriately named John V. Farwell and Company. Farwell's business success naturally led to other endeavors throughout his life, but it is essential to provide more background information before we dive into those topics.

John Villiers Farwell, pictured[65] to the right, was born in 1825 in Campbell, New York. The son of Henry and Nancy Farwell, he was

---

[64] Dale, John T. (1889). *The Secret of Success*, Page V.
https://nrrbook.com/DaleSecretofSuccess

[65] McKinney, Megan. (November 27, 2016). Farwells 1: A Gathering of Giants. *Classic Chicago Magazine*. https://nrrbook.com/FarwellGathering

always known as John V. or "Dutch" (never just John). In 1838, the Farwell family packed their belongings in a "prairie schooner" and began a journey from New York to Ogle County, Illinois, where Henry, perhaps influenced by John Deere's newly invented self-scouring steel plow, desired to farm. The first leg of the expedition was to Buffalo, New York, where the covered wagon boarded a steamship bound across Lake Erie for Detroit. From there, the family headed towards Chicago. At the time, Chicago was in its infancy, with a population of about 2,000. Finally, they continued west until reaching their destination near the Rock River, close to the town of Oregon in Ogle County, Illinois.

Henry immediately put John V. and his older brother, Charles (born July 1, 1823), to work. They split wood to build fences, and when that was complete, they were tasked with breaking the soil using teams of steers named Boz and Shakespeare, Polk and Dallas, Tippecanoe and Tyler Too, Martin Van Buren and Franklin Pierce, Zach Taylor and Millard Fillmore, and a team of oxen named Moses and Nebuchadnezzar.[66] Wheat was grown and hauled to Chicago to be sold for $.45 per bushel. The six-day round trip to Chicago used the same teams of steers and oxen to pull the load of wheat.

In John V.'s own words, *"It is impossible to draw even a word picture, true to the facts, to represent the hardships of making farms and homes in Illinois, when lumber wagons represented the only transportation facilities, and everything was wanting but a wilderness for open prairie."*[67]

He later added, *"Every improvement on the farm, resulting from labor was quite practicable, but anything that required money was out of the question. Forty-five cents per bushel for surplus wheat would hardly keep up taxes and buy the actual necessities*

---

[66] Farwell, John V. (1911). *Some Recollections of John V. Farwell*, Pages 19-20. https://nrrbook.com/RecollectionsofJVF

[67] Farwell, John V. (1911). *Some Recollections of John V. Farwell*, Page 20. https://nrrbook.com/RecollectionsofJVF

of life that could not be produced on the farm."[68] While life was not easy, a foundation of hard, honest work was being laid.

Farwell attended school in a country school known as the Elmira Academy. Before graduating, he asked the principal to teach a class on bookkeeping. The principal agreed, on the condition that John V. enlist at least two more students. Sure enough, Farwell met the recruitment quota, and he learned bookkeeping, which would prove to be a valuable skill in the future. At age sixteen, he would go on to attend Mount Morris College, which was known as one of the finest schools in Illinois at the time. Initially, Farwell was out of his element, but he soon found his footing. *"It may be true that those rough farmer boys were not, at first, very popular with the Chicago aristocrats at the school, who could plank down cash for their expenses and take the best rooms in the seminary building; but time and hard work in their studies soon compelled a respect that is always given to true merit."[69]*

At age twenty, John V. caught a ride on a load of wheat to Chicago, which had grown to a population of around 12,000. His only belongings were three dollars his father had given him and a Bible from his mother. Her parting words were *"My son, you will be known by the company you keep, and this Book - well read - will lead you into such companionships as will make life a blessing to yourself and others."[70]* With his training in bookkeeping, he quickly found a job in the City Clerk's office, where he earned $12 per month. Part of his duties included reporting the City Council's proceedings to a local weekly newspaper, but he was soon fired by a corrupt councilman who did not like that John V. reported the truth instead of the

---

[68] Farwell, John V. (1911). *Some Recollections of John V. Farwell*, Page 29. https://nrrbook.com/RecollectionsofJVF

[69] Farwell, John V. (1911). *Some Recollections of John V. Farwell*, Page 37. https://nrrbook.com/RecollectionsofJVF

[70] Farwell, John V. (1906). *Corner Stones of Character: Some Ways of Making Them*, Page 9. https://nrrbook.com/CornerStonesofCharacter

narrative the Council preferred to see published. Dirty politics were common, even then.

Farwell went on to get a job working 6:00 AM to 9:00 PM at a wholesale goods firm called Hamilton & White. His wages were $8 per month, plus boarding. A bonus at year's end would be paid if his boss felt it was deserved. *"Having kept the books, sold more goods than any other man in the store, as well as sleeping in the store after working till nine o'clock, and opening it in the morning, I asked the bargain boss at the end of the year how much more he thought I had earned, and found his opinion was against any bonus. I said 'Good morning, sir,' and found another position in less than half an hour, at three times his generous bargain and fulfillment."*[71] Sure enough, John V. started employment at Handin & Day, where he earned $250 per year.

Farwell started his next job with Wadsworth and Phelps in 1849, earning $600 per year. This firm would later become Cooley, Wadsworth, and Company, and John V. was eventually promoted to General Manager. In 1862, the firm became known as Cooley, Farwell, and Company when John V. became a partner. The original location was 205 South Water Street in Chicago. Due to massive growth, a new building, shown on the following page, was constructed at 42, 44, and 46 Wabash Avenue. This building measured 60 feet wide, 120 feet deep, and was six stories tall.

"The whole building is filled from cellar to roof, and the four large salesrooms are constantly thronged with buyers, while more than sixty clerks are kept thoroughly occupied in attending to them."[72]

Business was booming! Operations continued in this manner until 1865, when Cooley retired. Cooley's exit left Farwell in

---

[71] Farwell, John V. (1911). *Some Recollections of John V. Farwell*, Page 44. https://nrrbook.com/RecollectionsofJVF

[72] Cooley, Farwell & Co. *Chicagology*. https://nrrbook.com/CooleyFarwellCo

control of the company, and he partnered with Marshall Field and Levi Leiter to create Farwell, Field & Co. This partnership was short-lived, however, as Field and Leiter left the following year to establish Field, Palmer, Leiter & Co., which would eventually be known as Marshall Field & Co.

John V. Farwell & Co.

Wholesale

DRY GOODS!

NOTIONS,

AND WOOLENS,

42, 44 and 46 Wabash Ave.

CHICAGO.

We make largest sales, because we sell cheaper than our neighbors.

Orders will receive prompt and careful attention.

We do not interfere with the retailer by retailing ourselves, but are content to sell only at wholesale.

The business was renamed John V. Farwell & Company, and a new, larger building was constructed at 72, 74, and 76 Wabash in the late 1860s. This building was destroyed by fire in 1870, rebuilt, and sadly destroyed again by the Great Chicago Fire of 1871. By this time, annual sales had reached $10 million, and their customer base went *"east as far as Detroit, south and southeast to Cincinnati, and beyond St. Louis, west to the Pacific Coast, and north to the British possessions (Canada today)...Within this radius are included seventeen States and every territory in the Union."*[73]

Following the Great Fire, many prominent Chicago merchants convened to determine the best way to rebuild. Farwell was called to speak, and said, *"Let us first ascertain how each one*

---

[73] Farwell Block IV. *Chicagology*. https://nrrbook.com/FarwellBlockIV

stands, and then ask such an extension as corresponds with the condition of each, and then make the ashes of the fire the basis for rebuilding with fire-proof buildings as near as possible. Such a program will gain the confidence and support of creditors to any needed extent, while to sit down and cry over spilt milk would only acquire their contempt instead of their needed help."[74] John V. provided leadership at a time when it was badly needed.

While recovering from the Great Fire, John V. Farwell & Co. attempted to acquire adjoining property to rebuild a larger structure at their Wabash Avenue location. The attempt failed, and operations were temporarily moved to a shed at 167 Michigan Ave. Concurrently, Farwell acquired the burned-down remains of a two-story warehouse at 247 & 249 Monroe Street. Shortly thereafter, a five-story structure measuring 200 feet by 190 feet was built in its place. Once

---

[74] Farwell, John V. (1911). *Some Recollections of John V. Farwell*, Pages 70-71. https://nrrbook.com/RecollectionsofJVF

again, the company quickly outgrew its space, and a new building was planned, this time on the entire city block between Monroe and Adams Street, right along the south branch of the Chicago River.

With annual sales having grown to $20 million, a grand structure 400 feet wide, 280 feet deep, and 120 feet tall was constructed in 1883. Built at a cost of nearly $1 million,[75] the building had six stories above ground and two basement levels. This structure was built to last, with basement walls twenty-four inches thick, first and second story walls twenty inches thick, and third through sixth story walls sixteen inches thick. Fulfilling John V.'s promise to build as fireproof as possible, the building was constructed of stone and brick, and each floor contained a two-and-a-half-inch iron pipe fire-suppression system, powered by a dedicated pump in the basement. Sixty barrels of fire-resistant paint were used to coat two and a half million square feet of interior woodwork. Five fire escape routes were built, with outlets on each story.

A 250-horsepower Corliss engine with a 20-foot flywheel generated electricity. Twelve steam-powered elevators were used to move goods and people. The plumbing consisted of 50 tons of lead pipe and 50,000 feet of gas pipe. The boiler room housed eight smoke-consuming boilers, which, producing six hundred horsepower, could be used separately or together to heat the building and power the elevators. The floors were covered with over one million feet of maple flooring.

"It was faced with red pressed brick and stone trimming, pierced with a thousand plate-glass windows, presents a magnificent appearance and is the largest, best arranged, best lighted, and most notable building for commercial purchases ever erected in this country...It is built throughout in the most substantial manner...Perhaps no firm in the United States is better and more favorably known in this country than J.V. Farwell & Co, importers and jobbers of foreign and domestic dry goods. Within the past

---

[75] Using a rough inflation factor of 30:1 from 1883 to 2025, this equals an investment of $30,000,000 today.

year they have moved into their new building, the largest, most extensive, and best arranged for their business in the East or West. It is the general verdict of merchants who have been in every similar institution in the land that this is the case, and the extent and completeness of this house has become so universally known that thousands of people consider their visit to Chicago only half made without going through the Farwell building."[76]

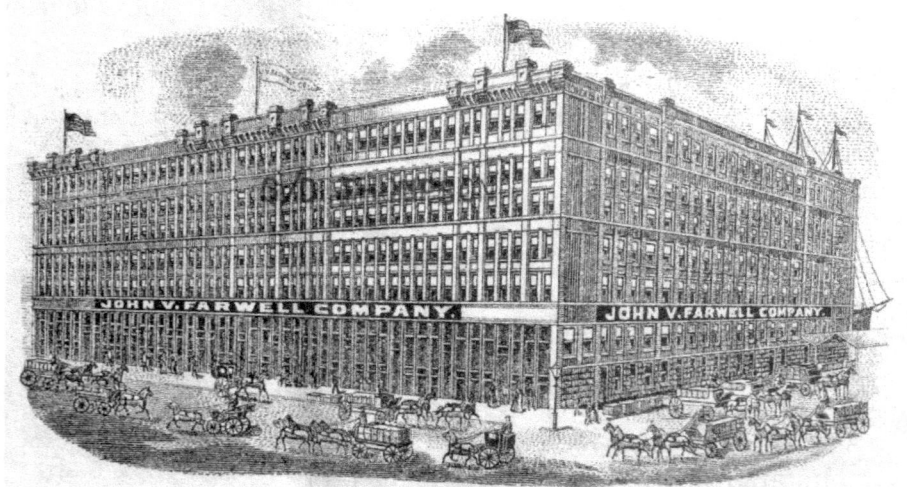

JOHN V. FARWELL COMPANY.
WHOLESALE DRY GOODS & CARPETS.
MONROE & MARKET STREETS.

Above: View of the 1883 building from the Market and Monroe Street intersection. Market Street is known as Wacker Drive today.

Farwell's new building was one of the largest buildings in the country at the time of completion. While most of the structure was occupied by John V. Farwell and Company, many of the storefronts were leased to other retailers. The west side of the building bordered the Chicago River, where ships could load and unload goods. A rail line was directly across the river, further assisting John V. Farwell and Company in the transportation of goods.

---

[76] Farwell Block IV. *Chicagology.* https://nrrbook.com/FarwellBlockIV

"It is questionable if there is another institution of the kind in this country that can make as good an exhibitor show a healthier growth, and is only one more illustration of the grand possibilities of Chicago's future."[77]

To put it simply, John Villiers Farwell had built a juggernaut. Late in his life, he would describe it as *"the greatest consuming center in the world for all the products in human industry."*[78]

Above: Looking southeast across the Chicago River, towards the northwest corner of the building,[79] circa 1910. A drawbridge was built here (Monroe St) in 1919 that still exists today. A freight depot sat across the Chicago River, directly opposite Farwell's building.

The company continued to operate out of this location for years to come. Annual sales reached $25 million (roughly $750 million in 2025 dollars after adjusting for inflation). John V. Farwell stepped down in the late 1880s to pursue other ventures, and his son, John V. Farwell, Jr., took his place. The

[77] Farwell Block IV. *Chicagology.* https://nrrbook.com/FarwellBlockIV

[78] Farwell, John V. (1906). *Corner Stones of Character: Some Ways of Making Them*, Page 276. https://nrrbook.com/CornerStonesofCharacter

[79] Farwell Block IV. *Chicagology.* https://nrrbook.com/FarwellBlockIV

change in ownership resulted in a minor name update to the John V. Farwell Company.

John·V·Farwell Company
CHICAGO

Operations continued under John V. Farwell, Jr.'s control until business began to decline. In September 1925, the company was sold to Carson, Pirie, Scott & Company (also known as Carson's). In 1953, the grand, 70-year-old building that made up the "Farwell Block" in Chicago was demolished. Notably, the Willis Tower, currently the tallest building in America outside of New York City, is situated diagonally across from where the John V. Farwell and Company building once proudly stood.

Carson's was acquired in 2006 by Bon-Ton, a holding company that owned multiple retailers. Bankruptcy followed, and the intellectual property was sold off. It later reopened as a virtual retailer known as BrandX, which still exists to this day.

*****

John V. Farwell was a highly successful businessman, but it is also worth discussing him on a personal level.

As noted earlier, Henry and Nancy Farwell instilled in their children the importance of hard work. More importantly, they instilled the value of a deep Christian faith. The family's first church service in Illinois was in 1839 at their doctor's cabin. *"The furniture was two double beds and some wood benches, and the organ was a live one- the doctor's wife. The minister was Luke Hitchcock, who drove twenty-one miles, and preached fifteen minutes, with a class meeting to follow. The audience was unique, more children than adults, but the music filled the room with a symphony of real worship that no hired choir can begin to equal, for it was a heart, as well as a vocal orchestra,* when *'Jesus, Lover of my Soul' was sung as only my mother could sing it."*[80]

The following year, a Christian camp was held in a grove near a clear spring, *"as if to remind thirsty ones of the Master's living water, springing up within them in answer to their request, like the woman's at Jacob's well, 'Give me of this water, that I thirst not, neither come hither to draw.' A large number drank of that living water, among whom were the Farwell boys, two of whom have gone where they 'thirst no more.' My own father led me to the altar the next day after I had heard my sainted mother praying for me before retiring for the night. They had learned their part of the sixth of Ephesians, 'Fathers, provoke not your children to wrath, but bring them up in the nurture and admonition of the Lord.' Blessed be their memory."*[81] At age 15, John V. gave his life to Jesus, and this would dramatically impact his future.

As you'll recall, John V.'s second job in Chicago was working for Hamilton & White, earning $8 per month. Of that, he gave $50 (more than half of his annual wages) towards the construction of the First Methodist Church of Chicago. In this church, he first met Dwight Moody, who had been spiritually mentored by Jerome Stillson (the same man who, years later, connected Farwell with the Hahns Peak Mining District). Initially, Farwell was annoyed that Moody would show up late for the sermon on a regular basis. However, guilt set in when he realized that Moody was faithfully out in the streets trying to gather people to attend the service. *"My criticism turned towards home with tremendous force, and why wasn't I doing something for others as well as this young man, was the basis of it. Judge not that ye be not judged, until investigation fixed the*

---

[80] Farwell, John V. (1911). *Some Recollections of John V. Farwell*, Pages 34-35. https://nrrbook.com/RecollectionsofJVF

[81] Farwell, John V. (1911). *Some Recollections of John V. Farwell*, Pages 35-36. https://nrrbook.com/RecollectionsofJVF

location of the beam in your own eye, instead of your brother's."[82]
Farwell and Moody would become very close, lifelong friends.

Above: Dwight Moody and J.V. Farwell stand behind 14 boys at their first Sunday School Class. The boys' "street names" were (Top, Left to Right) Red Eye, Darby the Gobbler, Smikes, Butcher Kilroy, Billy Bucktooth, Greenhorn, (Sitting, Far Right) Madden the Butcher, (Bottom, Left to Right) Indian, Jacky Candles, Black Stove Pipe, Sniderick, Old Man, Billy Blucannon, and Rag-Breeches Cadet.[83]

Moody went on to create and lead the largest Sunday School class in Chicago, known as the North Market Hall Sunday School. In 1860, Farwell was asked to be the Superintendent.

[82] Farwell, John V. (1911). *Some Recollections of John V. Farwell*, Page 101.
https://nrrbook.com/RecollectionsofJVF

[83] *Will it pay? D.L. Moody and J.V. Farwell's first Sunday school class, North Market Hall, Chicago, Ill.* The Library of Congress.
https://nrrbook.com/MoodyFarwellClass

He responded by attending a prayer meeting in Metropolitan Hall, standing before the large crowd, speaking his confession of Christ, and singing *"Praise God From Whom All Blessings Flow."* Moody's evangelism was contagious. After accepting the role, John V. traveled to New York for business. *"The trees and even the crooked rail fences seemed to be singing it with me, without interruption or intermission. Everywhere everything was vocal with its spiritual melody. The same intense religious interest prevailed in Hartford at the end of my journey, where at the first opportunity I gave this experience, emphasizing the necessity of confessing Christ at every opportunity before men, as the most effectual argument for Christianity, where coupled with witnessing of what He gives us in exchange for this simple act of saying - practically - that we have believed, and therefore, speak of faith's results."*[84]

Meanwhile, in 1858, the first Young Men's Christian Association (YMCA) in Chicago was formed and operated out of rented space on Randolph Street. Dwight Moody was heavily involved, even doing janitorial work, and eventually became President after Farwell himself had served two terms. As the organization grew, the need for its own building became apparent. In 1866, work began on a building at 148 Madison St, on a donated lot that was home to Farwell's previous residence. The cost of the building was $200,000, of which $30,000 was donated by John V. The remaining $170,000 was provided by sixty investors. Jerome Stillson served as the Superintendent of construction.

"The main hall building fronts on Broadway place. It has a depth of one hundred and twenty-one feet, with a width of eighty-one feet. This portion of the building is a plain, substantial structure, finished with the American building block. The cornice is of the same material, and gives a very imposing effect. There is another entrance from Broadway Place, nine feet wide, in addition to which there is a third entrance of a width of

---

[84] Farwell, John V. (1911). *Some Recollections of John V. Farwell*, Pages 102-103. https://nrrbook.com/RecollectionsofJVF

eight feet, on Madison Street, through a marble front building 45 feet wide by 100 feet deep, which was built by Mr. J.V. Farwell, in connection with the association buildings, and in the same general style. This gives three prominent entrances to the main hall, and all the other offices in various portions of the building. The hall stairways, being at three extreme corners, afford a most convenient exit, so that the hall can be vacated, when filled to its utmost capacity, in five minutes. The hall is capable of containing 3,500, giving to each person a convenient seat. The main hall floor occupies the whole space within the four walls of the building, and is of the dimensions 121 feet by 81 feet. The hall is 45 feet from floor to ceiling. The floor of the hall is level.

YOUNG MENS CHRISTIAN ASSOCIATION BUILDING.
Chicago

The galleries, of which there are two, incline greatly towards the platform, and are so arranged that all the seats have a good view of the speaker's position. The interior is plainly, but very neatly finished, and the ceilings are very tastefully frescoed. The galleries are finished with open balustrade fronts, and are furnished with stationary seats. The main floor will have two rows of stationary seats, with movable chairs between. The acoustic qualities of the hall are excellent. It is lighted from the ceiling by double reflectors.

The ground floor, beneath the hall, has space for five stores, while on the second floor are the library, reading room, lecture room, and other office rooms for the use of the association. On the floor above the hall are forty-two dormitories, intended for the use of young men who cannot afford more ample accommodations, besides a number of offices and a large hall which is now occupied by a gymnasium. The rooms of the whole building are heated by steam, well ventilated, and furnished with all the modern conveniences. The building is painted and grained throughout in imitation of oak and black walnut, alternative."[85]

The YMCA held a christening ceremony for its new building, the first dedicated YMCA structure in the world, on September 19, 1867. According to Farwell himself, *"I had intended to christen it 'Moody Hall' when the proper time came. But Moody got to his feet first and proposed with a modest speech that it be called 'Farwell Hall' - one of the mistakes of his life, for without his zeal in work for young men in the noon prayer meeting and elsewhere it never would have been erected."*[86]

And it was so. Farwell Hall was christened. While Farwell Hall was built to house the YMCA, it could also be rented out to religious or secular organizations for speeches, concerts, or other various purposes.

Tragically, disaster loomed.

On January 7, 1868, less than four months after opening, a fire broke out and destroyed Farwell Hall. *"A great calamity befell*

---

[85] Young Men's Christian Association Building (Farwell Hall). *Chicagology.*
https://nrrbook.com/YMCAFarwellHall

[86] Farwell, John V. (1911). *Some Recollections of John V. Farwell*, Page 109.
https://nrrbook.com/RecollectionsofJVF

DESTRUCTIVE FIRE.

The Young Men's Christian Association Building in Flames.

Farwell Hall and its Contents Reduced to Ruins.

Loss $347,100. Insurance $188,300

An Exciting Scene—Narrow Escape of More than Forty Persons from Death by Fire.

The Building Burning During the Entire Day—Surrounding Property in Danger.

Full Statement of Losses and Insurance.

Meetings of Stockholders and Pastors Yesterday and To-Day.

this city yesterday. The magnificent building known as Farwell Hall, which on Monday evening was filled with the beauty and fashion of the city, which gave back echoes to the strains of sweet music, lies this night a heap of broken bricks and powdered mortar."[87]

Only fifteen minutes after smoke was spotted coming out of windows on the top floor, the roof collapsed. The walls caved in shortly after that. The silver lining of the roof collapsing so quickly is that it pushed the fire down into the building's basement, where the brick foundation walls helped contain its spread.

As John V. would say just a few years later, after the Great Chicago Fire of 1871, there is no use crying over spilled milk. Immediately after the 1868 fire destroyed the building, a new Farwell Hall was constructed in its place, opening on January 19, 1869. *"The new building surpasses, in every respect, the old one. It is more substantially constructed, more care has been taken to remove it farther from danger by fire, and its beauty, capacity, and comfort are far greater. It is certainly a fine hall. Its dimensions are 120 feet long, 83 feet wide, and 57 in*

---

[87] Young Men's Christian Association Building (Farwell Hall). *Chicagology.* https://nrrbook.com/YMCAFarwellHall

height, from the main floor to the middle of the concave roof. Two tiers of galleries run all around the room. They are supported on iron columns, sufficiently near each other to insure strength and safety. The upper gallery has five tiers of seats on the sides, and six at the rear. The seats are so placed that from the very highest a full view of the platform and the middle of the main floor can be had...The roof is fire proof. There is no wood in it. It is a new style of roofing, formed of iron arches covered with iron wire in place of laths. The plastering fills in the intersects between the wires. There is no attic...The acoustic properties of the old hall were undoubtedly the best in the city, and as pains have been taken to construct the present room on strict scientific principles, it promises to be nearly as perfect...Such is the hall, the largest and finest in the United States, perhaps in the world."[88]

"The entire building will be heated by hot salt water circulating through tubes. In connection with the heating apparatus is a fan blower, to be used in creating a forced ventilation. The ventilating flues are judiciously arranged and distributed and the air ducts are roomy. By the use of the fan below, the room can be kept cool in the summer. The air in the main hall can be changed every twenty-three minutes, so that an audience can not suffer."[89]

Despite efforts to make the new Farwell Hall fire-resistant, it was again destroyed in the Great Chicago Fire of 1871. Moody was teaching there that evening. *"The night of the great Chicago fire found him in the Young Men's Christian Association hall, preaching from Paul's famous saying, 'This one thing I do, forgetting those things which are behind, and reaching forth unto those things which are before, I press toward the mark for*

---

[88] Young Men's Christian Association Building (Farwell Hall). *Chicagology.*
https://nrrbook.com/YMCAFarwellHall

[89] Young Men's Christian Association Building (Farwell Hall). *Chicagology.*
https://nrrbook.com/YMCAFarwellHall

the prize of the high calling of God in Christ Jesus.' In a few hours that hall and Chicago were in ashes."[90]

"One of the projectors of that enterprise, while the ruins were still smoking, wrote to a friend at the East concerning the great calamity that had fallen upon the city, declaring that 'those ashes were sown by our Heavenly Father, and that, therefore, the seed was good.' How has that prophesy been fulfilled in demonstration of the proposition therein contained? The burning of that building deprived the evangelists of their place of holding meetings in Chicago, and determined them to go to England until it should be rebuilt. The world knows the result in the spirit of revival that went with and followed them. And in the large cities of England and Scotland that seed has sprung up in magnificent buildings for Young Men's Christian Associations, as the legitimate fruit."[91]

Moody, whose home was also destroyed by the Great Fire, led the team that went to England for two years to evangelize. *"The destruction of this home, was as much perhaps, as that of the Y.M.C.A. building and the Illinois Street Church, the reason for Mr. Moody's great evangelistic tour in England. He left the ashes of one great city to make London - in due time (the greatest city in the world) the foundation as well as the capstone, physically speaking - of his evangelistic pyramid, which will last longer than the pyramids of Egypt, because built on Christ as chief cornerstone, with the unseen things of the spiritual kingdom in every living stone that has been, and will be built into it through his ministry, until time shall be no more."*[92]

While overseas, a third Farwell Hall was planned, and the core structure, measuring 180 feet by 190 feet, was built on the same

---

[90] Farwell, John V. (1906). *Corner Stones of Character: Some Ways of Making Them*, Page 41. https://nrrbook.com/CornerStonesofCharacter

[91] Farwell, John V. (1907). *Early Recollections of Dwight L. Moody*, Page 70. https://nrrbook.com/RecollectionsofMoody

[92] Farwell, John V. (1907). *Early Recollections of Dwight L. Moody*, Page 78. https://nrrbook.com/RecollectionsofMoody

site in only sixty days in 1874. *"Our young man (Farwell), in order to make the third Young Men's Christian Association building possible, gave the ground it occupies, which has kept on growing in value like the city and the association, until it has reached $750,000, thus making the last building possible with such a real estate basis for financing its erection; and with every prospect that within a quarter century or less it will be free from debt, and yield a princely income to carry on the work of educating young men in the building of character, that must help to mold society and the state under the influence of 'the inspiration of the Almighty Father', instead of the 'almighty dollar.'"*[93]

The famous hymn *"It Is Well With My Soul"* was performed for the first time in this building. This song was written by Horatio Spafford, who was a friend and financial supporter of Dwight Moody, after his four daughters, and nearly his wife Anna, drowned as the Ville de Havre steamship sank in the Atlantic Ocean in 1874 while en route to join Moody on his crusade in England. Horatio was delayed due to business commitments and planned to travel later. The French steamer, one of the most luxurious ships in the world, was returning from Philadelphia to France when it struck the iron-hulled Scottish ship Loch Earn and sank, killing 226. This tragedy was after Horatio and Anna suffered the death of their four-year-old son to scarlet fever, as well as devastating business losses from the Great Fire of 1871. Upon being saved and arriving in England, Anna sent a telegram to Horatio beginning *"Saved Alone. What shall I do?"* Horatio immediately boarded a ship to England to join his wife. There are conflicting reports on when Spafford penned the lyrics to his famous hymn. One account states that he wrote them while on board the ship to meet his wife. Another account says the lyrics were written two years later in his home. Phillip Paul Bliss, who was friends with Spafford, Moody, and Farwell, composed the music for the song and sang it for the first time at Farwell Hall on November 24, 1876. It remains a popular hymn to this day.

---

[93] Farwell, John V. (1906). *Corner Stones of Character: Some Ways of Making Them*, Page 38. https://nrrbook.com/CornerStonesofCharacter

OLD FARWELL HALL

Above: The interior of Farwell Hall, circa 1880s. Photo Credit to Encyclopedia of Chicago.

The third Farwell Hall was demolished in 1892 after the YMCA outgrew the space and moved elsewhere. *"For years this building was the headquarters of activities innumerable, and the influences which went out from the great center were potent factors in the moral and material upbuilding of the western metropolis...The hall was the assembly place for people interested in movements of all kinds, and the great concerts of the time were given there...Lectures and readings were given here without number...scores of men famous on the rostrum...But it is as a religious center that Farwell Hall will longest live in the memory of the people."*[94]

---

[94] Farwell, John V. (1911). *Some Recollections of John V. Farwell*, Pages 129-133. https://nrrbook.com/RecollectionsofJVF

Dwight Moody would go on to become one of the most well-known evangelists of all time. The Moody Bible Institute, founded in 1886, exists in Chicago to this day. Farwell was one of the original trustees.

Moody passed away in 1899 at the age of sixty-two. Speaking at the memorial service, Farwell made a touching tribute to his dear friend. He would later summarize his thoughts of that day with these words: *"It was a sad duty for me to stand on that platform, practically the creation of Mr. Moody's faith in God, and realize that the man, who under God was more to me than any other man that ever crossed my path, had gone out of the world forever, while so many, seemingly useless in comparison, were left behind. The only real refuge in such catastrophes is - Men Die, but God lives to perpetuate and complete the work of redemption for all men, through other men, who like Moody, can and will, consecrate their all to His service in that work."*[95]

As a successful and influential man in Illinois during the 1850s and 1860s, John V. naturally became acquainted with other prominent individuals, among them none other than Abraham Lincoln. After being elected President in November 1860, but before his inauguration in January 1861, Moody invited Lincoln to his church in Chicago, where he said this to 1,500 Sunday School children: *"There may be a president of the United States among these poor boys, depending on their learning and practicing well what is here taught."*[96] Lincoln and Farwell would cross paths again.

When discussing Lincoln and the 1860s, the Civil War naturally comes to mind. John V. Farwell, a significant supporter and supplier of the Union army, demonstrated his influence once again by becoming chairman of the Chicago-based Northwestern Branch of the United States Christian

---

[95] Farwell, John V. (1907). *Early Recollections of Dwight L. Moody,* Page 196. https://nrrbook.com/RecollectionsofMoody

[96] Farwell, John V. (1906). *Corner Stones of Character: Some Ways of Making Them,* Page 22. https://nrrbook.com/CornerStonesofCharacter

Commission, which had been established by the YMCA. This organization was created as a spiritual, secular, and medical ministry meant to boost the morale of Union soldiers. *"Besides visiting camps, maintaining diet kitchens, providing temporary lodging and employment bureaus, distributing tracts, Bibles, and secular reading material, the commission built a chapel at Camp Douglas for federal soldiers and prisoners. In all these activities John V. Farwell, who was a member of the United States Christian Commission, was a moving spirit, just as he had been in activities of the Y.M.C.A. His able and tireless confederates,[97] including Dwight L. Moody, Benjamin F. Jacobs, and Tuthill King, were instrumental in extending the usefulness of the commission and in aiding in the disbursement of over $100,000 for the comfort of soldiers."[98]*

John V. recalled one particular instance of helping the Union army: *"I remember buying at one time all the codfish in Chicago, as the best cure for prevalent bowel complaints in the army in the South, and at another all the woolen gloves and mittens for 'Pap' Thomas's army during a very cold snap in Tennessee. Neither of these purchases was regulation army rations or clothing, but they were much appreciated by sick and freezing soldiers."[99]*

Farwell's support of the Union army made him a target of Confederate soldiers. *"His activities were so well known that Confederate prisoners at Camp Douglas plotted to escape and to burn the John V. Farwell and Company store and the headquarters of the YMCA, supported by Farwell's philanthropy*

---

[97] The term "confederates" is used here to describe people that were working together. In this instance, it is not being used in affiliation with the Confederate Army.

[98] Pierce, Bessie L. (2007). *A History of Chicago*, Page 454.

[99] Farwell, John V. (1911). *Some Recollections of John V. Farwell*, Pages 73-74. https://nrrbook.com/RecollectionsofJVF

and headed by his evangelist friend Dwight Moody. Union soldiers discovered the conspiracy and thwarted it."[100]

Fast forward to 1864, and Lincoln was running for reelection. Farwell had been selected as an elector candidate from the 1st District of Illinois. As a potential elector, he felt called to write a letter of support for Lincoln.

"Having had my name placed before the people for Presidential Elector, without having sought the position, you will please allow me space in your columns to tell the people my views, without their having asked for them, so that no one shall have it to say, that he voted for an 'Abolitionist,' without knowing it. I always have been a 'Democratic-Republican Abolitionist,' though I never voted an Abolition ticket...I have a great love for the United States Government, because, as it is democratic in principle, republican in form, and now proposes that every man, woman, and child shall be free, from the bottom to the top of its population, I believe it is the only true exponent of liberty and progress for the human race...Its Constitution, and the Union of States under it, must be preserved at all hazards. Abraham Lincoln and the platform of principles he occupies are unequivocally pledged to this purpose; there, if the voice of the whole world were necessary to make him President, and I were empowered to cast the vote, I would cast it for this man, before all other good and true men who honor our times...We want no more a Buchanon in the White House, to allow his secretaries to steal our guns, our ships, our forts, and our money, as the price of his office. Professional politicians, and office-seekers, and brokers must be abolished. The people must learn to ask their best men to fill their offices, from justices of the peace to President of the Republic...If I am chosen as one of the Presidential Electors of the great state of Illinois, which has furnished the best President, and the best General, since the days of Washington, I herewith give notice to the voters that

---

[100] Lawrence, Ken. (April 2010). *The Farwell Brothers of Chicago: a postal and philatelic portrait.* Frajola. https://nrrbook.com/FarwellBrothers

shall so elect me, that I shall vote to place them securely in Abraham's bosom..."[101]

Lincoln won reelection in a landslide, winning 212 of the 233 possible electoral votes, including one from Farwell. Upon victory, Farwell wrote Lincoln from the Cooley, Farwell & Co. headquarters:

"Dear Sir— On thursday evening Bryan Hall was crowded, to rejoice over the 'Abolition victory,' & the tone of the meeting was decidedly executive & musical, & to my mind, suggested the idea that loyal Millions now demand one part, at least, of the music of the union, to be executed on one string — which 'reminded me of a story.' The pastor of a certain church (which had numerous elements of discord in it), was [illegible] for his constant exposition of Gospel goods — forgiving the full 'seventy times seven,' & some to spare, notwithstanding which a vote of the church always found the disorderly members against him, until finally an old gray headed exponent of the law requested prayer for the pastor that he might have 'grit added to his grace' in administering the affairs of the church, & then he was sure there would be entire harmony from the least unto the greatest— That is the point — the law as well as the gospel — grit as well as grace—

You are gloriously endorsed by the American people, with a timely suggestion underneath it, that grit & grace, go hand in hand, in dealing with home traitors, but especially grit— Give us general Jackson democracy for northern & southern leaders in the rebellion, & the gospel of peace will come in due-time, from the hands of their deluded followers, as well as from the hands of our boys in blue— The praying people of this & every other country; say now, & always have said, 'God bless Abraham Lincoln'— I expect the time will soon come — when your enemies, north & south, will utter the same prayer from honest hearts; — when time, that wonderful arbiter, with passing events for his arguments, shall have vindicated your character, as the

---

[101] Farwell, John V. (1911). *Some Recollections of John V. Farwell*, Pages 88-93. https://nrrbook.com/RecollectionsofJVF

*representative & father of the faithful band, who have pledged
their lives their property, & their sacred honor, for the
preservation of Washington's bequest to a grand & glorious
people — liberty & union, one & inseperable — for which
purpose, may God keep you, & the American people steadfast—
With the highest respect, I have the honor to subscribe myself,
one of the humble people, who always has, and always expects to
sustain you in your great work—*

*John V. Farwell
Elector 1st District — Ill—"*[102]

As the Civil War came to a close, the U.S. Christian Commission
was disbanded. A gathering of pastors and workers was held in
Chicago, with General Ulysses S. Grant presiding. John V.
Farwell was presented with a Bible and a letter signed by
Chicago's Christian workers, thanking him for his leadership of
that important ministry during the war. *"These are precious
memories of the results of work with Mr. Moody, for the Grand
Army of the Republic, in the most momentous era, in the making
of the world's history, in the maintaining of peace and good
government among all nations - beginning at Bunker Hill in 1776
and ending around Richmond in 1864."*[103]

On April 14, 1865, Farwell was in New York on business.
Meanwhile, Lincoln was in D.C., greatly strained by efforts that
ended the Civil War. *"At Mr. Lincoln's last cabinet meeting, and
just after the surrender of Lee's armies, he made the same
remark to one of his cabinet before the session, 'Something
terrible is going to happen. I had a dream last night just such as
I have had before all our greatest reverses.' The cabinet
proceeded with its business, and he was invited that day to go to
the theater in the evening, to divert his mind from the terrible*

---

[102] *Image 1 of Abraham Lincoln papers: Series 1. General Correspondence.
1833-1916: John V. Farwell to Abraham Lincoln, Saturday, November 12, 1864
(Congratulations and support).* The Library of Congress.
https://nrrbook.com/FarwellLincolnLetter

[103] Farwell, John V. (1907). *Early Recollections of Dwight L. Moody,* Page 48.
https://nrrbook.com/RecollectionsofMoody

strain (now relieved by victories) but depressed with this presentiment, and there met his death at the hands of an assassin."[104]

Lincoln's body would later lie in state in Chicago, and Farwell was in Springfield, Illinois, to see him buried.

"Washington built well, but he left the ugly artificial stone of slavery, built into the states' edifice, and in due time God sent Abraham Lincoln to remove with infinite patience and perseverance this rotten material from liberty's national temple, and put in its place 'liberty and equality for all,' before the law of love, and of the United States of America."[105]

A few years later, in 1869, Ulysses S Grant, now President, issued appointments to the Board of Indian Commissioners, which the Indian Appropriations Act had established. Created to reform government policy towards Native Americans and provide assistance to Native tribes, John V. Farwell was one of nine men from across the country appointed to this Board. Grant's appointees consisted of individuals known for their public service and high integrity, thus being unlikely to be bribed or influenced. Farwell certainly fit the mold.

In August 1870, John V. and his son, John V. Farwell Jr., aged eleven, traveled with Board of Indian Commissioners members John Lang and Vincent Colyer to southeast Kansas to persuade the Osage Indians to sign a treaty with the United States. The said treaty provided for the relocation of the Osage to a reservation in present-day Oklahoma in exchange for eight million acres of land in Kansas. Additionally, $1.25 per acre, or $10 million in total, would be held by the United States, with the income it generated going to the Osage.

---

[104] Farwell, John V. (1907). *Early Recollections of Dwight L. Moody,* Page 63. https://nrrbook.com/RecollectionsofMoody

[105] Farwell, John V. (1906). *Corner Stones of Character: Some Ways of Making Them*, Page 106. https://nrrbook.com/CornerStonesofCharacter

The group traveled by rail from Chicago to Topeka and then by prairie schooner to the Osage camp near present-day Independence, Kansas, where they joined Indian Agent Gibson and immediately began discussions with the Osage tribe. *"We had scarcely named our object, before the chief said to us 'White people are going there, same as here; if you can stop that, we will hold a council to consider the matter, and not otherwise.'"*[106]

Relations with the Osage were friendly, and a General Council was held where the terms of the treaty were presented. While there, Farwell received word notifying him that the John V. Farwell and Company store had burned down. *"While here a telegram came to me, informing me that the company's store at 72, 74 and 76 Wabash Ave had been burned up, not a very comforting piece of news, but success in our mission cured even this stroke of paralysis in business affairs."*[107]

Negotiations were held, and correspondence from the Osage was sent back to the President in Washington, D.C. *"We feel satisfied that it is your intention to deal fairly with us. We are assured that the bill is the work of our friends and not of speculators...We accept the bill as binding upon us and our people...the Government will bind itself to protect the Osages from intrusion upon their lands by treaty, as they have in the case of the Cherokee and other Indian nations."*[108]

The Osage, led by Chief Joseph, ultimately agreed to the terms and walked across the southern border of Kansas onto their 1.5 million-acre reservation in what would later become northeastern Oklahoma. In the early 1900s, significant oil deposits were discovered in the Osage territory, and the Osage

---

[106] Farwell, John V. (1911). *Some Recollections of John V. Farwell*, Pages 180-181. https://nrrbook.com/RecollectionsofJVF

[107] Farwell, John V. (1911). *Some Recollections of John V. Farwell*, Page 182. https://nrrbook.com/RecollectionsofJVF

[108] *Letter from the Secretary of the Interior, relative to the Osage Indians in Kansas.* The University of Oklahoma College of Law Digital Commons. https://nrrbook.com/OsageLetter1871

people became one of the wealthiest groups per capita on the planet.

Elsewhere, the Commission exposed rampant fraud by representatives of the U.S. Government towards the Indians. *"Our Commission sent detectives to the northern agencies to ascertain how vouchers were made up by the Indian agents. In one case, flour had been mixed with a white clay, rendering it unusable, and was rejected by the Indians. It was offered every delivery day, and vouchers made up, as thought it had been taken and used by the Indians. Cattle were driven over the scales several times so that a small drove became a thousand. A war was imminent, because of these cheats, and I wrote my brother, then a member of Congress, giving these facts, and stating that the Indian Office and Secretary of the Interior were certainly to blame for such action. These vouchers were paid after they had been rejected by our Commission, which resulted in the resignation of all but one of the members...The President soon had the resignation of the Secretary of the Interior, and there have been no Indian wars with the Northern tribes since then."*[109]

The evidence shows that John Villiers Farwell was a man of integrity and high regard, yet humble in nature. As a businessman, he was intelligent, capable, and resourceful. In his endeavors, he worked fairly and to the best of his abilities, treating those around him with respect. On a personal level, he was a man of deep faith, generous, and willing to help whenever and wherever he could. In short, John V. was a born leader. All of these qualities would be on display in the mountains of Colorado in the years to come.

---

[109] Farwell, John V. (1911). *Some Recollections of John V. Farwell*, Pages 185-187. https://nrrbook.com/RecollectionsofJVF

CHAPTER 3: BUGTOWN

"Success that involves moral bankruptcy may gain material kingdoms, and parcel them out - diminutively - to other failures in the process, but all must end in one common ruin, measured by the 'thou shalt' and 'thou shalt not' of the law of righteousness."[110]

-John V. Farwell

All mining companies need a camp for their employees. For Farwell's International Mining Company, this was International Camp, though it was commonly known as Bugtown, reportedly due to the company executives, or "Big Bugs," who resided there. It was also referred to as Amelia Town on a map drawn in 1876 by S.D.N. Bennett,[111] but Bugtown was the far more common nickname. While most historical references attribute this to Farwell and his executives, the Bugtown nickname traces its roots to the days of the Purdy Mining Company. *"Why it was called Bugtown deponent saith not, but the Purdy Mining Company of San Francisco and Denver are pretty proud of town, mines, name and all. It is situated about one mile and a half from Poverty Hill and covers a large number of valuable claims."*[112] From 1876 through 1878, the camp was further developed by Farwell. Wagon roads to the outside world were constructed, a sawmill was freighted in and put to work, and the seventeen-mile Farwell Ditch was dug with pickaxes, shovels, and dynamite. Bugtown was buzzing with activity!

---

[110] Farwell, John V. (1906). *Corner Stones of Character: Some Ways of Making Them*, Page 116. https://nrrbook.com/CornerStonesofCharacter

[111] "Map of Hahns Peak District, 1876" (July 4, 1900). *The Steamboat Pilot*, Page 4. https://nrrbook.com/SP-1900-07-04

[112] "Bugtown" (August 19, 1875). *The Laramie Daily Sentinel*, Page 3. https://nrrbook.com/LDS-1875-08-19

The exact location of Bugtown is unknown today, but we have some clues that can help us get pretty close. Historian Thelma Stevenson, in her book *Historic Hahns Peak*, had this to say: *"International Camp sprawled along the String Ridge between Way's and Nova Scotia Gulches northward to the bald mountain peak...At the same time Farwell's settlement was booming, a sister camp thrived about a mile westward by horse or foot travel. In those days it was called Poverty Flats...Today it is known as Hahns Peak Village..."[113]*

Similarly, the December 24, 1924, edition of the *Steamboat Pilot* said, *"It was a town of about twenty cabins located at the lower end of the ridge between Way's and Nova Scotia Gulches."[114]*

While Poverty Flats, labeled as Saphronia Town on Bennett's 1876 map,[115] was a typical rowdy mining town, Bugtown was nothing of the sort. John V. Farwell, true to his devout Christian faith, would not tolerate such debauchery. Drinking, gambling, dancing, and brothels were strictly forbidden. In fact, this camp was home to a Murphy Temperance organization,[116] a religion-based grassroots movement against alcohol consumption that emerged in the 1870s. We can assume that International Camp rules were similar to the

[113] Stevenson, Thelma. (2005, 4th Printing). *Historic Hahns Peak*, Page 14.

[114] Robert McIntosh, Pioneer Miner, Merchant and Rancher, is Dead. (December 24, 1924). *The Steamboat Pilot*, Page 5. https://nrrbook.com/SP-1924-12-24

[115] "Map of Hahns Peak District, 1876" (July 4, 1900). *The Steamboat Pilot*, Page 4. https://nrrbook.com/SP-1900-07-04

[116] "HOMEWARD BOUND. More About the Henn Peak Mines." (September 9, 1877). *Daily Rocky Mountain News*, Page 4. https://nrrbook.com/DRMN-1877-09-09

twenty-three rules later enforced at the legendary XIT Ranch[117] in Texas. Among these rules:

- Rule #12: Card playing and gambling of every description, whether engaged in by employees or by persons not in the service of the Company, is strictly forbidden on the ranch.

- Rule #13: In case of fire upon the ranch, or on lands bordering on the same, it shall be the duty of every employee to go to it at once and use his best endeavors to extinguish it, and any neglect to do so, without reasonable excuse, will be considered sufficient cause for dismissal.

- Rule #15: Employees are strictly forbidden from the use of vinous malts, spirituous, or intoxicating liquors during their time of service with the Company.

- Rule #20: Loafers, sweaters, deadbeats, tramps, gamblers, or disreputable persons, must not be entertained at any camp, nor will employees be permitted to give, loan, or sell such persons any grain or provisions of any kind, nor shall such persons be permitted to remain on the Company's land anywhere under any pretext whatever.

- Rule #22: It is the aim of the owners of this ranch to conduct it on principle of right and justice to everyone; and for it to be excelled by no other in the good behavior, sterling honesty and integrity, and general high character of its employees, and to this end it is necessary that the foregoing rules be adhered to, and

---

[117] The XIT Ranch was established in the 1880s on three million acres of land in the Texas panhandle given to John V. and Charles B. Farwell in exchange for constructing the Texas State Capitol building in Austin. With nearly 150,000 cattle, XIT became the largest ranch "under one fence" in the world. The XIT Ranch shut down operations in 1912, and parcels of land were sold off for decades, with the final piece selling in 1963. In 2022, John V. Farwell's great-great-great grandson, Drew Knowles, purchased land once owned by the original ranch and resurrected the XIT Ranch name.

the violation of any of them will be considered just cause for discharge.

- Rule #23: Every camp will be furnished with a printed copy of the rules, which must be nailed up in a conspicuous place in the camp; and each and every rule is hereby made and considered a condition and part of the engagement between the Company and its employees, and any employee who shall tear down or destroy such printed rules, or shall cause the same to be done, shall be discharged.

In short, company employees were expected to conduct themselves in a professional manner. Any rule-breaking would result in termination. As previously mentioned, if John V. expected this of his XIT Ranch employees in the 1880s, it is safe to assume he expected the same of his International Mining Company employees in the 1870s. The rules worked.

"One can but admire the excellent order prevailing here. The Sabbath is as quiet as that of a village in New England; the men are sober, intelligent gentlemen, and on Sunday dress up and go to church, whether they have a minister or not. The hour of worship is sacredly observed, and a prayer meeting of half an hour is held from 7:30 to 8 o'clock every evening. We have not seen, nor smelt, nor tasted liquor since we came here, and not being one of the dry kind, it has been a luxury to see in these wilds a community that is sober, industrious, and prosperous."[118]

International Camp was most certainly sober, industrious, and prosperous.

Naturally, one of the first buildings Farwell constructed in International Camp was a church. A reading room, which also served as a dining hall, was built and stocked with magazines

---

[118] Notes of Travel: Camp Life in Northwestern Colorado - Timber - Game - Resources, etc. - International and Hahns Peak Mining Camps. (July 27, 1877). *Daily Rocky Mountain News*, Page 4. https://nrrbook.com/DRMN-1877-07-27

and other reading material. Church services were held every Sunday.

"Religious services were conducted by Mr. Farwell, D.C. Stover and A.J. Bell, all being men connected with the company. They were not ordained ministers, but they conducted a Bible class each Sunday afternoon, and the miners assembled there to be instructed and to sing hymns and join in other forms of divine worship. This was a little out of the ordinary for a crude Western mining camp, but the services were well attended."[119]

"There was a boarding house with a dinner bell which also was used to call people to worship."[120]

Quick side note: In August of 1876, as the development of Bugtown and his mining company were underway, Farwell visited James Crawford, whose home was the only house in the area that would become Steamboat Springs. *"The Crawford family was the only family residing there, or within a radius of many miles...Mr. Farwell came down from his placer mines, and spent a couple of weeks at the Crawford home. While there he gave them many expositions and readings of the Scriptures, and afterwards sent them Sunday School literature and hymn books."*[121]

While Farwell and his Christian faith go hand in hand, so does his industrial spirit.

"International camp, we ought to have said sooner, has two framed houses, about twenty log cabins, a store wherein miners'

---

[119] Leahy, W. (March 24, 1915). Tales of Early Days. *The Steamboat Pilot*, Page 9. https://nrrbook.com/SP-1915-03-24

[120] Stevenson, Thelma. (2005, 4th Printing). *Historic Hahns Peak*, Page 14.

[121] Shelton, Ezekiel. (1906). *The Evolution of Christianity in Routt County*, Pages 4-6.

Note that this source is cited by Thelma Stevenson on page 18 of her book *Historic Hahns Peak*.

supplies are kept, a supply of drugs, and a physician, Dr. Durfee, of Chicago."[122]

International Camp was not just a camp. It was a full-fledged town. It would seem that Farwell, being the businessman that he was, would have set up, at a minimum, the general goods store as its own legal business entity. However, no records have been located to support this. The likely explanation is that the general goods store operated under the larger umbrella of the mining company. Two pieces of evidence support this. The first comes from the Historic Context of Routt County: *"John Farwell's International Camp, two miles from Poverty Bar, was an example of a company town."*[123]

The second piece of evidence supporting this is that Farwell lumped the sale of the general goods store with the rest of his mining operation when it was later sold. *"He made a proposition to James France, a banker of Rawlins, that if the latter would buy his store at invoice he would also give him a deed to all his Hahns Peak Properties."*[124]

More can be learned about Bugtown and the General Goods store from Joe Morin, who was a local involved in constructing the Farwell Ditch.

"Joe Morin, one of the old timers, reached the camp in 1877. He found at Bugtown a camp of 75 well-built log houses. There were big company stores and warehouses, one of the latter being 40x80 feet and filled with merchandise of all kinds...There were stacks of women's goods, when there were hardly three women in the country, one or two on Snake River and one at Steamboat Springs. There is probably not a store in Routt County at the

---

[122] Notes of Travel: Camp Life in Northwestern Colorado - Timber - Game - Resources, etc. - International and Hahns Peak Mining Camps. (July 27, 1877). *Daily Rocky Mountain News*, Page 4. https://nrrbook.com/DRMN-1877-07-27

[123] Historic Context of Routt County. (January 1994). Section 3-1. https://nrrbook.com/RouttHistoricContext

[124] Romantic Story of Hahns Peak's Golden Treasure. (March 18, 1932). *The Steamboat Pilot*, Page 5. https://nrrbook.com/SP-1932-03-18

present time which carries a larger stock of goods than Farwell put in nearly a quarter of a century ago. He was the pioneer road builder, ditch builder, city builder, saw mill man and merchant of what is now Routt County."[125]

We can assume the general store supplied not only Farwell's company but also all of the other people and miners in the area at the time. If there was one thing Farwell excelled at, it was selling goods.

The inhabitants of Bugtown and nearby Poverty Flats (known as Hahns Peak Village today) knew how to have a good time. The first recognition of Independence Day in Routt County took place in International Camp in 1877. With games, cannons, and a feast, it was a jubilant celebration!

"The first Fourth in the new county of Routt was observed with real earnestness. The miners from both these camps, Hahn's Peak and International, met at the latter place and spent the day as only earnest patriots can. At midnight it began in the free use of gun powder and anvils for cannons; at day-light a handsome flag was run up, furnished by A. J. Bell, of the International, who also tendered the men of both camps a dinner, which I need hardly say was accepted. Perhaps there is not often seen a more substantial bachelor dinner anywhere. At 10 a.m., the Declaration of Independence was read by Mr. Dibble, a miner, after which several toasts, among them the following:

Colorado— The Centennial State, gem of the mountain —May she lead in the production of the precious metals, as she does in the salubrity of her climate. Heaton, of Chicago, responding.

Routt County— The fairest of Colorado's many beautiful spots—May she be the banner county of the state. Response by S. C. Bassett.

---

[125] The New Camp of Farwell City: How J.V. Farwell Got Action on His Money. (June 6, 1900). *The Steamboat Pilot,* Page 5.
https://nrrbook.com/SP-1900-06-06

Hahn's Peak Mining Company— The Pioneer in this Park—May she Phoenix-like rise to greatness and wealth. Responded to by A. J. Bell.

Governor Routt — Colorado's wide-awake Executive—May he long live to enjoy the blessings he has so generously aided in bringing to all parts of the state. Response by Robert Hagar, of Chicago.

International Camp— May its generous promoters be successful in placing it in the front rank of mining enterprises. Response by D. C. B. Durper.

The Miners of the Rocky Mountains, hardy, earnest, true men— May every one of them reach the pay streak. Response by A. J. Bell.

There were others, such as the day, country, etc., with a vote of thanks for the generous dinner.

Then came the sports of the day—sack race, shooting (target), base ball; to wind up at the neighboring camp at night with a ball. Whatever may happen at night, one thing is quite evident, the absence of all liquor on this gala day was a source of great rejoicing to all friends of good order, and could our friend Governor Routt have been present, he would have felt proud of his namesake. While these mines are not the Black Hills, perhaps, nor in fact a poor man's camp, for the reason that it can only be developed by expensive hydraulic works, yet it now seems to be a settled fact that this county will take its place fairly among the mineral producing counties of Colorado, and has, we think, passed the time of dangerous experiment. So mote it be."[126]

Despite living in a remote part of Colorado, Farwell's employees were not shut off from the outside world. The Hahns Peak Post Office was established in 1876 in International

---

[126] ROUTT COUNTY. How the Fourth was Observed at Hahn's Peak. (July 11, 1877). *Daily Rocky Mountain News*, Page 4.
https://nrrbook.com/DRMN-1877-07-11

Camp, with Dr. Durfee serving as the original postmaster. Robert McIntosh took over this role in 1877. Harry Hernage was the mail carrier with weekly service to Rawlins, Wyoming.

Serving as further proof of its regional influence, International Camp was voted as the initial county seat, albeit briefly. Routt County was established on January 29, 1877, on land that was initially the western portion of Grand County. Hayden, a *"rural village of two cabins,"*[127] being roughly in the center of the new county, was named as the original county seat by governor-appointed county commissioners Thomas Iles, Gordon Smart, and A.J. Bell.[128] However, Section 41 of the Revised Statutes of Colorado 1868 states the following: *"Whenever any county shall be organized hereafter, the qualified voters thereof are hereby empowered to select the place of their county seat by a vote at the first election held in the county for the choice of county officers. For that purpose each voter may designate on his ballot the place of his choice for the county seat; and when the votes are canvassed the place having a majority of all the votes polled shall be the county seat; and public notice of said location shall be given within thirty days by the county commissioners, by posting up notices in three public places in the county."*[129]

Thus, a vote was held in the fall of 1877 to allow the people of the newly formed Routt County to choose their county seat. *"At the ensuing election in 1877, 96 votes were cast for county seat, divided as follows: Winsor, a location near the present site of Craig, 35; Steamboat Springs, 2; Hahns Peak, 12; International Camp, 47."*[130]

---

[127] Routt County - A Review of the Late Election, Etc. (October 16, 1877). *Daily Rocky Mountain News,* Page 4. https://nrrbook.com/DRMN-1877-10-16

[128] Leckenby, Charles. (1945). *Tread of Pioneers,* Page 99. https://nrrbook.com/TreadofPioneers

[129] *The Pacific Reporter,* Volume 42. (1896). Page 1,042. https://nrrbook.com/PacficReporterV42

[130] Leckenby, Charles. (1945). *Tread of Pioneers,* Page 99. https://nrrbook.com/TreadofPioneers

Despite receiving the most votes, county commissioners concluded that International Camp was not victorious, as it fell two votes shy of a majority. Section 43 of the 1868 Statutes states: *"If no place has a majority of all the votes polled in either of such elections for the location or change of the county seat, it shall be the duty of the county commissioners, within one month after any such election, to order a special election and give ten days' notice thereof, in each township in the county, at which election votes shall be taken by ballot, the same as at the general election, and if no place then have a majority of all the votes, the county seat shall not be changed until the next general election, when a vote may again be taken, as provided in section forty-one."*[131]

The special election was never held, however, and the subsequent vote took place the following year in 1878. Only 51 votes were cast, with 31 for Hahns Peak, this time including International Camp.[132] The voters had spoken, but it was not until the following spring that the move was formalized. *"Due to dissention between International Camp ("Bug Town") and Hahn's Peak residents...the move took place May 1, 1879. County records were tied in flour sacks and moved by saddle horse."*[133]

While Hahns Peak was the name listed on the ballot, county records were actually moved to International Camp. The first Commissioner meeting in the new location was held on May 5, 1879. Among the proceedings of that meeting was an order documenting the *"notice of the establishing county seat at Hahns Peak posted in three prominent places in the County."* In addition, *"Ordered that a warrant be drawn in favor of A.J. Reynold for service rendered in transportation of County*

---

[131] *The Pacific Reporter,* Volume 42. (1896). Page 1,043.
https://nrrbook.com/PacficReporterV42

[132] Robert McIntosh, Pioneer Miner, Merchant and Rancher, is Dead. (December 24, 1924). *The Steamboat Pilot*, Page 5. https://nrrbook.com/SP-1924-12-24

[133] *History of Routt National Forest 1905-1972.* (May 4, 2020). Page 16.
National Forest Service Library. https://nrrbook.com/HistoryofRNF

Records."[134] "Jimmy Dunn and William Leahy were on their way to Hahns Peak from the lower country and assisted Reynolds."[135]

County records were moved from International Camp to Hahns Peak in 1880, when International Camp was largely abandoned. *"When the records were moved from Hayden to International Camp in the spring of 1879, they had been installed in a small log cabin owned by the placer company, but formerly occupied by William Morgan. When they were taken to Poverty Bar they were located in a log cabin which was standing up to a few years ago, and probably is yet, being opposite the last Hahns Peak court house and until recent years used as a schoolhouse."[136]*

The story does not end there. As Steamboat Springs grew in population and influence, calls to move the county seat increased. In 1883, another county seat vote was held with the following results: Bear River Bridge, 16; Steamboat Springs, 12; Hahns Peak, 17; Mouth of Fortification Creek, 43; Yampa (now known as Craig), 5; and Hayden, 2. Mouth of Fortification Creek and Yampa were generally viewed as the same location, and their combined 48 votes constituted a majority (by one vote) of the 95 votes cast. Residents of those locations celebrated. However, the commissioners were still located in Hahns Peak, and they refused (likely playing political games) to acknowledge Mouth of Fortification Creek and Yampa as the same location. Thus, there was no majority winner, and Hahns Peak remained the county seat.

Another vote was held in 1887, again involving political games. This time, Hayden and Steamboat Springs were rivals. *"...the fight was so bitter between Steamboat Springs and Hayden that as a political move the nomination was thrown to Lay, it*

---

[134] Routt County Commissioner Meeting Minutes. (May 5, 1879). https://nrrbook.com/RCMinutes-1879-05-05

[135] Robert McIntosh, Pioneer Miner, Merchant and Rancher, is Dead. (December 24, 1924). *The Steamboat Pilot*, Page 5. https://nrrbook.com/SP-1924-12-24

[136] Robert McIntosh, Pioneer Miner, Merchant and Rancher, is Dead. (December 24, 1924). *The Steamboat Pilot*, Page 5. https://nrrbook.com/SP-1924-12-24

evidently being the intention to select a place so far down the river that it could not be successful, but even then it nearly succeeded. The upper country refused to support Lay. The election was held November 8, 1887, and resulted: Steamboat Springs 215, Hahns Peak 13, Lay 210, Hayden 2, Rosedale 1. No choice."[137] Steamboat Springs fell six votes short of a majority, and Hahns Peak again remained as the county seat, despite only receiving thirteen votes.

In March of 1894 (more than sixteen years after the original 1877 election), Ephus Donelson filed a lawsuit to have the county seat moved back to Hayden. He believed that since a special election was not held following the 1877 election, the 1878 election was invalid. Furthermore, because the 1877 election did not have a majority winner, the county seat should still be Hayden.

Robert McIntosh was called as a witness in the case, along with James Crawford, Dave Miller, and Alfred McCargar. *"By them it was shown that Poverty Bar, Bugtown, International Camp and Whisky Gap were all generally regarded as Hahns Peak. Mr. McIntosh said he was postmaster in 1877, that the office was called Hahns Peak, but that it was located at International Camp. He said he came to the county in 1876 and that some time in January, 1877, the Hahns Peak post office was established at International Camp 'done by Chicago people; done by Andrew Jackson Bowles; he was the main instigator.' He said Dr. Durfee was the first postmaster and that he (McIntosh) succeeded him. In the winter the post office was moved into his cabin, while in the summer, while he was in the hills, it was moved into the store. No permission was asked of the government to make these changes. But in 1880, when Mr. McIntosh moved over to take charge of the Poverty Bar workings he asked and was granted permission by the government to move the post office from*

---

[137] Leckenby, Charles. (1945). *Tread of Pioneers*, Pages 100-101.
https://nrrbook.com/TreadofPioneers

International Camp to what then became the town of Hahns Peak."[138]

Donelson's lawsuit failed, as it was ultimately determined that votes cast for International Camp and Hahns Peak in 1877 were votes cast for the same location due to their close proximity. *"This leaves the sole inquiry whether, when the voter cast his ballot for International Camp, he intended to vote for Hahn's Peak, as did the voter who put that name or designation on his ballot...We should therefore conclude that, in 1877, Hahn's Peak had been chosen by the voters as the permanent location of their county seat, and that the votes which were cast for Hahn's Peak and International Camp were cast for the same place, and should have been counted by the board, and that they had the authority under the acts then in force to locate the county seat at that spot."[139]*

A similar case elsewhere in Colorado was used as the basis for this opinion. *"The Colorado Supreme Court decided that votes cast for Grand Lake and Grand Lake West Side should be counted as having been cast for the same place, and that any spot on Grand Lake could be selected by the commissioners as the point for the erection of the county offices and the location of the records."[140]*

With this result, the original 1877 vote was affirmed as having chosen a winner, as the 59 combined votes for International Camp (47) and Hahns Peak (12) were a clear majority of the 96 votes that had been cast.

Yet another county seat battle ensued in 1898. *"The petition for a vote on the county seat was presented to the county*

---

[138] Robert McIntosh, Pioneer Miner, Merchant and Rancher, is Dead. (December 24, 1924). *The Steamboat Pilot*, Page 5. https://nrrbook.com/SP-1924-12-24

[139] *The Pacific Reporter,* Volume 42. (1896). Page 1,043. https://nrrbook.com/PacficReporterV42

[140] *The Pacific Reporter,* Volume 42. (1896). Page 1,043. https://nrrbook.com/PacficReporterV42

commissioners on July 8, and after a full investigation the commissioners found that 130 legal tax payers had signed said petition more than was necessary or requisite in calling an election, and therefore the county clerk was ordered to give due notice of a county seat election to be held on November 8."[141] The results of the vote were as follows: Steamboat Springs, 654; Hayden, 558; Hahns Peak, 147; Trull, 3; and Maybell, 1. Once again, there was no majority, and Hahns Peak survived.

The numerous battles over the county seat location ultimately led to the division of Routt County. *"Senator John S. Cary, representing the 13th District, introduced a measure in the 18th General Assembly creating the County of Moffat with Craig as the county seat. It was duly passed by senate and house, L. Boyd Walbridge of Meeker then being the representative in the lower house, and was approved by Governor Shafroth February 27, 1911. The county (Routt) seat matter was again brought to a vote in the general election of 1912 and Steamboat Springs was an easy winner."*[142] After thirty-three years, Hahns Peak's reign as county seat was over.

Sadly, International Camp disappeared as quickly as it formed. In 1879, a massive forest fire, started by the Utes, ravaged the area. J.B. Donaldson, Superintendent for Farwell's company at the time, wrote in a letter to the U.S. General Land Office *"the forest fire that began near Sand Mountain early in May last, has been burning ever since, and has finally culminated, after sweeping all over that section of country, in a grand attack on our mining property on String Ridge, sweeping all before it, and causing us very serious expenses to keep it out of this camp. Besides, it is now sweeping everything before it along the line of our 17-mile ditch, on which we have several miles of fluming. The fire is so hot and the smoke is so dense that we cannot reach*

---

[141] ELECTION IS ORDERED. (July 13, 1898). *The Steamboat Pilot,* Page 1. https://nrrbook.com/SP-1898-07-13

[142] Leckenby, Charles. (1945). *Tread of Pioneers,* Page 102. https://nrrbook.com/TreadofPioneers

many of our flumes to know at present how many of them are destroyed. If any are left it will be nothing short of a miracle."[143]

While the camp itself was saved (Rule #13 surely came into play), Farwell decided, for various reasons (details to come in Chapter 6), that it was time to move on. He sold his operation, including the general goods store, to banker and general goods merchant James France of Rawlins, Wyoming, and J.B. Donaldson of Denver. France and Donaldson then leased it to Robert McIntosh, who extended the ditch one mile to Little Mountain. At this time, Bugtown was largely abandoned. Miners moved to Poverty Flats (present-day village of Hahns Peak). The post office relocated there, as well. *"During this transition, houses were moved from abandoned Bugtown to Poverty Flats. The Hahns Peak Post Office was relocated there and a three-gabled, log building was purchased to house the court records and activities."*[144]

A forest fire in 1899 destroyed what remained of Bugtown. *"Bugtown soon fell into decay. Some of the houses were moved over to Poverty Bar, now Hahns Peak. The ruins of others were destroyed by fire last year, thus wiping out the last evidence of the rise and fall of Bugtown."*[145]

The mining camp that once held the majority of Routt County's population was no longer just deserted, but totally destroyed, only twenty-three years after Farwell arrived in the area.

---

[143] *History of Routt National Forest 1905-1972.* (May 4, 2020). Page 44. National Forest Service Library. https://nrrbook.com/HistoryofRNF

[144] Stevenson, Thelma. (2005, 4th Printing). *Historic Hahns Peak*, Page 15.

[145] The New Camp of Farwell City: How J.V. Farwell Got Action on His Money. (June 6, 1900). *The Steamboat Pilot,* Page 5. https://nrrbook.com/SP-1900-06-06

Above: Hahns Peak Post Office. Photo credit to the Hahns Peak Historical Society.

Above: Original three-gabled Routt County Courthouse in Hahns Peak. Image Credit to Hahns Peak Historical Society.

CHAPTER 4: HANS PEAK WAGON ROAD COMPANY

"How foolish to choose self first as the center and circumference of all our mental, moral and business aims, instead of Christ and His work, when one gives us a hundred-fold more of the enjoyments of this life and the life everlasting, while the other, even to a man who trusts in Christ for personal salvation, and does nothing for others, loses the best riches of this world and of the next, because his quest was only for self, and not like that of the good Samaritan, who spent time and money for a needy man, while the priests and Levites passed by on the other side of the road - priests and Levites only in name. Such will have no bank account in Heaven."[146]

-John V. Farwell

John V. Farwell knew that International Camp and his gold-mining enterprise would fail without two crucial connections to the outside world. First was the Hahns Peak Post Office, discussed in the previous chapter. Established in 1876, this post office provided weekly service, presumably on horseback, to Rawlins, Wyoming. Second, infrastructure was needed for the efficient transportation of people, goods, and materials to and from the mining district. To address this, Farwell envisioned wagon roads connecting the mining district to Laramie, Wyoming, and to a supply route linking Rawlins, Wyoming, to the White River Indian Agency. Why Laramie?

The answer seems simple enough. On May 4, 1868, Union Pacific completed railroad tracks to Laramie, connecting it to a vital east-west route that extended to Cheyenne, Omaha,

---

[146] Farwell, John V. (1906). *Corner Stones of Character: Some Ways of Making Them*, Pages 275-276. https://nrrbook.com/CornerStonesofCharacter

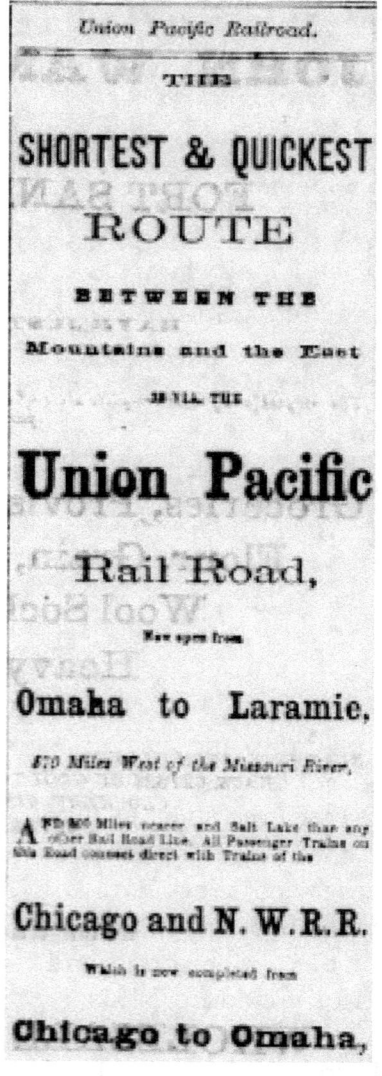

Chicago, and beyond. The first passengers arrived that very day, and regular service began the following week.

This route promised to *"save 300 miles stage travel and 48 hours time"*[147] for passengers crossing the Great Plains. Additionally, "Pullman's Palace Sleeping Cars" were promised for night trains. These cars were luxurious units, *"wider and taller than anything that came before and used trucks with rubberized springs to reduce bouncing and shaking. Thick curtains or silk shades covered the windows and chandeliers hung from the ceiling, which was painted with elaborate designs. The walls were covered in a rich dark walnut, the seating was covered in plush upholstery, and the fixtures were brass. During the day, the sleeper looked like a regular, if especially lavish, passenger car, but during the night it transformed into a 2-story hotel on wheels. Seats were unfolded into lower sleeping berths, while upper berths, instead of lowering from the ceiling on pulleys, folded out from it. Sheets and privacy partitions were installed by Pullman Porters to complete the effect."*[148]

---

[147] Union Pacific Advertisement. (May 19, 1868). *The Frontier Index,* Page 1. https://nrrbook.com/FI-1868-05-19

[148] Stamp, J. (December 11, 2013). Traveling in Style and Comfort: The Pullman Sleeping Car. *Smithsonian Magazine.* https://nrrbook.com/Pullman

This new connection to Laramie was of particular interest to those shipping goods across the plains towards the Rockies. From the same ad: *"The attention of shippers of freight for the Mountains is particularly called to the opening of the great Platte Valley Route to Laramie and its connections. 500 miles of 'wagon transportation' is saved in sending goods via Omaha. Reliable freight lines are at all times prepared to transport goods from the western terminus of this road to all points in the Mountains. General handling and quick time guaranteed. Rates always as low, and changes fewer, than by any other route."*

Fast forward to the mid-1870s, and Laramie was the nearest railroad hub for John V., who undoubtedly experienced many luxurious rides across the Midwest aboard the famous Pullman cars. Similar to a direct flight today, the Union Pacific route from Chicago to Laramie was the quickest, most efficient method of travel for Farwell.

Above: Laramie, Wyoming, circa 1875.[149]

Ever the businessman, John V. Farwell sought to minimize operating and shipping costs for his growing company and town. A direct route, capable of accommodating freight

---

[149] Laramie in 1875. Cavalryman Steakhouse. https://nrrbook.com/Laramie1875

wagons to the Hahns Peak Mining District from Laramie, promised to provide lower shipping costs than alternative destinations such as Rawlins, Wyoming, or Georgetown, Colorado.

"Freight from Laramie can be hauled for two and one half cents per pound - from Rawlins five cents, besides saving 130 miles railroad carriage and several toll bridges...We have been informed that the miners here chiefly sought an outlet to Laramie instead of Rawlins or Georgetown because they are unanimously determined that they will not pay enormous tolls to get their gold to market and their supplies here. Two thousand dollars more will make the road to Laramie good, and reduce freight to about 1 ½ cents per pound, and that will be accomplished by the liberality of Laramie and the enterprise of Routt County. The trade from this county will steadily and rapidly increase and Laramie will reap a rich reward. She has all now and can easily control it for many years. The motto of Routt County is 'Free Roads to Market.' That she has, and is determined to hold it. Clear Creek county, Colorado and Denver may as well give it up entirely or build a good free road from the end of the Georgetown branch of the C.C. road to Hahn's Peak, that, or not one cent of trade is the fixed policy of miners here."[150]

Farwell took it upon himself to construct this connection to Laramie and established the Hans Peak Wagon Road Company to make it happen. The spelling of Hans is what was used in the legal documents establishing this company, further documenting the evolution of the use of Henn, Hans, Hahns, Hann, etc.

Two entities were established under the name Hans Peak Wagon Road Company: one in Wyoming and one in Colorado. Both were formed on July 5, 1876, just one day after the deal with the Purdy Mining Company was signed. The swiftness of these actions serves as evidence of John V.'s commitment to

---

[150] Notes of Travel: Camp Life in Northwestern Colorado - Timber - Game - Resources, etc. - International and Hahns Peak Mining Camps. (July 27, 1877). *Daily Rocky Mountain News*, Page 4. https://nrrbook.com/DRMN-1877-07-27

his new venture. Company officers for both wagon road entities were Andrew J. Bell, Daniel C. Stover, John W. Bell, and James H. Stover.

Hans Peak Wagon Road Company executives presented their vision for this new route to Laramie businessmen on September 5, 1876, and it was immediately apparent that this road would provide access to potentially huge economic benefits for them. Per the 1870 census, Laramie's population was only 2,957. It was a small but growing town, and the proposed wagon road offered tremendous potential. A direct road to one of the first industrial enterprises on the western slope of the Rockies would surely pay dividends long into the future.

"An impromptu meeting of a large number of our business men was held in Col. Downey's office Tuesday evening to hear a report from Messrs. Bell and Stover, who are in from the Hans Peak mines. These gentlemen have been for some time engaged in opening and working the extensive placer mines in that region.

They stated that their nearest point out to the railroad, and best point from which to receive supplies, was Laramie City, and they asked the aid of our citizens to build a road between here and there. They estimated that it would be fifty miles nearer to this point than to Rawlins, with a much better road, and great advantages as an outfitting point. Mr. Bell, who is a thoroughly reliable man, submitted an estimate of the cost and the amount of aid they required from us. Nearly this whole amount was contributed in a minute by those present - Messrs. Ivinson, Holliday and Downey contributing a hundred dollars each.

We have before called attention to this matter, and we regard it as the most important enterprise ever brought to the notice of our city (note - big words considering the Union Pacific railroad came to town just eight years earlier!). *The distance from here to Hans Peak is estimated to be seventy-five or eighty miles. It not only opens direct connection with the placer mines, but will open a much shorter and more direct route clear to the White*

River agency. It also runs all the way through a rich mining and pastoral region, including the mines on the Big Laramie, the North Park, the Middle Park, Hot Sulphur Springs, etc.

The region through which this road will pass is destined to support a large population, and will be a permanent and lasting resource to our city. We were especially gratified at the public spirit and generosity manifested on that occasion, and the disposition to establish friendly relations and extend a helping hand to those who are laboring to develop the resources which surround us. All this is rich seed which will bring forth rich fruit in the near bye and bye."[151]

The perceived economic potential of the Hahns Peak area cannot be overstated. The August 18, 1875 edition of the *Rocky Mountain News Daily* stated: *"Millions in Sight, but Thousands Needed for Development - A Country Within Three Days Travel from Denver that will 'Discount' the Black Hills for Everything - Past and recent discoveries - A Region Rich in Wild Fruits and Game...It is simply that in years to come there will be one of the most important placer mining camps at the foot of Hann's Peak America has ever known. The gold is here in quantity, and will be taken out in quantity."[152]*

Proving their excitement about this opportunity (in addition to the estimated costs being covered in one minute) was the fact that Laramie businessmen immediately began planning this road. How quickly did this happen? The report of their initial planning work was printed in the very newspaper that reported the proposal for the road itself.

"We have spoken before of the fact that active measures were being taken toward securing at once the shortest and most practicable route to the miners in the North Park, and now the matter is satisfactorily arranged so that there is no longer any

---

[151] A New Opening for Laramie. (September 11, 1876). *Laramie Weekly Sentinel*, Page 1. https://nrrbook.com/LWS-1876-09-11

[152] "The Snake River Mines" (August 18, 1875). *Daily Rocky Mountain News*, Page 4. https://nrrbook.com/DRMN-1875-08-18

doubt about its successful operation. Mr. Bell, who has been giving the subject his undivided attention here for some time, yesterday sent Mr. M.N. Grant of this place, with instructions to start a party from the Hans Peak mine immediately upon his arrival to construct a good road as they come towards Laramie. Money has already been raised here among our business men to defray all necessary expenses, and Mr. Bell has telegraphed for all goods to be sent here for his mines, and from this point they will be sent over the new route, to their destination. It is now estimated that at the outside the party will be here from the North Park with a wagon road completed behind them in ten days. The opening of this new source of business to our mere hands was recognized as an important one at a glance, as is witnessed by the prompt action taken by them as soon as the subject was presented to them by Mr. Bell, and this road to the mines with which he is connected will only be the starting point toward securing the trade with mines in that neighborhood and near the route, all of which will ultimately become tributary to Laramie. Not only is this new arrangement advantageous to us, but it will be of great value to those who own mines in the North Park, assisting those who are already operating, and those who have waited until something of this kind should be done to assist them in getting supplies to their camp as speedily, and at as small cost to themselves as possible. Every avenue of this kind opening up a new country of known resources, bringing those sections into ready communications with us is a permanent source of assistance to Laramie, and one that will return a good rate of interest for every dollar invested. Of course this is but one step, but is unquestionably a step in the right direction, and will serve to assist materially in bringing to notice the superior natural advantages of the Park."[153]

A week later, a report in the *Laramie Weekly Sentinel* stated: "*W.H. Holliday and W.O. Downey have located the bridge for the new route to the Hans Peak mines, and Mr. Downey will go out today to make the necessary estimates. The bridge will be*

---

[153] Enterprise. (September 11, 1876). *Laramie Weekly Sentinel*, Page 4.
https://nrrbook.com/LWS-1876-09-11

located at the crossing of the Big Laramie, near Leroy's Ranche."[154]

An update was reported in the paper the following week: *"A meeting of the citizens was held at Col. Downey's office yesterday, to bear the report of M.N. Grant, in relation to the Snake River Road. Mr. Holliday acted as chairman. Mr. Grant reported between here and the west side of North Park, there was required from 260 to 300 feet of corduroy*[155] *and about three quarters of a mile of grading done. The following resolution was on motion adopted:*

Resolved, That the Road Committee be instructed to procure the necessary teams, employees and supplies, and proceed at once to locate and construct the road from Laramie toward Hauntz' Peak Mines (note - another new spelling!), *and proceed until the party of construction working from the other terminus of the route is met, when the portion of the road, from the meeting point west, shall be passed over by the said committee, who, upon their return shall make a report of the condition of the whole road and an estimate of the relative expense of each portion of construction, when the Executive Committee shall adjust the appropriation money to be paid.*"[156]

To recap, in the span of three weekly editions of the *Laramie Weekly Sentinel*, reports of the initial proposal for a road, a follow-up meeting of Laramie's business leaders, a scouting trip to determine the location of a key bridge, and a resolution to approve the road and begin construction were all printed. The speed at which this happened is unfathomable in today's world!

---

[154] From the Daily of Wednesday. (September 18, 1876). *Laramie Weekly Sentinel*, Page 2. https://nrrbook.com/LWS-1876-09-18

[155] Corduroy road construction consisted of laying logs perpendicular to the direction of travel. This method was used to create a stable surface when traversing wet or unstable terrain.

[156] The Hans Peak Road. (September 25, 1876). *Laramie Weekly Sentinel*, Page 3. https://nrrbook.com/LWS-1876-09-25

One interesting note from the September 25, 1876, *Sentinel* article discussed John W. Bell's zeal for evangelism while in Laramie. Similar to John V., the wagon road company executives were devout Christians. *"A newspaper puff (in the ordinary acceptation of the term) of a man for his christian zeal and piety would be, to him who possesses these qualities, one of the most repugnant things to which he could be subjected, and it is perhaps impossible to refer to the subject at all so as not to cause an unpleasant feeling. Once when the Rev. Rowland Hill had preached an excellent sermon, as he was leaving the church one of his parishioners took occasion to remark to him - 'Mr. Hill, that was a most wonderful discourse.' 'Yes' - replied the good man, half sorrowfully - 'the devil informed me of that fact before I left the pulpit.'*

Mr. Bell has gone away now and left us, and we trust we shall not wound his feelings, by congratulating the religious portion of the community upon the valuable acquisition to their ranks of his talents, ability and zeal. Mr. Bell comes into our city from out in the wilderness, comes as a miner, not as a minister, comes on matters purely of a business nature. He brought no nuggets of gold or specimens of quartz, but he brings with him his familiar and well worn bible, and his zeal for his Masters service does not permit him to be idle for a moment.

For less than two weeks he has been among us and in that short time he has called together the christian people of this community not less than six times to talk with them about their Father and their Home in Heaven. There are many here who could tell, better than we could tell for them, how much their hearts have been rejoiced, their faith strengthened, and their hopes brightened by his brief labors and shining example.

We expect such work from ministers. They have been selected out from the mass, are educated for their profession and paid to preach the gospel. And we honor and would on no account detract from their high and holy calling. Mr. Bell is not a minister - merely a private in the ranks of the great army that have enlisted under the Banner of Emmanuel. But he fully recognizes the divine authority of the commission which says: 'Let him that heareth say come' - and he has 'heard' and he says to all he meets 'come! and partake of the water of life.'

And it is such work by such men as he that counts."[157]

John W. Bell was not the only Bell in town. The same article stated, *"Mr. A.J. Bell and family left last evening for a brief trip to California. He will return here about the 5th of Oct., and make a trip over the new road..."* Several entries like this can be found in the *Sentinel* in the late 1870s, along with notes of Farwell himself coming and going.

Excitement for the road continued to build. *"We hate to speak of the bridge across the Platte again, but there are so many reasons why it should be built that we can't help it. There are now five mining districts along this Hahn's Peak road, all calling loudly for a road, so that they can not only trade with us and turn all business from that neighborhood into Laramie, but they are very desirous to have a mail service established from here to Hahn's Peak some time during the next summer at least. In addition to the miners, who are receiving constant accessions to their numbers, there are a great many men who are connected with the cutting and hauling of ties, and who would be greatly benefited by this road. From Captain McMahon, who was in the city yesterday, we learn that the mines are all doing first-rate. The claim at Independence Mountain furnishes some of the finest placer gold we have ever seen, being 935 fine. Some very fine nuggets have been found there, one of the party finding a $2.50 chunk in grass roots. This comes the nearest to the fabulous of anything we have heard, unless it be the yarn about the South American discovery years ago. This mine will do some tall work next spring, as everything is in readiness for operations as soon as a supply of water can be obtained next season. The 'Pay Streak' was struck just as the water gave out this season. There are many reasons why this road should be completed now*

---

[157] The Hans Peak Road. (September 25, 1876). *Laramie Weekly Sentinel*, Page 3. https://nrrbook.com/LWS-1876-09-25

that it has been so well begun. Denver and Rawlins are both leaving no stone unturned to secure the growing trade from this promising region. Why should we not complete the arrangement, so long as all the miners are anxious that this route should be established in preference to any other?"[158]

The January 22, 1877, edition of the *Laramie Weekly Sentinel* had this to say: *"Messrs. Bell, Stilson & Farwell, of Chicago and the Hahn's Peak Mines, are making an effort for the establishment of a military road and mail route from this city west through the North Park Hahn's Peak Mining company to the White River Ute Indian Agency. The entire feasibility of the route has been demonstrated, and it is some fifty miles nearer from Laramie City, and by a much better route, than from any other point on the Union Pacific railroad.*

Such a road would open up a country the most rich in resources of any region on the whole continent. It passes through one continued succession of mining, pastoral, timber and agricultural lands, from the very beginning to the end of the route. A hundred thousand men would find constant and profitable employment in the mines along this road. A hundred thousand head of cattle can find the best of summer and winter grazing along the route, while the best timbered region between the Missouri River and the Pacific Coast is opened by it.

It is a matter of the most vital importance to our city to have this vast store-house of wealth opened and developed. It is the region to which our city must look for its future resources in the way of commerce and business. Let us once get this region developed, and we can successfully compete with Denver and Salt Lake City in the matter of growth and business importance.

Our citizens here owe a great debt of gratitude to these gentlemen, who are working in our interest in this matter, and

---

[158] From the Daily of Thursday: What is Needed. (November 20, 1876). *Laramie Weekly Sentinel*, Page 3. https://nrrbook.com/LWS-1876-11-20

we must give them all the assistance and encouragement in our power."[159]

Without a doubt, this road was expected to have a massive economic impact.

The Wyoming Articles of Association for the Hans Peak Wagon Road Company state, *"the object of the company shall be to construct and maintain a wagon road in the county of Carbon and Territory of Wyoming. Commencing at a point in the Rawlins and Snake River County Road west of the Big Muddy River, about three miles north of the Snake River crossing of Said Road, thence running east on the most practicable and eligible ground to and through the claim of Charles Perkins, thence on the most practicable and eligible ground to and through the claim of Noah Reader, thence east and up the Snake River on the most suitable and practicable route to a point at or near where the said Snake River crosses the Southern line of Said Territory."*[160]

Meanwhile, the Colorado entity's Articles of Association state, *"the object and purpose of the company shall be to construct and maintain a wagon road in Grand County Territory of Colorado as follows - beginning at a point at or near where the northern line of said Territory crosses Snake River. Thence running east up and along said river on the most eligible and practicable ground on either side of said river crossing and recrossing the same as may be necessary through the Hahns Peak Mining District in a southerly direction, to Steam Boat Springs on Bear River."*[161]

---

[159] Our Western Resources. (January 22, 1877). *Laramie Weekly Sentinel*, Page 3. https://nrrbook.com/LWS-1877-01-22

[160] Hans Peak Wagon Road Company - Wyoming Articles of Association. (July 5, 1876). Wyoming State Archives. https://nrrbook.com/HPWRCWyoming

[161] Hans Peak Wagon Road Company - Colorado Articles of Association. (July 5, 1876). Colorado State Archives. https://nrrbook.com/HPWRCColorado

As described in both Articles of Association, we can fairly easily track a route from north of present-day Baggs, Wyoming, east along the Little Snake River, then southeast towards the Hahns Peak Mining District, and ultimately to Steamboat Springs. This route was developed into the Snake River Wagon Road, from Hahns Peak to the north, and the Steamboat Springs Wagon Road, from Hahns Peak to the south. Each road can be partially seen on both the Hahns Peak Mining District Map,[162] produced in 1896 by J.J. Argo and A.C. Ostrom, and the USGS Hahns Peak Topography Map,[163] created in 1911. This wagon road has stood the test of time, and today it is generally known as County Road 129 in Colorado, as well as Highway 70, County Road 702, and County Road 16 in Wyoming. Perhaps this route should be known as Farwell Road!

Notably, the Snake River Wagon Road is nowhere close to Laramie. However, it did connect the Hahns Peak Mining District with the Rawlins and Snake River County Road,[164] which traveled south into Colorado to the White River Indian Agency near present-day Meeker. One piece of the plan to connect Laramie to the Hahns Peak Mining District and White River Agency was complete.

The other part of the plan was the wagon road from Laramie to the Hahns Peak Mining District. For reasons unknown, the planned route for this road was not explicitly called out in the Articles of Association for the wagon road company. However, some bits of information help us determine the path of this road.

---

[162] Hahns Peak Mining District Map. (1896). https://nrrbook.com/HPDistrictMap1896

[163] USGS Hahns Peak Topography Map. (1911). https://nrrbook.com/HPTopoMap1911

[164] Johnson, D. (May 20, 2024). The Rawlins to Baggs Wagon Road. *Wyoming Historical Society*. https://nrrbook.com/RawlinsBaggsRoad

According to historian Thelma Stevenson, *"To find substantial stretches of the Old Laramie Trail is almost impossible today except for a real old timer. A few of them will say, 'I can remember when Ellis Freight-wagon Road was called the Laramie Trail.' Quite likely it's true. There seems little doubt, after reading historic references and familiarizing one's self with trails north, east and west of Hahns Peak, that Laramie Trail was but a footpath and horseback route until it was improved for freight wagons by John V. Farwell of Hahns Peak Mining District in 1877...Common sense would have dictated that he use at least parts of Old Laramie Trail...Farwell's employees hewed a wagon passage over Park Range Continental Divide. His freighter, John Gordon, reined freight teams along rocky creek beds, he maneuvered sidling ridges upward through the beautiful white quartz outcroppings along Whiskey Creek, wound over marshes, boglands and random swift drainages down to the meadows and wide gravel bars of Encampment's old Indian crossing. Thence the Laramie Trail went eastward across North Park, turned north into Wyoming."*[165]

A separate account states, *"One of the earliest roads in Routt County was built in 1877 from Hahns Peak to Laramie via Hog Park. John A. Gordon did the freighting for the Farwell Company."*[166]

Likewise, an article from the July 27, 1877, *Rocky Mountain News Daily* states, *"The road from Laramie goes nearly south to the cropping at Walden's, thence southwest, though it winds round so many peaks and spurs that we are not yet straight with nature...The road is new, but fair for a mountain road newly made."*[167]

---

[165] Stevenson, Thelma. (2005, 4th Printing). *Historic Hahns Peak*, Pages 101-103.

[166] *History of Routt National Forest 1905-1972*. (May 4, 2020). Page 12. National Forest Service Library. https://nrrbook.com/HistoryofRNF

[167] Notes of Travel: Camp Life in Northwestern Colorado - Timber - Game - Resources, etc. - International and Hahns Peak Mining Camps. (July 27, 1877). *Daily Rocky Mountain News*, Page 4. https://nrrbook.com/DRMN-1877-07-27

In general, it is believed that the Laramie Wagon Road followed the approximate path of these present-day roads:

1. From Laramie: Highway 230 to the Colorado border, where this turns into Highway 127. According to an 1883 map of Wyoming, present-day Highway 230 was formerly known as the North Park Road.[168]
2. 127 turns south onto County Road 6E, towards present-day Cowdrey.
3. Near Cowdrey, west onto County Road 6W, and then 6B towards Hog Park and the Encampment River. This section passes over the Sierra Madre range, and at one time, it was proposed to call it "Bell's Pass" after A.J. Bell.[169]
4. From here, the wagon road crossed present-day Hog Park Reservoir (likely the site of the marshes and boglands referenced by Thelma Stevenson) and then tied into 550 (follows Whiskey Creek, per Stevenson).
5. Follows 550 to its intersection with 500, where it turns east and then south on 1155 (Ellis Trail).
6. Follows the Ellis Trail south to where it ties in with FS 417, and shortly after that, FS 409.
7. Takes FS 409 west across String Ridge and into Hahns Peak (village, not mountain).

Another piece of evidence to support this route comes from T. Allnutt Brassey's travel diary, which was later published as a book in 1888 called Sixteen Months' Travel: *"We crossed the divide at the same place as on Sunday, then swung to the left towards Grand Encampment Creek, leaving our old camp to the right. We followed the creek till we struck the Hans Peak road,*

---

[168] Holt's New Map of Wyoming. (1883). https://nrrbook.com/WyomingMap1883

[169] Notes of Travel: Steamboat Springs, Routt County, Colorado. (July 28, 1877). *Daily Rocky Mountain News*, Page 4. https://nrrbook.com/DRMN-1877-07-28

and four miles farther brought us to the north end of Hog Park at 8 o'clock."[170]

Just as amazing as the speed at which the road was approved, the entire Hahns Peak Wagon Road system was constructed and operational in mere months. From May 7, 1877: *"Lamphler and his party are building a good, substantial bridge across the Platte, on the Hahn's Peak and White River Road. They have the piles all driven, and expect to have the bridge completed by Thursday of this week."*[171]

A May 28, 1877, report stated, *"The road from Laramie City to Hahn's Peak and White River Agency is now complete, and the Platte River bridge in North Park finished. A good deal of travel is going into the mines in that region."*[172]

Less than nine months after being proposed, the entire route was constructed and put into operation. John V. Farwell had planned his work, worked his plan, and his infrastructure vision was complete.

According to the September 17, 1877, *Laramie Weekly Sentinel,* *"J.W. Bell arrived from Hahn's Peak mines this morning, with two freight wagons, which he will load with supplies, and return in a few days. Mr. Bell's family, which has been spending a portion of the summer at Hahn's Peak, has returned to the city."*[173]

---

[170] Brassey, T. Allnutt. (1888). *Sixteen Months' Travel*, Page 9. https://nrrbook.com/SixteenMonthsTravel

[171] News From the North Park. (May 7, 1877). *Laramie Weekly Sentinel*, Page 2. https://nrrbook.com/LWS-1877-05-07

[172] From the Daily of Thursday. (May 28, 1877). *Laramie Weekly Sentinel*, Page 4. https://nrrbook.com/LWS-1877-05-28

[173] From the Daily of Thursday. (September 17, 1877). *Laramie Weekly Sentinel*, Page 4. https://nrrbook.com/LWS-1877-09-17

Completion of the road also enabled tri-weekly mail service from Laramie to the mining district, replacing the weekly route from the Hahns Peak Post Office to Rawlins.[174]

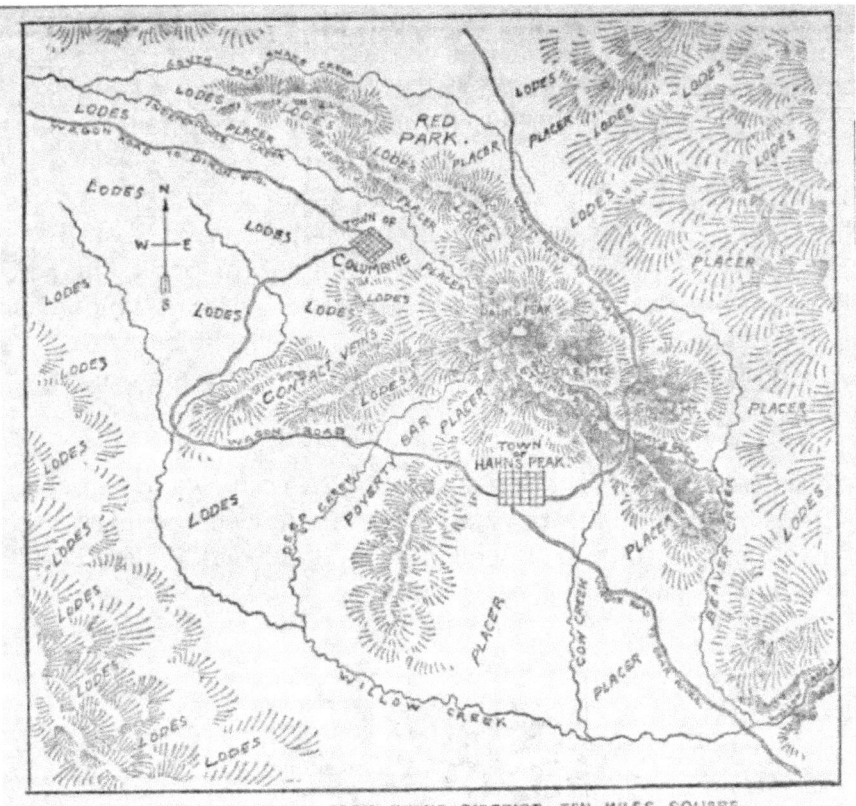

PORTION OF HAHNS' PEAK MINING DISTRICT—TEN MILES SQUARE.

Above: This map of the Hahns Peak Mining District, including wagon roads, was posted in the November 30, 1895, edition of the *Rocky Mountain News*.[175] The December 9, 1895, edition of the same paper reported judges saying this map was "almost perfect."[176]

---

[174] Our Territory. (August 27, 1877). *Laramie Weekly Sentinel*, Page 2. https://nrrbook.com/LWS-1877-08-27

[175] Portion of Hahns' Peak Mining District. (November 30, 1895). *Rocky Mountain News*, Page 2. https://nrrbook.com/RMN-1895-11-30

[176] The Home: The State Press. (December 9, 1895). *Rocky Mountain News*, Page 4. https://nrrbook.com/RMN-1895-12-09

The Hans Peak Wagon Road Company was likely commissioned to build more roads than those noted in this chapter, but details are scarce. The Articles of Association filed in Colorado stated the company was formed for the purpose of constructing wagon roads (plural). The 1896 Hahns Peak Mining District Map shows multiple generic "Wagon Roads" that likely trace their roots back to the 1870s and the Hans Peak Wagon Road Company.

The roads discussed in this chapter have been plotted on the CalTopo map referenced at the beginning of the book, and linked to below. I emphasize that these are estimated plots, as we can't know if today's roads precisely track the original wagon roads, but they do represent the approximate wagon road locations.

It is a little-known fact that several of the county and forest service roads in the North Routt region today can be directly traced back to John V. Farwell and the Hans Peak Wagon Road Company.

www.nrrbook.com/map

Check out the map!

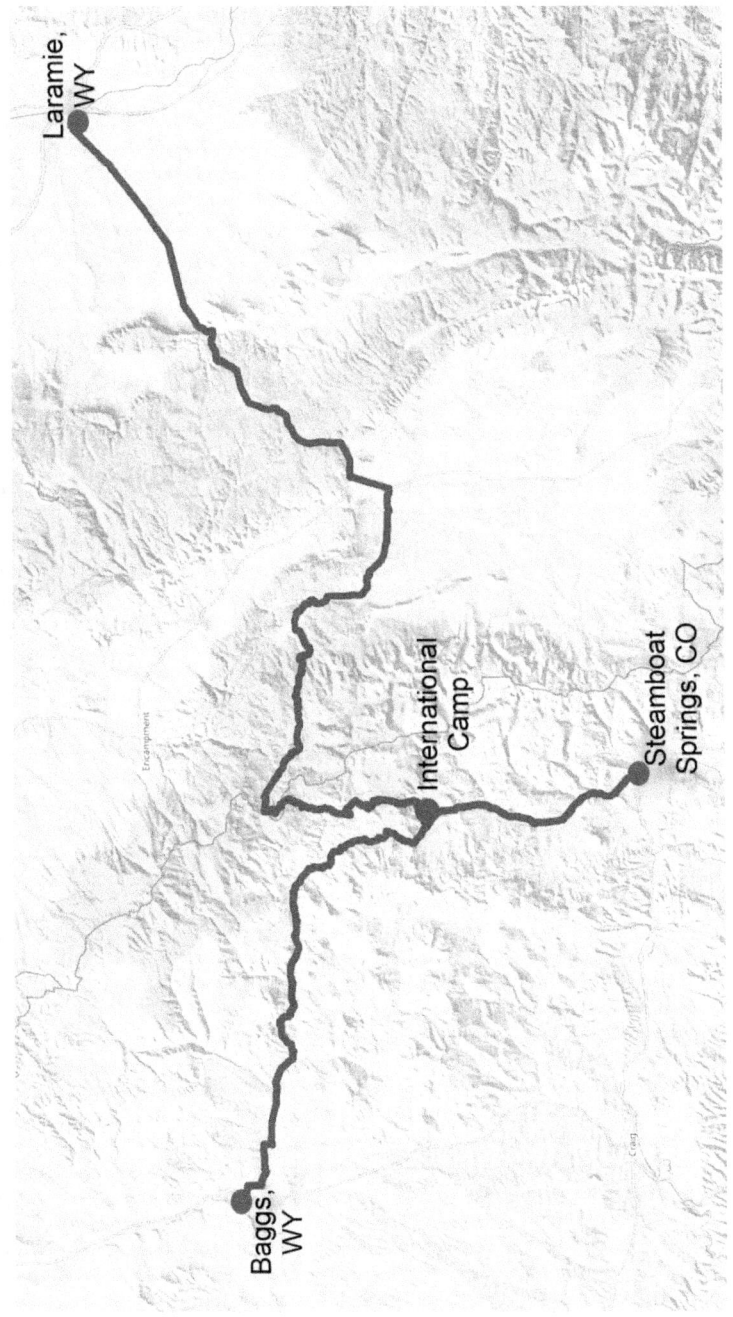

Above: Approximate routes of the Laramie, Snake River, and Steamboat Springs Wagon Roads.

CHAPTER 5: FARWELL DITCH

"Job built well in his day, and with Satan's hosts turned against him to test the fibre of his character, his wife calling on him to curse God and die, he maintained his integrity, and God gave him double as his reward."[177]

-John V. Farwell

The International Mining Company held *"an immense amount of land, including the lower end of Way's gulch, Nova Scotia gulch, String Ridge, and the ground up and down Beaver Creek for several miles."*[178]

As noted in Chapter 1, Beaver Creek itself could not supply a sufficient amount of water for its claims, especially late in the mining season. John V. Farwell intended to develop the ditch from the Elk River that had been planned and surveyed by the Purdy Mining Company in 1875. On July 17, 1876, a water claim[179] was filed in Grand County for a fork of the Main Elk River that is known as Trail Creek today:

"We claim the waters of this entire Stream for the purposes of Placer Mining and Hydraulic purposes with the right of way to carry it by ditch five feet wide on the bottom and seven feet wide at the top to run on most feasible route to Beaver Creek, thence across the same to Ways Gulch allowing it to again pass into its natural channel with the waters of Beaver Creek. And we hereby

---

[177] Farwell, John V. (1906). *Corner Stones of Character: Some Ways of Making Them*, Page 105. https://nrrbook.com/CornerStonesofCharacter

[178] Robert McIntosh, Pioneer Miner, Merchant and Rancher, is Dead. (December 24, 1924). *The Steamboat Pilot*, Page 5. https://nrrbook.com/SP-1924-12-24

[179] This record was filed in Grand County because Routt County was not established until January 29, 1877 with land that had been the western portion of Grand County.

give public notice that we will with due diligence prosecute the work of taking in said water appropriating the same according to the laws of the United States giving us the right to appropriate water for mining purposes."[180]

It is important to note that the 1866 Mining Act granted individuals the right to preempt or appropriate water for mining purposes. Section Nine of the Act states, *"And be it further enacted, That whenever, by priority of possession, rights to the use of water for mining, agricultural, manufacturing, or other purposes, have vested and accrued, and the same are recognized and acknowledged by the local customs, laws, and the decisions of courts, the possessors and owners of such vested rights shall be maintained and protected in the same; and the right of way for the construction of ditches and canals for the purposes aforesaid is hereby acknowledged and confirmed.*"[181]

The Colorado Constitution, which was drafted on March 14, 1876, approved by voters on July 1, 1876, and took effect on August 1, 1876 (when Colorado formally became a state), reiterated this right. Article XVI Section 7 states the following: *"All persons and corporations shall have the right of way across public, private and corporate lands for the construction of ditches, canals, and flumes for the purpose of conveying water for domestic purposes, for the irrigation of agricultural lands, and for mining and manufacturing purposes, and for drainage, upon payment of just compensation.*"[182]

Farwell needed a contractor to build his big ditch, and he had the perfect man for the job. Supervising the project was Robert McIntosh, a contractor from Chicago. *"Father (McIntosh) had been a contractor in Chicago before the fire and*

---

[180] Main Elk River Water Claim. (July 17, 1876). Grand County Clerk and Recorder's Office. https://nrrbook.com/FarwellDitchClaim

[181] 1866 Mining Act. https://nrrbook.com/1866MiningAct

[182] The Constitution of the State of Colorado. (March 14, 1876). Page 42. https://nrrbook.com/COConstitution

had been associated with the Farwells in various projects...He liked the wild and primitive and had been a sort of nonconformist in a Scottish-Canadian family of established ideas, so he was easily persuaded to come west."[183] According to historian John Burroughs, McIntosh was responsible for building the Rock Island Depot, McVicker's Theater, and the original Palmer House Hotel in Chicago. Despite his great success as a contractor, the Great Fire of 1871 took its toll on him, and he jumped at the opportunity for a fresh start in Colorado.

Having accepted Farwell's offer, McIntosh, who was a *"young Scotchman of powerful build,"*[184] traveled from Chicago to Laramie, Wyoming, in June of 1876. From there, he set out on foot for the Hans Peak Mining District (the wagon road described in the previous chapter did not yet exist). *"He got off the train in Laramie and traveled south to the Peak. Deep snows were melting and running off. He walked most of the way and says he bridged every gulch between Laramie and the Peak."*[185]

Upon his arrival, McIntosh expected to put his contracting expertise to immediate use. However, an associate of Farwell named James Steele was deathly ill, and McIntosh was tasked with nursing him back to good health. *"One of the first things that my father did was to nurse Mr. Steele through a serious illness. I have no illusions of father as a nurse. The hospital was a log cabin. The food was coarse, and medicines consisted of epsom salts, castor oil, mustard, baking soda, bear's oil, vaseline, and whiskey. Nevertheless, Mr. Steele recovered, and Mr. Farwell said that Father nursed him as 'tenderly and gently' as a woman."*[186]

---

[183] Morgan, Helen. (1970). *Snake River Profiles, Volume 1*, Page 44.

[184] Leahy, W. (March 24, 1915). Tales of Early Days. *The Steamboat Pilot*, Page 9. https://nrrbook.com/SP-1915-03-24

[185] Morgan, Helen. (1970). *Snake River Profiles, Volume 1*, Page 44.

[186] Morgan, Helen. (1970). *Snake River Profiles, Volume 1*, Page 44.

McIntosh then got to work on three main projects:

1. Expanding International Camp - The general store, church, post office, and cabins for the miners would all need to be constructed.

2. Constructing and operating the sawmill - The sawmill was freighted in from Rawlins, Wyoming, and set up on the south side of Farwell Mountain. In its first year of operation, 300,000 feet of lumber were sawn for use as building materials at International Camp, as well as for fluming to carry water.

3. Building the Farwell Ditch.

"McIntosh built the aforementioned canal. Setting up a sawmill, he got out the necessary boards and timbers for the flumes and for the trestle-work which supported them. In addition...he built a town to accommodate his large crew of workmen."[187]

Construction of the Farwell Ditch began the very day the water claim was filed: July 17, 1876.[188] It is estimated that between 150 and 200 men were employed to dig the ditch using shovels and pickaxes, earning $5 to $7 per day.[189] Rocky sections were blasted through with dynamite. Notably, there are no reports of injuries or deaths among the laborers.

While it is believed that most of the employed men were locals (most being newcomers to the area), there are old rumors that suggest Chinese immigrants supplied labor. Though generally false, there is a logical reason for these claims. The Hans Peak Gold & Silver Mining Company (mentioned in Chapter 1)

---

[187] Burroughs, John. (1962). *Where the Old West Stayed Young*, Page 99.

[188] Farwell Ditch Water Right Notice. (July 17, 1876). Grand County Clerk and Recorder's Office. https://nrrbook.com/FarwellDitchNotice

[189] A Tale of Early Days. (August 26, 1896). *The Steamboat Pilot*, Page 3. https://nrrbook.com/SP-1896-08-26

planned to use Chinese labor to work their Poverty Hill mine in 1875. *"A new company, called Hahn's Peak Gold & Silver Mining Company, propose to introduce Chinese miners next season, to work a strip of gulch ground known as Poverty Flat."*[190] Keep in mind that the Hans Peak Gold & Silver Mining Company consisted of miners from San Francisco, where Chinese immigrants were very common. By some accounts, they made up 10% of California's population in the 1870s. It is possible that some of these Chinese laborers were still in the Hahns Peak area in 1876 and were employed by Farwell; however, there is no evidence to support this claim.

Most, if not all, of the laborers were local settlers or pioneers of the area. *"Most of the early pioneers of Routt county worked at some time or another at Hahn's Peak. Some of them came to mine and then took ranches, while others came to be ranchmen but took this means to earn wages during the summer so as to improve their land."*[191]

"McIntosh urged the newcomers to stay as work soon would begin on the ditch and there would be no trouble in finding employment."[192]

Farwell was highly unlikely to have allowed his employees to unionize. Although he recognized the improved wages and working conditions that unions had generally provided, his experience dealing with unions in Chicago led him to believe that they were led by corrupt union leaders who prioritized their own interests over those of their members.

"I am just as free to say that properly managed labor unions would be quite beneficial as I am to say that as they are now

---

[190] Laramie Daily Sentinel. (October 5, 1874). *Laramie Daily Sentinel*, Page 3. https://nrrbook.com/LDS-1874-10-05

[191] Leahy, W. (March 31, 1915). Tales of Early Days. *The Steamboat Pilot*, Page 7. https://nrrbook.com/SP-1915-03-31

[192] Leahy, W. (March 24, 1915). Tales of Early Days. *The Steamboat Pilot*, Page 9. https://nrrbook.com/SP-1915-03-24

managed they are an unmitigated curse both to capital and labor, but especially to labor. Eighty per cent of the men in the unions are honest, but they are led by officers and walking delegates for purely selfish ends.

Strikes without just cause and unrelenting war on non-union men will either destroy unionism or invite a reasonable arbitration law that will end all labor troubles in the near future. May God speed the day in the interests of all, but especially of labor in industrial enterprises.

...

'Sluggers' were hired by this union to put out of business any union teamster that did not obey its orders. Can anyone imagine anything more devilish, and all in this 'land of the free and home of the brave?'"[193]

We do have the names of a handful of locals employed by Farwell:

- Joe Morin and William Leahy[194]
- Norris Brock and a Mr. Whiting[195]
- Matt Lemmons[196]
- Joe Lucien[197]

---

[193] Farwell, John V. (1906). *Corner Stones of Character: Some Ways of Making Them*, Page 261. https://nrrbook.com/CornerStonesofCharacter

[194] Robert McIntosh, Pioneer Miner, Merchant and Rancher, is Dead. (December 24, 1924). *The Steamboat Pilot*, Page 5. https://nrrbook.com/SP-1924-12-24

[195] Leahy, W. (March 31, 1915). Tales of Early Days. *The Steamboat Pilot*, Page 7. https://nrrbook.com/SP-1915-03-31

[196] Romantic Story of Hahns Peak's Golden Treasure. (March 18, 1932). *The Steamboat Pilot*, Page 5. https://nrrbook.com/SP-1932-03-18

[197] A Tale of Early Days. (August 26, 1896). *The Steamboat Pilot*, Page 3. https://nrrbook.com/SP-1896-08-26

Farwell, being a very religious man, had a unique way of awarding contracts. William Leahy, who worked as a contractor on the ditch, said, *"It became a standing joke - and perhaps there was a degree of truth in it - that if you wanted a good ditch contract or any other lucrative employment from the Farwell company it was nine points in the game to be a regular attendant at the Sunday services...Ditch contracts were let in twenty-rod section and the company reserved the right to reject any bids, always insisting that the successful one be a responsible party. This was the way the contractors got the idea that to be responsible it was necessary to attend church services and show a little interest. Whether this was true or not, it is certain that the Farwell people solved the problem of how to succeed with a church in a new mining camp, for interest and enthusiasm grew wonderfully when contracts were being let."*[198]

Farwell wanted responsible men of high character working for him. He also wanted them to attend church. His method in awarding contracts helped achieve both goals. As noted in Chapter 3, the rowdy lifestyle of a typical miner was not tolerated. Those caught sneaking over to Poverty Flats for "entertainment" had their employment terminated.

Just as Farwell demanded the best of his employees, he demanded the finest of equipment. *"They are putting in the very best machinery, flumes, etc. and Mr. R Haskins, an expert and inventor from California is here now examining the property and making suggestions and changes that we hope will add greatly to the efficiency of the entire works."*[199]

James Dunn was another man hired by Farwell. He filed a receipt[200] with Grand County on August 11, 1876, documenting

---

[198] Leahy, W. (March 24, 1915). Tales of Early Days. *The Steamboat Pilot*, Page 9. https://nrrbook.com/SP-1915-03-24

[199] Notes of Travel: Camp Life in Northwestern Colorado - Timber - Game - Resources, etc. - International and Hahns Peak Mining Camps. (July 27, 1877). *Daily Rocky Mountain News*, Page 4. https://nrrbook.com/DRMN-1877-07-27

[200] James Dunn Labor Receipt. (August 11, 1876). Grand County Clerk and Recorder's Office. https://nrrbook.com/DunnReceipt

that he had been paid $20 for labor from August 8th through the 11th. Specifically, this labor involved assisting Robert McIntosh in building the dam on the Elk River (now known as Trail Creek), which would eventually divert water into the ditch.

From the dam and headgate, the ditch tracked south, gradually separating from Trail Creek, which, like all rivers and streams, followed the terrain to lower elevations. Meanwhile, the Farwell Ditch was brilliantly constructed to be almost perfectly level. Starting at an elevation of approximately 9,300 feet, it would drop, on average, only six feet per mile, allowing the flow of water to be controlled to minimize the washout of ditch walls. After meandering just over one mile through both open meadows and thick forest, the ditch reached a Dakota Sandstone ledge[201] on the southeast flank of Dome Peak known as Sand Rock Point. On the south wall of this ledge, nearly 100 yards of wooden, boxed-in fluming was built to carry the water west until flat ground was reached again. To construct this fluming, it is believed that the ditch builders would hang from ropes anchored above the ledge. In 1897, this fluming was replaced with a tunnel through Sand Rock Point, which will be discussed in detail in Chapter 8.

www.nrrbook.com/map

Check out the map!

A wastegate[202] was installed in the lower wall of the ditch just before Sand Rock Point. This allowed water to be released from the ditch, where it would naturally drain back towards Trail Creek if maintenance or repair were required on

---

[201] *General Geology of the Hahns Peak and Farwell Mountain Quadrangles, Routt County, Colorado, Geological Survey Bulletin 1349.* (1972). Page 54.
https://nrrbook.com/HahnsFarwellGeology

[202] William Flick vs. The Hahns Peak & Elk River Canal & Placer Mining Company, Colorado Court of Appeals Number 2024. (1899). Page 181.
https://nrrbook.com/FlickCase

the fluming (or the tunnel in later years), and the flow of water needed to be temporarily diverted.

Above: This photo is <u>not</u> of the Sand Rock Point Fluming, but rather a hanging flume constructed by the Montrose Placer Mining Company in Dolores Canyon in 1891. The fluming constructed at Sand Rock Point likely looked very similar to this. Photo credit to History Colorado and www.coloradoencyclopedia.org.

From Sand Rock Point, the ditch continued to wrap around Dome Peak. Much of the terrain in this section is wide open, which likely made construction easier; however, the lack of trees and roots to stabilize the ground made the ditch more vulnerable to erosion. Thus, portions of this section were lined with boulders to stabilize the ditch walls. After reaching and crossing Hinman Creek (which, at this point and elevation, is dry for most of the year), the Farwell Ditch turned south towards Hinman Canyon. High along the western wall of the canyon, the ditch was cut through a thick evergreen forest until reaching an area where the surface was solid rock. Here, fluming was constructed to carry the water over the rock, as blasting a ditch through the rock would have been very labor-intensive.

The Farwell Ditch continued to track south above Hinman Canyon, eventually reaching, roughly five miles in, a point on the southeast flank of Farwell Mountain known as Tunnel Hill. The terrain here was very steep, and wrapping the ditch around this point would be nearly impossible. Instead, a tunnel was planned through this point. Joe Lucien, mentioned earlier, secured the contract and decided to make things interesting with one of his partners.

"Joe and a gang started in on one side of the hill and his partner started in on the other, it being their intention to meet in the center. When all had been completed but sixty feet, Joe bet the price to be secured for the work with his partner that he would shake hands with him through the tunnel in ten days. The wager was agreed to and the work began.

Laboring men were scarce at that time and when two men took sick their places could not be filled, so Joe and one man found themselves working alone on their end of the tunnel. To make matters worse his partner began to play off in order to have a sure thing on the bet. It took them a whole day to put in a shot, and they were in all respects taking life very easy. A week passed in this way, and at the end of that time Joe had made twenty feet and his partner only ten - only half of the work done and three days was all there was left to complete it in order to win the bet. 'Then,' says Joe in telling the story, 'I concluded to win out anyhow not because I wanted the money, but just for meanness.'

Then some rock work began such as has never been known before or since. Night and day, Joe and his men labored at the breast of the tunnel. They broke rock like mad men, they put in shots so deep and heavy that their detonation could be plainly heard at camp, nineteen miles away. Without food and without sleep they pushed their resistless way through the mountain. At last only half a day remained. Thousands of dollars hung on the result. They were uncertain as to the distance yet to go but as a last despairing hope they drilled a hole ten feet straight into the breast of the tunnel. Into this they loaded stick after stick of giant powder and placed a 'snuff' under the fuse. Then they rushed out to the entrance to await the discharge. It seemed an ave in coming, and in less than half an hour the ten days would be up. At last the explosion came with a report which seemed to rend the mountain asunder and the earth shook with the awful discharge. They rushed in to see the result of the blast.

There was no smoke in the tunnel and up in the breast a little glimmer of light could be seen. Working with might and main they soon cleared away the rock from the opening, which was long and narrow, and Joe crawled in. It was a tight squeeze but he finally got in far enough to reach his hand through to his astonished partner on the other side and shouted out: 'Shake; I win.'

'Not by a h— of a sight,' returned the man on the other side. 'I won't shake. You made your bet that I would. Time'll be up in five minutes. I win.'

'And sure enough he did,' as Joe tells the story. 'I couldn't make him shake hands but I call that a darned mean trick just the same. It was low down and sneaking after me and my man had broken thirty feet of rock in three days. I'm proud till yet of that piece of work though and don't believe it was ever equalled in the state.'

Joe always winds up his Hahns Peak stories with the remark: 'If you don't believe that just ask Robert McIntosh; he was there.'"[203]

The tunnel at Tunnel Hill was approximately 4 feet wide, anywhere from 4 to 6 feet tall inside, and 120 feet long. The terrain here, especially on the west (outlet) side, is extremely steep, and the men who worked here almost certainly had to rope themselves to a tree or solid rock to prevent tumbling down the mountain.

---

[203] A Tale of Early Days. (August 26, 1896). *The Steamboat Pilot*, Page 3. https://nrrbook.com/SP-1896-08-26

Left: The entrance to the Tunnel Hill Tunnel, where Joe Lucien's handshake bet took place. This tunnel is at approximately 9,270 feet of elevation.

For as legendary as Joe Lucien's handshake bet story is, the engineering of the Farwell Ditch has it beat. Upon exiting the tunnel, the ditch continued westward approximately one mile along the southern face of Farwell Mountain until it reached present-day Coulton Creek. It was at this point that the Upper Level of the ditch fed water into the Coulton Creek drainage. The water then dropped nearly 450 feet in elevation to the start of the Lower Level of the ditch, marking the completion of the transition from the Upper Level to the Lower Level.

This was no small trickle of water falling down the face of Farwell Mountain. Recall that the water claim described a ditch *"five feet wide on the bottom and seven feet wide at the top."* There was a serious amount of water flowing through this ditch, and a drop of 450 feet would have made for a spectacular sight.

Separating the ditch into two levels was a brilliant engineering feat. As noted earlier, the headgate of the ditch at Trail Creek was at approximately 9,300 feet of elevation. Meanwhile, the water needed to be at around 8,700 feet to feed into the hydraulic giants in the mining district. If the ditch maintained a constant grade over its entire length, the slope would be too great, and the water would rush out of control. The ditch walls would erode very quickly, rendering it useless. The only way to control the water was to have a nearly level ditch. And the only way to have a nearly level ditch, when the source was 600 feet higher in elevation than the outlet, was to split the ditch into two levels and engineer a controlled drop of the water. The southeast flank of Farwell Mountain was the perfect site for this, as the terrain was well-suited for dropping the water into the Coulton Creek drainage. In 1897, the transition from the Upper Level to the Lower Level was reengineered, and a man-made waterfall was constructed directly underneath the Tunnel Hill Tunnel outlet. As a result, the Lower Level of the ditch was extended roughly one mile to the east to catch the water. This renovation will be discussed in more detail in Chapter 8.

Continuing, the Lower Level headed southwest, carrying water around the south side of Farwell Mountain. We must pause briefly here because this peak was obviously not always known as Farwell Mountain. A little-known fact is that it was known as East Mountain until John V. Farwell arrived in the area. We know this from James Dunn's testimony in the Thomas Brooks lawsuit mentioned in Chapter 1. Being interrogated, Dunn was asked, *"How are the waters of the Main Elk and the west branch of the Elk separated?"* Dunn's response: *"By a dividing ridge a spur running East from East Mountain, sometimes called Farwell Mountain, and continuing down between Scott's Run and the West branch on the West and the Main Elk on the East."*[204]

---

[204] Thomas W Brooks vs John V. Farwell & B.F. Jacobs, Denver, CO District Case Number 4026. (1879). Page 126. https://nrrbook.com/FarwellBrooksCase

Wrapping around Farwell Mountain, the Lower Level of the ditch traversed all types of terrain. Near Tunnel Hill, it was cut into a steep, rocky slope containing several spots that required blasting with dynamite. As it continued, thick pine forests, aspen groves, and open meadows were all crossed. To enable access to the ditch and the Tunnel Hill sandbox, a wagon road was built just below the ditch along much of its path around Farwell Mountain, before separating and following Scott's Run towards Diamond Park.

Near where the road and ditch came together was where Farwell's sawmill was located. Per William Flick's testimony in 1899: *"...and at a point we call the 'Old Saw-mill,' where the wagon road strikes the ditch and passes along."*[205] Keep in mind, Flick was contracted to refurbish the ditch twenty years after Farwell had it constructed, so his reference to "Old Saw-mill" would be referencing Farwell's sawmill. The sawmill was strategically placed here for a few reasons:

- The forest is very thick here; thus, lumber was plentiful. Especially important were the tall, straight pine trees that could be milled into various sizes and shapes of boards and beams.

- It was at the rough halfway point of the ditch.

- International Camp was accessible via a wagon road, allowing lumber to be easily transported there for the construction of homes, cabins, and other buildings.

The ditch continued around the southwest flank of Farwell Mountain and turned to the north, still following the lay of the land and maintaining its nearly flat grade. The forest is incredibly thick in this area, and the amount of manual labor required to cut down massive trees and dig their roots out of the ditch's path is mind-boggling. The ditch tracked into and

---

[205] William Flick vs. The Hahns Peak & Elk River Canal & Placer Mining Company, Colorado Court of Appeals Number 2024. (1899). Page 290. https://nrrbook.com/FlickCase

out of several thick drainages along its route and eventually
began a northward arc around Beaver Basin.

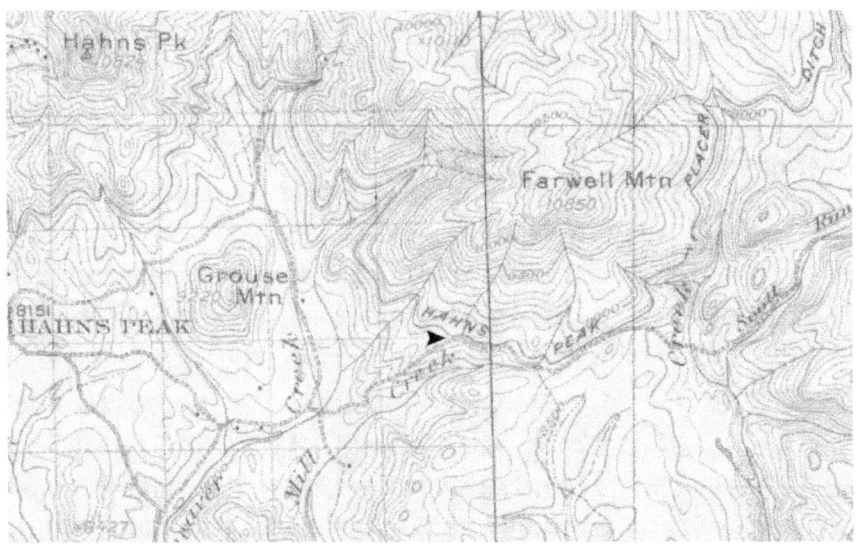

Above: The approximate location of the sawmill is marked with the
arrow, near where the ditch and wagon road came together.
Interestingly, what is now known as Lester Creek is marked as Mill
Creek on the map, further supporting the belief that the sawmill was
located in this general area. This map, from 1911, referred to the
Farwell Ditch as the Hahns Peak Placer Ditch. The break in the ditch
on the southeast flank of Farwell Mountain is the tunnel at Tunnel
Hill. If you look closely, you can see the quick drop in elevation of the
ditch coming out of the tunnel, which is consistent with the
reengineered waterfall that was built there in 1897. This map can be
viewed in the linked CalTopo map.

Near the point where it crosses present-day FS 409 are the
remains of an old cabin and some old metal pipe. It is believed
the cabin was home to either a ditch maintainer or, potentially,
a miner. The eastern fork of Beaver Creek flowed right below
this cabin.

Approximately half a mile beyond the old cabin, the ditch
approached a rock outcropping where a second tunnel, known
as the Beaver Creek Tunnel, was constructed. This tunnel,
approximately sixty feet long, was similar in construction to

the Tunnel Hill Tunnel, measuring about four feet wide and ranging from four to six feet tall inside. Upon exiting the tunnel, the ditch continued its path, wrapping around the north side of Beaver Basin.

At this point, the ditch was in its final stretch to String Ridge, following the terrain toward present-day Beryl Mountain. In several places, metal piping carried water across very steep side-hill sections that would have made it nearly impossible to build a ditch. As the ground flattened back out, the pipe, having been anchored underground on each end, fed water back into the ditch. Per Joe Morin, contractors *"received $1 a section for putting together piping, making about $15 a day."*[206]

After rounding Beryl Mountain, the ditch wrapped around present-day Anderson Mountain (formerly known as Doyle Mountain[207]), which stood above Ways Gulch. This section of ditch today is FS 417.1B, having been bulldozed at some point into a road. String Ridge soon followed, with its upper end located where Anderson Mountain and Little Mountain meet.

From atop String Ridge, the ditch fed water into pipes that dropped in elevation, narrowing in diameter as it went, thus building immense pressure as it fed into water cannons known as giants or monitors. The giants were used to blast the earth away in Ways Gulch and Nova Scotia Gulch, creating a slurry that was fed into sluice boxes. In these boxes, the heavier gold particles settled into riffles while clean water rinsed away the waste material. The amount of pay dirt that could be processed using this system of hydraulic mining dwarfed the simple methods used in the early days of the mining district.

At this point, Farwell's International Mining Company had successfully created a sufficient water source to enable

[206] The New Camp of Farwell City: How J.V. Farwell Got Action on His Money. (June 6, 1900). *The Steamboat Pilot,* Page 5. https://nrrbook.com/SP-1900-06-06

[207] Portion of Hahns' Peak Mining District. (November 30, 1895). *Rocky Mountain News*, Page 2. https://nrrbook.com/RMN-1895-11-30

hydraulic mining on a large scale. Still, it needed a system to release the water after it had run through their operation. This was accomplished through a water right-of-way filed in Grand County on July 20, 1876:

"We claim the right of way for a bedrock flume from a point in Ways Gulch where A.J. Bell has a ditch or cut and where the waters of Ways Gulch is into Nova Scotia Gulch thence down Beaver Creek in most feasible route of sufficient width and with room enough for work and excavation, to intersection of Beaver and Willow Creek. Thence with the main stream passing through narrow Gorge or Canyon three thousand feet below where the water leaves the Park at a point of Rocks in the angle of the stream in head of said gorge or canyon which three thousand feet we claim mainly for dumping purposes."[208]

After entering the narrow canyon, Willow Creek water flows towards and drains into the Elk River along present-day Seedhouse Road. Thus, Farwell Ditch water was originally claimed from a fork of the Elk River (Trail Creek), and it ultimately drained back into the Elk River.

Maintaining a ditch of this length required constant attention and care. Much of the ditch was formed with walls made from the very dirt that was dug out of the ground. It was common for these dirt walls to soften, erode, and break away, thus allowing water to escape. The remedy was often to "flume," or line, these sections with wooden boards.

During the spring and early summer months, only the Lower Level of the ditch was needed. The snowmelt off Farwell Mountain and the peaks wrapping around Beaver Basin and String Ridge supplied ample water to feed Farwell's operation. The Upper Level was tapped during the dry season, which spans the late summer and fall months. This engineering marvel was designed and constructed to enable the

---

[208] Ways Gulch Water Right-of-Way. (July 20, 1876). Grand County Clerk and Recorder's Office. https://nrrbook.com/WaysGulchWaterRight

International Mining Company to have a significantly longer mining season than would typically be possible.

Above: While the exact location of where this photo was taken is unknown, it comes from the Hahns Peak area and portrays the pipe and water cannon in action. Photo Credit to the Hahns Peak Area Historical Society.

The final cost of constructing the ditch is unknown, but it far exceeded the $50,000 estimated by Purdy Mining Company in 1875. A report from 1877 stated, *"The International Camp has expended about $60,000, and will expend nearly as much more before being ready to operate on the scale intended."*[209] Other reports range from $125,000 to $200,000. In today's dollars, that equates to roughly $3.75 to $6 million. In addition to the financial commitment, the ditch took two years to construct, being completed in August 1878. John V. Farwell invested a fortune in time and money, clearly expecting that hydraulic

---

[209] Notes of Travel: Camp Life in Northwestern Colorado - Timber - Game - Resources, etc. - International and Hahns Peak Mining Camps. (July 27, 1877). *Daily Rocky Mountain News*, Page 4. https://nrrbook.com/DRMN-1877-07-27

mining would yield piles of gold, which he would need to make a profit. With gold priced at roughly $20 per ounce in 1877, it would take anywhere from 6,000 to 10,000 ounces of gold just to cover the cost of the ditch. That does not include the mining expenses to recover the gold itself, which drives the actual break-even amount even higher.

However, the hype was real: *"Here the tourist can any day see what the writer has - from twenty-five to eighty grains of gold taken from one pan of dirt; not selected dirt either."*[210] As noted in the previous chapter, the Hahns Peak Mining District had expectations of becoming a gold mining epicenter.

Unfortunately, the expected returns did not materialize. At their best, gold yields were fair. *"Some very rich placer gold was found at Nova Scotia, but it was very erratic and pockety. Many nuggets to the value of $25 were taken out."*[211]

Additionally, the 1897 Hahns Mining District Report, when talking about the history of Farwell's operation, stated, *"it is known that the ground is rich and generally believed that a profit yielding product was obtained."*[212]

More commonly, however, the reports were less favorable:

"Work continued there all of the season of 1879, and it became evident that results were not satisfactory."[213]

---

[210] "Bugtown" (August 19, 1875). *The Laramie Daily Sentinel*, Page 3. https://nrrbook.com/LDS-1875-08-19

[211] The New Camp of Farwell City: How J.V. Farwell Got Action on His Money. (June 6, 1900). *The Steamboat Pilot,* Page 5. https://nrrbook.com/SP-1900-06-06

[212] Hahns Mining District Report. (1897). Page 1. https://nrrbook.com/HahnsMiningReport1897

[213] Leahy, W. (March 31, 1915). Tales of Early Days. *The Steamboat Pilot*, Page 7. https://nrrbook.com/SP-1915-03-31

"J.B. Donaldson, superintendent for J.V. Farwell at the International mine, has shut down work for the season and gone to his home in Denver. Mr. Donaldson is a thorough business manager, and, after thoroughly testing the ground, the result not being sufficient to justify a continuance of the work immediately shut down and stopped the further useless outlay of money."[214]

"...John Farwell had spent a fortune without finding much gold...Grapevine reportings are that String Ridge had been salted, that Hahn's early gulches were exhausted before Farwell invested."[215]

"It was intended primarily to use this water in working String Ridge, an immense bar of gravel which Farwell's experts had told him would run $1.25 a yard, altho it is evident some of the early prospectors had 'salted' the experts."[216]

The possibility of Farwell's claims being "salted" with gold was not just grapevine reporting. A.J. Bell, the original Superintendent for Farwell & Jacobs, very likely believed this to be true. While being interrogated for the Thomas Brooks lawsuit about his scouting visit in 1876, he said this about nearby Poverty Bar: *"...I was favorably disposed towards Poverty Bar, a part of the Hans Peak Companies property of which plaintiff was the title Superintendent and which property adjoins and near to the plaintiff's property as mentioned in Kean's deed. Great pains were taken to make a good showing and they took about 35 pounds of gold dust out of a few rude sluice boxes running as the result of 15 days washing with two ordinary pipes under light pressure. Plaintiff (Thomas Brooks) assured me that his was a better property and richer gravel was*

---

[214] Central Wyoming. (July 20, 1879). *The Cheyenne Daily Sun*, Page 2. https://nrrbook.com/CDS-1879-07-20

[215] Stevenson, Thelma. (2005, 4th Printing). *Historic Hahns Peak*, Page 14.

[216] Robert McIntosh, Pioneer Miner, Merchant and Rancher, is Dead. (December 24, 1924). *The Steamboat Pilot*, Page 5. https://nrrbook.com/SP-1924-12-24

more abundant and had an abundance of water, and I thought if these statements were true that it would be a good purchase. Anything I may have said or written was based upon these representations by Plaintiff, but all his representations as to richness of gravel & area & extent, when in fact in every particular were absolutely false upon examination."[217]

Bell clearly believed that Brooks had misrepresented the claims he was trying to sell to Farwell and Jacobs. While they did not purchase anything from Brooks, this does not rule out the possibility that the land they did acquire had also been salted. When the results came in lower than hoped, it would have been only natural to wonder if that were the case.

Meanwhile, some reports state that Farwell believed Bell was mismanaging the company. *"A.J. Bell was let out of the management of the Farwell company and a man by the name of Holt was placed in charge."*[218] Another report stated, *"...it is alleged that gross mismanagement disrupted the company..."*[219] In Bell's defense, gold in the Hahns Peak Mining District was not always easy to mine. *"The gold is generally very fine dust, and the utmost skill and care is required to extract it without losing greatly."*[220]

At a later point, J.B. Donaldson was named Superintendent for Farwell. Work continued in 1879, and results did not improve. Despite not mining for even one full season with his big ditch and water cannons, Farwell had seen enough and made a deal

---

[217] Thomas W Brooks vs John V. Farwell & B.F. Jacobs, Denver, CO District Case Number 4026. (1879). Page 85. https://nrrbook.com/FarwellBrooksCase

[218] Romantic Story of Hahns Peak's Golden Treasure. (March 18, 1932). *The Steamboat Pilot*, Page 5. https://nrrbook.com/SP-1932-03-18

[219] Hahns Mining District Report (1897). Page 1. https://nrrbook.com/HahnsMiningReport1897

[220] Notes of Travel: Camp Life in Northwestern Colorado - Timber - Game - Resources, etc. - International and Hahns Peak Mining Camps. (July 27, 1877). *Daily Rocky Mountain News*, Page 4. https://nrrbook.com/DRMN-1877-07-27

to sell his mining claims, water rights, and all other assets tied to his company.

While it may seem like poor results are the sole reason for John V.'s sudden exit, and indeed most old reports (which likely piggyback off each other) state this as the cause, there is much more to the story. Why would Farwell, who invested a tremendous amount of money and patiently waited more than two years for his big ditch to be constructed, pull the plug and take a financial loss so abruptly? As a highly successful businessman, he surely had experience in weathering the ups and downs of running a company.

The truth is that very few people could have endured the events of the 1879 mining season, which, for Farwell, paralleled some of the most significant challenges he faced in life.

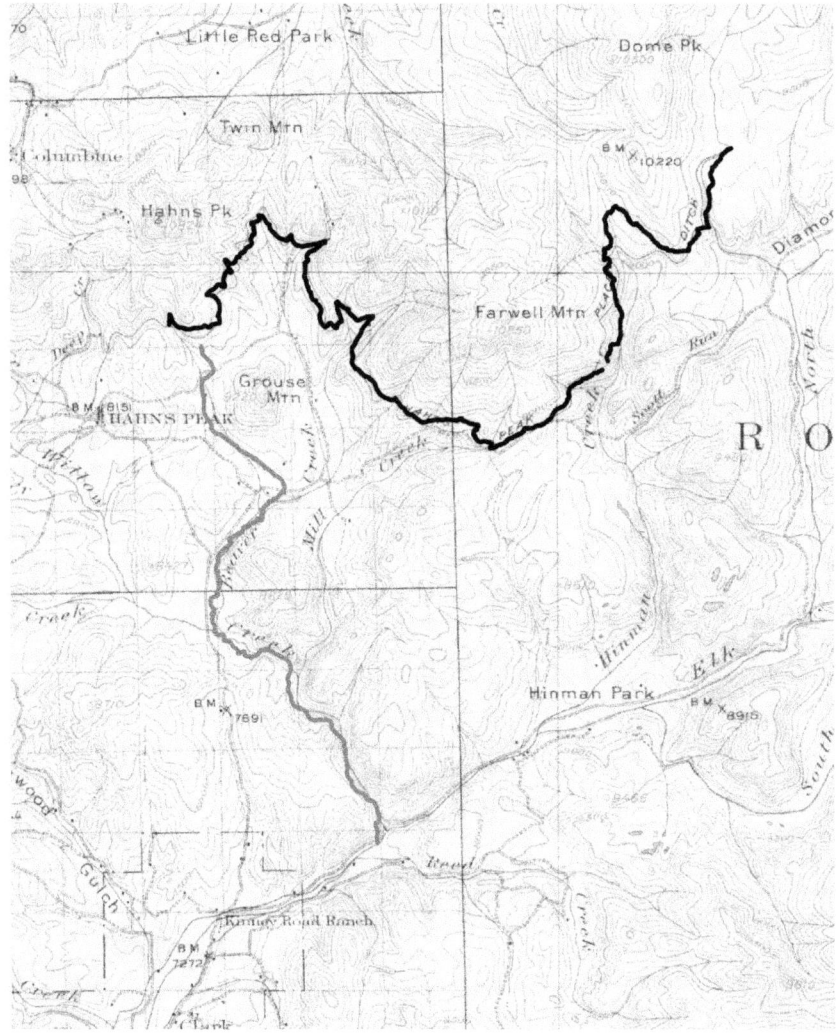

Above: The dark line is the track of the original seventeen-mile Farwell Ditch, from Trail Creek (fork of the Elk River) in the top right, to String Ridge near Farwell's mining operation. The lighter line represents the right-of-way the water followed to be released back into the Elk River.

CHAPTER 6: INFERNO

"Behold the difference, young man, between leaving all for the King's service with an undying enthusiasm to follow Him wherever He leads, and leaving Him to follow the vanities of this world, all of which turn into the smoke of torment, when 'the fire shall try every man's work' to reveal its true character in the crucible of eternity."[221]

-John V. Farwell

Not all was well in the Hahns Peak Mining District in the late 1870s, as relations with the nearby Utes were quickly deteriorating and spiraling into chaos due to decades of broken promises by the United States Government.

Until the early 1860s, relations between the Utes and American settlers were largely friendly. It was common for members of these groups to barter and trade with one another, exchanging goods such as animal pelts for guns & ammunition, iron goods, textiles, and liquor. Nevertheless, there were occasional skirmishes that cascaded into a series of treaties between the Utes and the U.S. Government. The boundaries created by these treaties are marked on the map found at the link to the right.

www.nrrbook.com/map

Check out the map!

Following the Mexican-American War (1846-1848), the first treaty between the Utes and the United States was signed on December 30, 1849, and ratified on September 24, 1850, by President Millard Fillmore.[222] This treaty was necessary because the war resulted in the United States acquiring land

---

[221] Farwell, John V. (1906). *Corner Stones of Character: Some Ways of Making Them*, Page 98. https://nrrbook.com/CornerStonesofCharacter

[222] Ute Treaty of 1849. https://nrrbook.com/UteTreaty1849

that would later become the states of Texas, New Mexico, Arizona, California, Utah, and Colorado. The Utes called much of this land home. The main points of this treaty were:

- Article 1: The Utes acknowledged they were now under the jurisdiction of the U.S. Government.
- Article 2: Hostilities between the contracting parties will cease.
- Article 3: All captives and stolen property would be returned.
- Article 4: The contracting parties agree to the laws that are in force and acknowledge that new laws may be passed.
- Article 5: U.S. Citizens shall have free passage through Ute territory.
- Article 6: The U.S. Government would establish agencies and military posts wherever it deemed necessary.
- Article 7: The U.S. Government would establish defined territorial boundaries for the Utes, mainly consisting of their "accustomed homes or localities," and the Utes would agree to remain within their territory unless granted special permission.[223]
- Article 8: In exchange for the Utes' faithful adherence to the terms of the treaty, the U.S. Government would provide them with donations, presents, and implements.
- Article 9: The treaty shall be binding upon all parties after being signed.

While the 1849 treaty was intended to formalize a friendly relationship between the Utes and the U.S. Government, the dynamic shifted with the Gold Rush of 1858-1859 and the Homestead Act of 1862. As thousands of prospectors and settlers flooded into the region, tension began to increase, and in 1863, Colorado Territorial Governor John Evans proposed a

---

[223] This section of the treaty specifically calls for the Utes "to cease the roving and rambling habits which have hitherto marked them as a people."

new agreement. The Ute Treaty of 1863[224] was signed only by Chief Ouray and his Tabeguache band of Utes. The six other bands (Muache, Capote, Weeminuche, Yampa, Grand River, & Uintah) did not sign on or adhere to its terms. The articles of this treaty are summarized as:

- Article 1: Acknowledge the Tabeguache band of Utes resides in U.S. territory and admit the right of the U.S. to regulate trade with them.
- Article 2: Establish new Tabeguache Ute boundaries, which replace land formally ceded to the United States (by this band only).
- Article 3: The United States maintains the right to build roads, railroads, and military posts on its territory. Additionally, *"The right of any citizen of the United States may mine without interference or molestation in any part of the country hereby reserved to said Indians, where gold or other metals or minerals may be found, is hereby also conferred and guaranteed. And for all other purposes, excepting as herein stipulated, settlement by other persons than Indians is hereby prohibited."*[225]

  This article clearly allowed U.S. citizens to prospect and mine for gold on Tabeguache Ute land, though they could not settle on it.

- Article 4: The Tabeguache band of Utes gives its consent that the Muache band may also be settled with them.
- Article 5: The Tabeguache will grant safety to all persons passing through their territory.
- Article 6: Affirm peaceful relations between the Tabeguache and U.S. Citizens and spell out the consequences for hostilities.

---

[224] Ute Treaty of 1863. https://nrrbook.com/UteTreaty1863

[225] Chief Ouray's view on this was to let the prospectors take the gold, but leave the land.

- Article 7: The Tabeguache will not supply another band of Indians with weapons in the event of a war against the United States.
- Article 8: For a period of ten years, the Tabeguache will receive $10,000 worth of goods and $10,000 worth of provisions from the United States.
- Article 9: The Tabeguache will receive five American stallions for the purpose of improving their breed of horses.
- Article 10: If the Tabeguache pursue agricultural development, the United States will provide 150 cattle annually for five years, 1,000 sheep annually for two years, and 500 sheep annually for the following three years. These provisions will only continue if the tribe continues to pursue agriculture in good faith. Additionally, the United States will build and maintain a blacksmith shop to repair guns and agricultural implements.

The 1863 treaty was ratified on December 14, 1864, by President Abraham Lincoln. Unfortunately, it was doomed to fail, since the Tabeguache were the only band that signed on. American settlers continued their westward advance, and calls to take more territory from the Utes increased.

In 1867, Colorado Territory Governor Alexander Hunt, in a Governor's Message issued before the assembly of the 7th state legislature, called for the U.S. Government to significantly increase money, goods, and supplies for the Utes. In addition, he called for the Utes to "receive instruction, properly tendered, in the ways of civilization."

"In this connection it is proper to advert to the Ute nation, whose friendship and uniform good conduct is a subject for universal congratulation, and should commend these worthy people to the favorable consideration of the parent government. During the

bloody conflict that has passed with the tribes of the plains,[226]
*they have steadily maintained their allegiance to treaty
stipulations. They have mingled freely with our citizens without
the slightest collision, until they have come to be regarded not
only as friends but allies, and their necessities cheerfully
relieved by private contributions.*

*But something more is necessary. The general government, while
caring for the interests of those whose record is written in the
blood of our people, should certainly extend its beneficent offices
to those who are manifestly entitled to the first place in its
confidence. Through the occupancy of their lands by the white
settlers, all opportunity for self maintenance by the only means
they know how to employ is sacrificed, having them greedily
dependent on charity for support. Life annuities similar in
extent to those granted other bands referred to, should be
provided by congress, and their distribution regularly and
honestly made. The Utes are now in a condition to receive
instruction, properly tendered, in the ways of civilization.
Agencies established among them, upon reservations wisely
chosen for their adaptation to agricultural and pastoral
pursuits, and missionaries appointed to teach them these new
duties would, I am convinced, be followed by immediate good
effects.*"[227]

The following year, Chief Ouray, who had visited Washington,
D.C., and witnessed the power of the U.S. Government during
the Treaty of 1863 negotiations, begrudgingly participated in
negotiating the Ute Treaty of 1868,[228] knowing resistance was
futile. Ouray was viewed as the de facto Chief of all Ute bands
by the U.S. Government and negotiated on their behalf, despite
being the Chief of only the Tabeguache band. *"The agreement*

---

[226] The U.S. Army fought Cheyenne, Arapaho, and Lakota Sioux in the Colorado
War from 1864-1865.

[227] Governor's Message. (December 4, 1867). *The Rocky Mountain News*,
Page 2. https://nrrbook.com/RMN-1867-12-04

[228] Ute Treaty of 1868. https://nrrbook.com/UteTreaty1868

an Indian makes to a United States treaty is like the agreement a buffalo makes with his hunter when pierced with arrows. All he can do is lie down and give in."[229] This treaty consisted of:

- Article 1: All the terms of the 1863 Treaty with the Tabeguache band that do not conflict with this treaty are reaffirmed and deemed to apply to the other Ute bands.
- Article 2: Establishes new territory lines, defined as:

"Commencing at that point on the southern boundary-line of the Territory of Colorado where the meridian of longitude 107° west from Greenwich crosses the same; running thence north with said meridian to a point fifteen miles due north of where said meridian intersects the fortieth parallel of north latitude; thence due west to the western boundary-line of said Territory; thence south with said western boundary-line of said Territory to the southern boundary-line of said Territory; thence east with said southern boundary-line to the place of beginning."

Effectively, the new boundaries were a vertical rectangle, with the southern boundary being the southern Colorado border, the eastern boundary being the 107th meridian west, the northern boundary being a line fifteen miles north of the 40th parallel, and the western boundary being the western Colorado border. In general, all bands of Utes were moved west of the Continental Divide, and prime mining territory was opened up for U.S. Citizens, including the Hahns Peak region. The northeast corner of the reservation was now, as the crow flies, approximately fifty-five miles southwest of where Joseph Henn (Hahn), William Doyle & George Way had mined Willow Creek just a few short years earlier.

---

[229] *Ute Removal and the Hunt Treaty - The Agreement a Buffalo Makes When Pierced with Arrows.* Denver Public Library. https://nrrbook.com/HuntTreaty

Critically, Article 2 also contained this provision: *"...and the United States now solemnly agree that no such persons, except those herein authorized so to do, and except such officers, agents, and employees of the Government as may be authorized to enter upon Indian reservations in discharge of duties enjoined by law shall ever be permitted to pass over settle upon, or reside in the Territory described in this article, except as herein otherwise provided."*

Thus, U.S. Citizens were banned from mining on Ute land. On paper.

- Article 3: All previous Ute territory is relinquished.
- Article 4: The United States will build two agencies on the reservation, each consisting of a warehouse, agent residence, buildings for a carpenter, farmer, blacksmith, miller, schoolhouse, sawmill, gristmill, and shingle mill. One agency will be located on the White River and the other on the Rio de los Pinos.

The White River Indian Agency would later be connected to the Hahns Peak Mining District and also to Laramie, Wyoming, by John V. Farwell's Hans Peak Wagon Road Company in 1877, as detailed in Chapter 4.

- Article 5: United States Indian Agents will reside on the agencies and keep an open office at all times.
- Article 6: Crime will be tried and punished according to the laws of the United States.
- Article 7: If the head of a family wishes to pursue farming, he will be given 160 acres of land within the reservation that is his exclusive property as long as he continues to farm. Likewise, a single man at least 18 years of age can claim 80 acres as his own for the same purpose.
- Article 8: Ute children between the ages of 7 and 18 will attend school. For every thirty children, a schoolhouse and a teacher will be provided.

- Article 9: Those who claim land to farm will be provided with seed and equipment and access to the farmer for instruction.
- Article 10: After ten years, the farmers, carpenters, blacksmiths, and millers can be withdrawn from the agencies. In exchange, an annual sum of $10,000 (in addition to the promised money from the 1863 treaty) will be provided for educational expenses.
- Article 11: An annual sum for thirty years of up to $30,000 worth of clothing, blankets, and other articles of utility.
- Article 12: An annual sum of up to $30,000 worth of food.
- Article 13: Each head of family will be provided a gentle American cow to promote a civilized, self-sustaining lifestyle.
- Article 14: The U.S. retains the right to build roads and railroads through the reservations.
- Article 15: All teachers, blacksmiths, carpenters, millers, and blacksmiths will be furnished.
- Article 16: No treaty for the cession of land provided in this agreement will be valid unless signed by at least three-fourths of the adult male Indians on the reservation.
- Article 17: All appropriations from previous treaties will be divided proportionally among the seven bands (Tabeguache, Muache, Capote, Weeminuche, Yampa, Grand River, and Uintah) named in this treaty.

The articles of the 1868 Treaty were a checklist of items suggested by Territory Governor Hunt. It was signed in phases, with the final Ute approval taking place on September 24, 1868. The progression of these treaties followed a theme: less land for the Utes in exchange for more money and supplies from the U.S. Government, eventually resulting in the concept that the Utes should be educated and converted to the "white man's" way of life. Like its predecessors, the 1868 Treaty was short-lived.

Unsurprisingly, the new boundary lines were ignored, and miners and prospectors continued to enter Ute territory in search of gold, now primarily in the San Juan Mountains of southwest Colorado. Ouray grew frustrated that the U.S. citizens were not keeping their end of the bargain. Miners came in, were removed by U.S. soldiers, and immediately returned. As more gold deposits were discovered, calls for Ute removal intensified, and pressure mounted to negotiate yet another new treaty. The Utes, meanwhile, regularly traveled off the reservation to their former lands.

In 1872, a council was held at the Rio de Los Pinos Indian Agency. Colorado Governor Edward McCook, authorized to negotiate another treaty, discussed options with the Utes, but sought their voluntary agreement to new terms. McCook felt the Ute Reservation was too large and should be downsized, but the Utes were not interested in making a new deal and wanted the 1868 Treaty upheld. *"Ouray spoke for the rest when he stated, 'We do not want to sell a foot of our land - that is the opinion of all.' Nothing came of this negotiation."*[230]

Meanwhile, miners became more aggressive, forming a union that threatened to fight against the U.S. soldiers if they tried to push them out of the San Juans again. The U.S. Government relented and pulled its soldiers out of the area. As a result, more miners poured into the San Juans.

Tension continued to build, which led to another council in 1873. Initially deadlocked, the Utes eventually agreed to the terms of a new treaty when Ouray changed his mind, breaking a stalemate. The Ute Treaty of 1873[231] contained these terms:

- Article 1: A portion of the land from the 1868 Treaty, specifically a rectangle covering the San Juan Mountains, would be ceded back to the United States.

---

[230] *Ute Removal and the Hunt Treaty - The Agreement a Buffalo Makes When Pierced with Arrows.* Denver Public Library. https://nrrbook.com/HuntTreaty

[231] Ute Treaty of 1873. https://nrrbook.com/UteTreaty1873

- Article 2: The Utes are allowed to hunt on their lands as long as there is plentiful game and they are at peace with the "white people."
- Article 3: The United States will set aside money in perpetual trust to provide $25,000 per year, forever, for the use and benefit of the Utes.
- Article 4: An agency will be constructed on the southern portion of the reservation.
- Article 5: All provisions of the 1868 Treaty not altered by this agreement are reinforced, with the provision in Article 2 dealing with U.S. citizens not being allowed on Ute land (except those specifically authorized), being "expressly re-affirmed."
- Article 6: Chief Ouray would receive a salary of $1,000 per year for 10 years, or as long as he remains Chief of the Utes and there is peace with the United States.

  Money talks, and this likely explains why Ouray, who previously declared the Utes would not sell one foot of land, flipped and decided in favor of the treaty.

- Article 7: The agreement is subject to ratification by the U.S. Congress and the President.

Ratification occurred on April 29, 1874. More money. Less land. Boundaries still ignored.

The subsequent years did not go any better. The agencies were designed to convert the Utes to the white man's agricultural way of life, but were ineffective in doing so. Meanwhile, the United States was regularly late in delivering the promised money and supplies as stipulated by the treaties, and turnover was high among the staff at the agencies.

"The White River Agency had a history of problems. Since its establishment in 1868, the agency had seen several agents come and go. Most left in total frustration. The next to last agent, the Reverend E.H. Danforth, quit because the government failed to deliver the promised annuities on schedule. The Indians deeply

resented the fact that goods such as flour, blankets, and other supplies sat in the depot at Rawlins, Wyoming, and rotted."[232]

With Edward Huntington Danforth vacating his position, a new agent was needed at the White River Agency, and John V. Farwell had someone in mind. He wrote a letter to politician William Henry Smith in support of his employee, John W. Bell.

"Dear Sir:

I write you in regard to John W. Bell's application for the Ute Indian agency. Myself & party have very large interests in that region & are therefore deeply interested in having peace with the Indians – There is much discontent among them now owing to insufficiency of the agent – Their goods now lie at Rawlins that should have been delivered last fall.

Mr. Bell's father, with us and others, are therefore very anxious for the safety of our investments & don't know what better guarantee the government could have of good management, than this appointment would give. I am quite conversant with the whole question and was delighted to see the course Secretary Shulz is pursuing in this office, as it augurs a clearing up of a very murky sky in the part of our governmental affairs.

I can almost guarantee that if John W. Bell is appointed, that there will be no trouble growing out of the management of the agency, as I deem him remarkably well qualified for the position, aside from his personal interest in treating them well.

A. J. Bell, his father, is a friend of Secretary McCrary & served with him in the Iowa Legislature. I hope therefore that you may be able to secure his appointment.

Very Truly,

---

[232] Athearn, Frederic J. (1981). *An Isolated Empire: A History of Northwestern Colorado,* Page 49. https://nrrbook.com/AnIsolatedEmpire

John V. Farwell"[233]

Farwell's Superintendent, A.J. Bell, also penned a letter to Smith in support of his son John:

"Mr. Smith

Dear sir: John W Bell of whom Mr. Farwell speaks of for White River Agency Ute Indians, is a man 33 years old. Of large experience among Indians having spent much of his life on the frontier and had to do with the Sioux always peacefully, he is a man of good moral habit, and I think I can say he can refer to C.B. or J.V. Farwell as to his capability in such a fashion.

Mr. Farwell is largely interested in maintaining peaceful relations with the Ute Indians. At present there is certainly danger to be apprehended from them, and it does seem just that those having the largest monied interest in the county ought to be consulted to some extent in matters in which they have so much interested.

A.J. Bell"[234]

In addition, A.J. Bell wrote a letter to his friend, U.S. Secretary of War George McCrary:

"To the Honorable Secretary of War, Mr. George W. McCrary

Presuming our old acquaintance and former friendship in Iowa, I venture to ask you to aid us a little in regard to the White River Agency of Ute Indians.

In connection with Mr. J.V. Farwell of this city we have large mining interests so near the Utes that we are directly interested

---

[233] John V. Farwell Letter of Support for J.W. Bell. National Archives Microfilm M808, Roll 13. https://nrrbook.com/JVFforBell

[234] Letter from A.J. Bell to Mr. Smith. National Archives Microfilm M808, Roll 13. https://nrrbook.com/BelltoSmith

in keeping peace with those Indians and there is real danger to be apprehended if great care is not taken to treat them fairly.

The Messrs. Farwells who have the largest interest there recommend J.W. Bell for agent and from their personal knowledge are sure he is the man for the place, and he is in their employ now and like them directly interested in peace with the tribe.

I might add he was soldier nearly three years in the Sioux Country as the National Guard Member 910th assembly of Iowa and he is 33 years of age.

Yours truly

A.J. Bell"[235]

Farwell and his team believed that, as the most significant industrial enterprise operating near the White River Agency, they should have some influence over who the next White River Agent would be. They had no interest in turning the Utes into farmers, but they did have an interest in maintaining fair and peaceful relations that could potentially benefit everyone in the region. This vision aligned with John V.'s friendly experience with the Osage eight years prior, which led to a peaceful, mutually beneficial agreement.

Unfortunately for them, Nathan Meeker had also thrown his hat in the ring. His opinion of the Utes was clear: *"They are savages, having no written language, no traditional history, no poetry, no literature...their constructive and investigative faculties have never been exercised. They are not a powerful people, nor are they war-like...they remain a race without ambition, and also a race deficient in the inherent elements of progress...vermin abound on their persons...It might not be too late to reform and Christianize them, but past efforts had failed*

---

[235] Letter from A.J. Bell to Hon. George W. McCrary, Secretary of War. National Archives Microfilm M808, Roll 13. https://nrrbook.com/BelltoMcCrary

from want of a strong and wise government, and second, from a defect in the character of the teachers or missionaries."[236]

Meeker viewed the Utes as a flawed people in need of more intentional efforts to convert them to a Christian, agricultural way of life. This mindset, combined with endorsements from P.T. Barnum[237] (famous for his "Greatest Show on Earth") and Governor John Routt,[238] among others, ultimately won Meeker the appointment to the White River Agency from President Rutherford B. Hayes in April 1878. Farwell was notified[239] of this appointment directly by the Department of the Interior. *"It was into this culture conflict that Nathan Meeker maneuvered himself. He was a typical 19th century American who believed in all the principles of Indian welfare and conversion. The Utes, at first, gracefully accepted and tolerated him, but he demanded too much too fast, and the cultural changes that were required by him proved overly demanding for the Ute people."*[240]

Meeker's first course of action was to move the White River Agency a few miles west to Powell Park, which contained fertile land used by the Utes as a horse pasture and race track. New agency buildings were constructed, including a personal home for Meeker's family. During the summer of 1878, several irrigation ditches were dug and fences were built with Ute labor to aid in farming; however, they gradually lost interest and reverted to their traditional hunter-gatherer ways by

---

[236] Decker, Peter. (2004). *"The Utes Must Go!": American Expansion and the Removal of a People,* Page 96.

[237] P.T. Barnum Letter of Support for Nathan Meeker. National Archives M808, Roll 13. https://nrrbook.com/BarnumforMeeker

[238] Routt Letter of Support for Nathan Meeker. National Archives M808, Roll 13. https://nrrbook.com/RouttforMeeker

[239] Department of Interior Letter to John V. Farwell. National Archives M808, Roll 13. https://nrrbook.com/DOItoFarwell

[240] Athearn, Frederic J. (1981). *An Isolated Empire: A History of Northwestern Colorado,* Page 47. https://nrrbook.com/AnIsolatedEmpire

leaving the reservation to hunt. In response, Meeker withheld the Utes' rations of food and supplies to keep them near the agency.

Tension escalated. In May of 1879, after the winter snow had melted off, the Utes defiantly set several forest fires, including one near Sand Mountain next to the Hahns Peak Mining District. *"The Utes went on a rampage, rebelling against the effort of Agent Meeker to make them work. They set the entire country on fire and millions of dollars worth of timber were destroyed. The smoke hung like a pall over the country for days and the sun was almost clouded, appearing only as a red ball in the heavens."*[241]

Governor Frederick Pitkin,[242] who campaigned on the slogan of "The Utes Must Go," was furious and sent a telegram on July 5th to Commissioner of Indian Affairs Ezra Hayt:

"Reports reach me daily that a band of White River Utes are off the reservation, destroying forests and game near North and Middle Parks. They have already burned millions of dollars of timber, and are intimidating settlers and miners. Have written Agent Meeker, but fear letters have not reached him. I respectfully request you to have telegraphic order sent troops at nearest post to remove Indians to their reservation. If general government does not act promptly the State must. Immense forests are burning throughout Western Colorado, supposed to have been fired by the Utes. I am satisfied there is an organized effort on the part of Indians to destroy the timber of Colorado. The loss will be irreplaceable. These savages should be removed to the Indian Territory, where they can no longer destroy the finest forests in this state."[243]

---

[241] Leahy, W. (March 31, 1915). Tales of Early Days. *The Steamboat Pilot*, Page 7. https://nrrbook.com/SP-1915-03-31

[242] Federick Pitkin was sworn in as Colorado's Governor on January 14, 1879.

[243] Santala, R.D. (1955). *The Ute Campaign of 1879: A Study in the Use of the Military Instrument*, Page 51. https://nrrbook.com/UteCampaign1879

A.H. Smart of Hayden stated this when describing the situation: *"All the country from the divide on the north side of the Bear (Yampa) River to the Hahn's Peak mines are burnt, that is from 12-15 miles, and all hands have been fighting fire for two days to save the buildings, so I am told by the mail carrier. The fire extends over 40 miles in length. All of Twenty Mile Park is burnt, and all the range of mountains to the east and northeast of it. That fire alone has burnt thousands of acres of timber.*

I do not know how much country is burnt over below here, but some five or six fires have been burning for weeks. The air is so full of smoke you can scarce see half a mile, and at times you cannot see two hundred yards. I have not seen the sky for four weeks to tell whether it was cloudy or not.

From the canyon to the mouth of the Elk River a large width of country is burnt and thousands of acres of timber have been destroyed by the fires which the Utes originated over three months ago, as far as I can learn.

Nearly all fires have been set by the Utes. I could tell when they moved camp and what way they were going by the fires they left. They burnt all my meadow lands below here with the Johnson house. Then above all the bottom lands from here to the canyon six miles above, with a great deal of the timber on the islands. A large bunch of timber is burnt between Steamboat Springs and Rock Creek, and thousands of acres of country burnt over that I saw while in Middle Park last July. How much was burnt in North Park I cannot learn, but thousands and thousands of acres of land has been burnt over, and millions of dollars' worth of timber has been destroyed by fire."[244]

Mr. Deering (first name unknown) ran into Chief Colorow of the Utes outside of Steamboat Springs, where this brief conversation occurred:

---

[244] Miscellaneous Documents of the House of Representatives for the Second Session of the Forty-Sixth Congress, 1879-80, Volume 4, Ute Indian Outbreak, Pages 136-137. https://nrrbook.com/UteOutbreak

"I asked Colorow why they had kindled the fires; he said it was 'to make heap grass next spring for ponies.' I directed his attention to the fact that most of the fire was burning in the mountains where no grass grew, and he declined to answer any questions upon that subject. I told him then that I was satisfied, and had been for two or three years, that they were trying to destroy the value of the country for the white man; which he did not deny. I had been satisfied for two or three years before that they were systematically burning the timber outside the reservation."[245]

Relations ultimately boiled over in early September when Meeker decided to plow the Utes' beloved racetrack for use as farmland. Several days later, on September 10th, Chief Johnson (whose real name was Cavanish) met with Meeker to discuss the incident. Meeker refused to listen to Johnson, and out of anger, Johnson shoved Meeker into a hitching post. As a result, Meeker urgently sent a message to the Bureau of Indian Affairs requesting military assistance to help restore order:

"Sir: We have plowed eighty acres, and the Indians object to any more being done, and to any more fencing. We shall stop plowing. One of the plowmen was shot at last week. On Monday I was assaulted in my own house, while my wife was present, by a leading chief named Johnson, and forced out doors and considerably injured, as I was in a crippled condition, having previously met with an accident, a wagon falling over on me. The employees came to my rescue. I had built this Johnson a house, given him a wagon and harness, and fed him at my table many, many times. The trouble is, he has 150 horses, and wants the land for pasturage, although the agency was moved that this same land might be used, and the agency buildings are on it. I have had two days' council with the chiefs and headmen of the tribe, who concluded, after a sort of a way, that I might plow, but they will do nothing to permit me to, and they laugh at my being forced out of my house.

---

[245] Miscellaneous Documents of the House of Representatives for the Second Session of the Forty-Sixth Congress, 1879-80, Volume 4, Ute Indian Outbreak, Page 151. https://nrrbook.com/UteOutbreak

I have no confidence in any of them, and I feel that none of the white people are safe. I know they are not if we go on to perform work directed by the Commissioner of Indian Affairs. Here are my wife and daughter in this condition.

Confer with General Pope, Commissioner, and Senator Teller. At least 100 soldiers ought to come hither to protect us, and to keep the Utes on their reservation - should be more.

Don't let this application get in the papers, for I know the Indians will hear of it in a few days. Of course, what the Indians have done is a matter of news.

Truly,

N.C. Meeker"[246]

As a result of this urgent plea, Major Thomas Thornburgh, along with 153 soldiers and 25 civilians, departed from Fort Steele, Wyoming, on September 22nd to restore order to the White River Agency. Thornburgh, though, had doubts about how serious the situation truly was. *"He knew only of the need to make arrests and of Meeker's stubborn, inflexible management of his Indians. He had learned over the summer to mistrust the agent's reports. Had the agent, to protect his authority with the Utes and his reputation with the government, exaggerated his trouble and lied again?"*[247]

Meanwhile, the fire that was set ablaze near Sand Mountain had spread to the Hahns Peak Mining District and was burning wildly out of control. On September 19th, Farwell's

---

[246] Miscellaneous Documents of the House of Representatives for the Second Session of the Forty-Sixth Congress, 1879-80, Volume 4, Ute Indian Outbreak, Pages 107-108. https://nrrbook.com/UteOutbreak

[247] Decker, Peter. (2004). *"The Utes Must Go!": American Expansion and the Removal of a People,* Page 121.

Superintendent, J.B. Donaldson, penned a letter to Jason Thompson of the General Land Office in Washington, D.C.

"Dear Mr. Thompson:

Your favor of September 6 received. The forest fire that began near Sand Mountain early in May last has been burning ever since and has finally culminated, after sweeping all over that section of the country, in a grand attack on our mining property on String Ridge, sweeping all before it, and causing us very serious expense to keep it out of this camp. Besides it is now sweeping everything before it along the line of our 17-mile ditch, on which we have several miles of fluming.

The fire is so hot and the smoke so dense that we cannot reach many of our flumes to know at present how many of them are destroyed. If any are left it will be nothing short of a miracle.

Thousands of acres have been burned, and who can say where it will stop? Our sawmill and timber, I think, may go, unless we get rain or snow within the next three days. We keep men night and day battling it where we can, but man is almost powerless against such a destructive element when once set in action.

Frank Hinman asked the Utes when he was on Snake River, why they set the timber in our section on fire and they replied: 'In order that their ponies could travel. Now, too much timber.'

Jim Baker, the scout, who lives on Snake River, was out with a surveying party, and says the Utes started a fire in the timber in two different places, not far from their camp. I am not acquainted with any of the Utes, and of course they will not converse with a stranger, but I do know they were in our vicinity when these fires were started in the spring, and there had been no hunters around or we should have known, because the mining camps are their market for meat.

About the quantity of timber and grazing land burned over, I cannot give it in acres, but it is immense. It can only be measured by miles, and at this date it is growing more fierce every day. Nothing can now stop it but a storm of rain or snow.

Very truly yours,

J.B. Donaldson"[248]

The same day, with the situation at the White River Agency still at a boiling point, Meeker sent a telegram to Governor Pitkin:

"Dear Sir: Yours received. I have a dispatch from the Indian Commissioner giving directions as to course to pursue when troops arrive, viz, arrest the ringleaders and hold them until further orders. I think it high time these Indians should be taught to behave themselves equally with white people, and I might as well try them on as anybody else. Things are quiet because we have stopped plowing and fencing.

N.C. Meeker"[249]

Meeker sent another telegram to Governor Pitkin on September 24, 1879:

"Dear Sir: Yours of the 19th received. I learn that the soldiers from Middle Park, after reaching Bear River, turned back. I hear some are coming from Fort Steele, or were to come, but nothing further.

Things are quiet because I have ceased to make improvements, and the agency is run as the Indians wish.

So far as I can gather, a large number are getting ready to go north to the Sweetwater country to hunt buffalo, and among

---

[248] *History of Routt National Forest 1905-1972.* (May 4, 2020). Page 44-45. National Forest Service Library. https://nrrbook.com/HistoryofRNF

[249] Miscellaneous Documents of the House of Representatives for the Second Session of the Forty-Sixth Congress, 1879-80, Volume 4, Ute Indian Outbreak, Pages 108-109. https://nrrbook.com/UteOutbreak

them are more or less from Los Pinos. They have urged me with might and main to distribute annuity goods now, but as a part of the goods are behind I cannot. Unless turned back they will, until next July, cover the whole country north of the reservation. If soldiers come in, depredators will be arrested, but I judge this should be done by legal process, the military enforcing it.

N.C. Meeker"[250]

All the while, Thornburgh and his troops continued their march towards the White River Agency, reaching Fortification Creek on September 25th, where they camped. Thornburgh, via courier, messaged Meeker:

"In obedience to instructions from the General of the Army, I am enroute to your agency, and expect to arrive there on the 29th instant, for the purpose of affording you any assistance in my power in regulating your affairs, and to make arrests at your suggestion, and to hold as prisoners such of your Indians as you desire, until investigations are made by your department.

I have heard nothing definite from your agency for ten days and do not know what state of affairs exists, whether the Indians will leave at my approach or show hostilities. I sent this letter by Mr. Lowery, one of my guides, and desire you to communicate with me as soon as possible, giving me all the information in your power, in order that I may know what course I am to pursue. If practical, meet me on the road at the earliest moment."[251]

After crossing Fortification Creek and dispatching the letter to Meeker, Thornburgh's unit encountered Ute Chief Jack (real name Nicaagat), who demanded to know what the soldiers

---

[250] Miscellaneous Documents of the House of Representatives for the Second Session of the Forty-Sixth Congress, 1879-80, Volume 4, Ute Indian Outbreak, Page 109. https://nrrbook.com/UteOutbreak

[251] Santala, R.D. (1955). *The Ute Campaign of 1879: A Study in the Use of the Military Instrument*, Page 5. https://nrrbook.com/UteCampaign1879

were doing and warned them that crossing into the Ute reservation would result in war. Thornburgh told the Ute Chief that he would reconsider, but ultimately followed his orders and continued his advance to the agency.

The Utes, now aware of the approaching army, began preparing for battle. Meeker began to fear the worst and sent a response to Thornburgh on September 27th:

"Understanding that you are on the way hither with United States troops, I send a messenger, Mr. Eskridge, and two Indians, Henry (interpreter) and John Ayersly, to inform you that the Indians are greatly excited, and wish you to stop at some convenient camping place, and then that you and five soldiers of your command come into the Agency, when a talk and a better understanding can be had.

This I agree to, but I do not propose to order your movements, but it seems for the best. The Indians seem to consider the advance of the troops as a declaration of real war. In this I am laboring to undeceive them, and at the same time to convince them they cannot do whatever they please. The first object is to allay apprehension."[252]

Thornburgh responded to Meeker on the 28th:

"Sir: I shall move with my entire command to some convenient camp near and within striking distance of your agency, reaching such point during the 29th. I shall then halt and encamp the troops and proceed to the agency with my guide and five soldiers, as communicated in my letter of the 27th instant.

Then and there I will be ready to have a conference with you and the Indians, so that an understanding may be arrived at and my course of action determined. I have carefully considered whether or not it would be advisable to have my command at a point as distant as that desired by the Indians who were in my

---

[252] Santala, R.D. (1955). *The Ute Campaign of 1879: A Study in the Use of the Military Instrument*, Page 6. https://nrrbook.com/UteCampaign1879

camp last night, and have reached the conclusion that under my orders, which require me to march this command to the agency, I am not at liberty to leave it at a point where it would not be available in case of trouble. You are authorized to say for me to the Indians that my course of conduct is entirely dependent on them. Our desire is to avoid trouble, and we have not come for war.

I requested you in my letter of the 25th to meet me on the road before I reached the agency. I renew my request that you do so, and further desire that you bring such chiefs as may wish to accompany you."[253]

Reports of exactly what happened next vary, though it is certain Thornburgh continued his advance with his entire unit, reaching and fatefully crossing the generally accepted boundary of the Ute Reservation, Milk Creek, on September 29th. There are differing reports as to why this happened:

- Thornburgh changed his mind about leaving his unit behind, believing he would be led into an ambush. Thus, he chose to advance offensively with his entire unit. *"Thornburgh and his officers believed that leaving their full force beyond reach of the agency was too risky, so they devised a cautious plan to invade the reservation."*[254]

- Thornburgh intended to follow through with the plan, but ignored suitable sites to stop and camp. Upon reaching and crossing Milk Creek, it was too late. *"Some of the major's officers and scouts later testified that their commander had inexplicably ignored a number of adequate camp sites outside the reservation and crossed*

---

[253] 1879 Annual Report of the Commissioner of Indian Affairs, Page XXXII. https://nrrbook.com/1879Report

[254] Battle of Milk Creek. Colorado Encyclopedia. https://nrrbook.com/MilkCreek

Milk Creek with two cavalry companies behind reconnaissance patrols."[255]

- Thornburgh expected to replenish his water supply at Milk Creek before crossing and advancing with the small delegation. However, Milk Creek had run dry, so he decided to advance to Little Beaver Creek, which was located within the Ute boundaries. *"But about midday of their arrival on Sept. 29, because of the lack of pasture and water in the dry Milk Creek at his command camp, Thornburgh decided, on the advice of a scouting party, to move his camp south to Little Beaver Creek, just inside the reservation. From there, he planned to travel unarmed with five men to the agency, as agreed to with Nicaagat.*"[256]

Regardless of how or why it happened, Thornburgh's team had crossed into Ute Territory and was in grave danger.

"Led by Jack and Colorow, several dozen Utes waited behind rocky outcroppings on the heights above Milk Creek, armed with rifles. About fifty more waited with their mounts below, just off the main wagon road that led to the agency. If the soldiers crossed the creek, in violation of the 1868 treaty, the Utes would fight.

At the agency on the morning of September 29, Meeker assured Douglas that Thornburgh would not enter the reservation. But Thornburgh had already made his decision. The major crossed dry Milk Creek with all his troops, leaving behind only his cumbersome wagons. The lead unit promptly ran into Jack's Utes, and even though both sides signaled that they wanted to talk, a shot was fired—it is not known by whom—and the battle began."[257]

---

[255] Davis, R. (June 10, 2013). Bloody Siege at Milk Creek. *True West Magazine.* https://nrrbook.com/BloodySiege

[256] Cooney, T. (2023, June 24). At Milk Creek, Northern Utes defend their territory. *Aspen Journalism.* https://nrrbook.com/UtesDefendTerritory

[257] Battle of Milk Creek. Colorado Encyclopedia. https://nrrbook.com/MilkCreek

The Battle of Milk Creek and the Meeker Massacre were underway.

"By noon, Thornburgh's entire expedition struggled desperately for their lives. From a line of cedar trees, scrub oak and serviceberry bushes at the base of Yellow Jacket Pass blew a hail of rifle bullets. Gauging from the volume of shots and smoke, some soldiers later stated that the Utes outnumbered their men three to one. The cavalry's reconnaissance patrols began a fighting retreat.

The Utes, utilizing the high ground to their left, immediately maneuvered to outflank the cavalry and cut them off from where Lt. James V.S. Paddock's D Company guarded the wagon supply train on a nearly level butte above the Milk Creek. Hearing the shots, Paddock immediately circled the wagons. This action, coupled with a disciplined withdrawal of the forward detachment, literally saved the day.

But Maj. Thornburgh lay dead somewhere in the tangle of sagebrush leading up to the tree line on Yellow Jacket Pass. His body would lie there for the next five days. Captain J. Scott Payne, Thornburgh's second in command, had only just narrowly escaped death himself from a bullet wound to his left side and shoulder. Payne's and Lawson's companies won the race back to the wagons."[258]

Nearly fifty men would be killed or wounded, though Joe Rankin[259] managed to escape and fled for help. *"Rankin managed to procure a horse and, changing mounts at various cow camps en route, made one of the greatest rides in the history of the West, covering the 160 miles to Rawlings, Wyoming, in something less than twenty-eight hours."*[260]

---

[258] Davis, R. (2013, June 10). Bloody Siege at Milk Creek. *True West Magazine*. https://nrrbook.com/BloodySiege

[259] Joe Rankin served as a scout and messenger for Thornburgh.

[260] Burroughs, John. (1962). *Where the Old West Stayed Young*, Page 48.

Receiving word of the attack at Milk Creek, Chief Douglas (real name Quinkent) led twenty-five to thirty Utes on an attack at the White River Agency. Meeker and ten others were killed, and the agency was burned to the ground. Meeker's wife, Arvalla, and daughter, Josephine, were among five women taken captive as hostages.

As a result of Rankin's urgent dash to Rawlins, Captain F.S. Dodge and his 9th U.S. Cavalry (known as the Buffalo Soldiers) met up with the besieged forces at Milk Creek on October 2nd, where they helped turn the tide of the days-long battle. Three days later, Colonel Wesley Merritt arrived from Russell, Wyoming, along with infantry and cavalry, and the Utes, now vastly outnumbered, laid down their arms and fled. Soon after, Merritt's forces traveled to the White River Agency, where they learned the fate of Meeker and his employees. *"The body of Mr. Meeker was found about two hundred yards from his house, with a log chain around his neck, one side of his head smashed, and part of a barrel-stave driven through his body."*[261]

"The captivity of the women was discovered and Colonel Merritt contacted the War Department and Bureau of Indian Affairs for direction. Charles Adams, retired Ute agent at Los Pinos and trusted friend of Ouray, was chosen to negotiate return of the hostages. Ouray, himself, sent out pleas for the fighting to stop and for the prisoners' safe release.

Adams was successful in his mission. On October 21, 1879, he secured the captives' release near Douglass' camp on the plateau between the present sites of DeBeque and Palisade, Colorado. The good offices of Chief Ouray greatly aided Adams' work."[262]

---

[261] Burroughs, John. (1962). *Where the Old West Stayed Young*, Page 48.

[262] Mehls, Steven F. (1982). *The Valley of Opportunity: A History of West-Central Colorado,* Page 41. https://nrrbook.com/ValleyofOpportunity

The battle was over, but relations between the Utes and the United States remained turbulent.

Back in International Camp, John V. Farwell was distraught. After two years of construction, Farwell had finally put his big ditch and giant water cannons into operation the previous fall. While the 1879 mining season should have been a time of hope and optimism, ideally marking the beginning of a good return on his investment, in reality, it was nothing short of a disaster. The threat of attack, ever-worsening fire that surrounded and destroyed much of his operation, and nearby conflict between the United States and the Utes had to make the Hahns Peak Mining District, once compared to Eden,[263] feel more like Hell.

For the fifth time since 1868, John V. faced a major fire that destroyed property in which he had invested substantially. Unlike the previous fires, however, this inferno was intentional. Farwell had recovered from earlier fires in Chicago by rebuilding bigger and better, and certainly could have done the same here, but to what end? Would the Utes start another fire in the future if he were to rebuild?

The level of panic intensified when International Camp received a message from the Governor. Pitkin, upon hearing of the massacre, sent an urgent notice to mining camps near the reservation. *"Immediately upon receiving news of this outbreak, I dispatched couriers to all the frontier mining camps near the reservation, to notify the settlers of the condition of affairs, in order that they might guard against possible dangers. The alarm which was felt throughout the western half of the State, on the receipt of the news of these Indian atrocities, was intense and widespread."[264]*

The despair and destruction of 1879, combined with the uncertainty of what Ute relations would be in the future, made

---

[263] The Snake River Mines. (August 19, 1875). *The Laramie Daily Sentinel*, Page 3. https://nrrbook.com/LDS-1875-08-19

[264] Frederick Pitkin 1881 Biennial Message to the Colorado Legislature. (January 5, 1881). Page 36. https://nrrbook.com/PitkinMessage

operating a business next to impossible. Reports state that Farwell's mining results were below expectations, and while this may be true, the International Mining Company never truly had a fair chance. Given the time spent fighting fires and worrying about safety, rather than sluicing gold from the dirt, it is only natural that the results were disappointing. Under normal conditions, a businessman with John V.'s expertise and resources would be perfectly capable and willing to weather a short-term economic struggle, especially when he had committed a vast amount of time and money to build it, and it would be irrational to abandon ship so soon. However, this was no ordinary economic struggle. Making things even worse, Farwell was caught up in litigation with Thomas Brooks over their failed contract in 1876. Pitkin's message was the final straw.

Enough was enough. Instead of crying over spilled milk, John V. sold his operation[265] at a steep loss to a party consisting of James France of Rawlins, Wyoming, and former Superintendent, J.B. Donaldson. France and Donaldson received all the business's assets, including mining claims, the Farwell Ditch, equipment, and the general store's inventory (valued at $32,000) for a total price of $60,000. France, who had purchased[266] the neighboring Hans Peak Gold & Silver Mining Company operation in July of 1878, now controlled virtually all of the mining ground around Poverty Bar and String Ridge in the Hahns Peak Mining District.

John V. likely had the words of his friend Horatio Spafford's *"It Is Well With My Soul"* on his mind as he witnessed the destruction of his International Mining Company and arranged for its sale. Penned by Spafford after immense personal tragedy, and performed by Phillip Paul Bliss in Farwell Hall in Chicago for the first time only three years prior, the lyrics tell

---

[265] John V. Farwell Sale to James France & J.B. Donaldson. (December 17, 1879). Book C Page 4. Routt County Clerk and Recorder's Office. https://nrrbook.com/JVFSale

[266] Our Rawlins Letter. (June 27, 1878). *Cheyenne Weekly Leader*, Page 8. https://nrrbook.com/CWL-1878-06-27

of finding peace and contentment through faith in Jesus during times of suffering:

When peace, like a river, attendeth my way,
When sorrows like sea billows roll;
Whatever my lot, Thou hast taught me to say,
It is well, it is well with my soul.

> *Refrain:*
> *It is well with my soul,*
> *It is well, it is well with my soul.*

Though Satan should buffet, though trials should come,
Let this blest assurance control,
That Christ hath regarded my helpless estate,
And hath shed His own blood for my soul.

My sin—oh, the bliss of this glorious thought!—
My sin, not in part but the whole,
Is nailed to the cross, and I bear it no more,
Praise the Lord, praise the Lord, O my soul!

For me, be it Christ, be it Christ hence to live:
If Jordan above me shall roll,
No pang shall be mine, for in death as in life
Thou wilt whisper Thy peace to my soul.

But, Lord, 'tis for Thee, for Thy coming we wait,
The sky, not the grave, is our goal;
Oh, trump of the angel! Oh, voice of the Lord!
Blessed hope, blessed rest of my soul!

And Lord, haste the day when my faith shall be sight,
The clouds be rolled back as a scroll;
The trump shall resound, and the Lord shall descend,
Even so, it is well with my soul.

Surely, Farwell had to wonder if things would have gone differently if his preferred pick for the White River Agency,

John W. Bell, had gotten the job instead of Meeker. We will never know, but Bell's appointment could have dramatically altered the history of Colorado in many ways, and it is natural to wonder "What if?" *"It was recognized that the whole affair might have been prevented had those on the scene been better acquainted with Indian nature and superstitions."*[267]

Chief Ouray knew that the massacre would lead to the loss of more land, and in November 1879, a Peace Commission was held at the Los Pinos Agency. Failing to reach an agreement, the participants were summoned to Washington, D.C., where negotiations continued. A treaty was signed on March 6, 1880, resulting in these relocations:

- The White River Utes (northern bands) were relocated to the Uintah Reservation in Utah. This was accomplished by sending the rations and land payments to the Uintah reservation, thus luring the Utes in. A military post was planned to keep them there.

- The Tabeguache Utes could relocate to either agricultural plots of land where the Gunnison River and Grand (Colorado) River meet (present-day Grand Junction) or to a newly created reservation adjacent to the Uintah reservation in Utah. They ultimately chose Utah, with their new land commonly being known as the Ouray reservation.

  The Tabeguache were forced to march by the U.S. Army to their new reservation in August of 1881. Chief Ouray did not live to see this, as he died in 1880.

- The Southern Utes (Muache, Capote, Weeminuche) were relocated to a vastly reduced reservation in the southwest corner of Colorado, which remains in existence to this day.

---

[267] Leckenby, Charles. (1945). *Tread of Pioneers*, Page 34.
https://nrrbook.com/TreadofPioneers

Despite dealing with everything the events of 1879 could throw at him, Farwell was not done mining in Colorado. He, partnering with brother Charles B. Farwell, among others, moved on to other gold mining operations near Georgetown, Leadville, and most notably Independence,[268] which today is a ghost town near Aspen. Operating under the umbrella of the Farwell Consolidated Mining Company, this company owned numerous properties,[269] including:

Lode Mining Claims

The Bennington, Big Chief, Boston, Boston No. 2, Beebe, Bennett, Camp Bird, California, Cholar, Climax, Dutchman, Dolly Varden, Five-twenty, Friday, Fourth-of-July, Ferdinand, Gatton, Golden Champion, Gold Dollar, Golden Champion No. 2, Home Stake, Independence, Last Dollar, Legal Tender, Little Betsey, Last Dime, Little Annie, Little Tillie, Lancaster, Muscatine, Little Chief, Little Elsie, Mammoth, Mount Hope, May E., Minnie, Minnie W., Overman, Pacific, Pinafore, Seek-no-further, Syndic, Sheba, Sitka, Steuben, Salmon, Tam O'Shanter, and the Zoa.

Placer Mining Claims

The Burton, Bell, Independence, Johnson, Wilson-Buck, and the Gold.

---

[268] For a short period of time, the mining town of Independence was known as Farwell. The remains of several buildings still stand today. This site was added to the National Register of Historic Places in 1973 to help protect it from further deterioration.

[269] Lease Agreement: W.B. Dickerman, Receiver of the Farwell Consolidated Mining Company To William L Davis. (May 12, 1885). Colorado State Archives. https://nrrbook.com/DavisLease

Mill Sites

The Brown, Brown No. 2, Farwell, Farwell No. 2, Golden Champion, Marrs and Middleton, Mount Hope, and the Ward.

Water Claim Structures

The Marrs and Middleton Dam, Water-Ditch and Water Rights, also the Shinn Tunnel and Boston No. 2, Tam O'Shanter Tunnel and Tunnel Site, the Brown Claim and Tunnel Site; also the Ditch and Water Rights and Water Privileges staked or claimed on the south side of Independence Gulch in Pitkin County.

In 1885, the assets and equipment of the Farwell Consolidated Mining Company were leased[270] to William L. Davis in exchange for a 15% royalty on all gold produced in the first six months, and a 20% royalty for the remainder of the two-year term. This lease marked the end of John V. Farwell's direct involvement in gold mining in Colorado, allowing him to devote his time and resources to form a syndicate that financed the construction of the State Capitol building in Austin, Texas. In return, Farwell and his partners, including brother Charles B. Farwell, received more than 3,000,000 acres of land in the Texas panhandle, which they developed into the legendary XIT Ranch, destined to become the largest ranch "under one fence" in the world.

---

[270] Lease Agreement: W.B. Dickerman, Receiver of the Farwell Consolidated Mining Company To William L Davis. (May 12, 1885). Colorado State Archives. https://nrrbook.com/DavisLease

CHAPTER 7: OLD MAC

"Any man who contends that Christianity is not the handmaid of real success in business life, does not know either the meaning of success that is worthy of the name, nor the meat and drink contained in God's promises."[271]

-John V. Farwell

Following the turmoil of 1879, only nine men stayed in the Hahns Peak area for the winter, likely due to the alarm caused by Governor Pitkin's message. With Farwell gone and the March 6, 1880 Ute Treaty promising to move the Utes permanently out of the area, John V.'s trusted lieutenant, Robert McIntosh, and new partner, Ed Cody (presumably two of the nine that stayed), seized the opportunity to mine in peace, and leased the Poverty Bar and String Ridge claims now owned by James France and J.B. Donaldson. The Farwell Ditch, which McIntosh had supervised the construction of in previous years, was now under his control.

Believing the gravel deposits of Poverty Bar had greater potential than Ways and Nova Scotia Gulches, McIntosh & Cody, along with approximately thirty employees, extended the Farwell Ditch one mile from String Ridge to a sandbox on Little Mountain in 1880. Here, the sandbox fed most of the Farwell Ditch water into a pipe that dropped over four hundred feet on its way to Poverty Bar. The diameter of the pipe narrowed as it descended the mountain, thereby causing the falling water to build immense pressure and feed the water cannons. The remaining water collected by the sandbox was released down the southern face of Little Mountain in a controlled manner, also towards Poverty Bar, where it was

---

[271] Farwell, John V. (1906). *Corner Stones of Character: Some Ways of Making Them*, Page 119. https://nrrbook.com/CornerStonesofCharacter

captured and fed through sluice boxes to wash gold from pay dirt. Hydraulic mining with the giants at Poverty Bar produced immediate results.

"The first year Father's share was around forty thousand dollars. The gold dust was carried in small containers on skis to Snake River and then by stage to Rawlins, where it was delivered to James France and expressed by him to the Denver mint."[272]

Note that $40,000 in 1880 is worth approximately $1.2 million today. The "McIntosh Bonanza" did not stop there! In 1881, production at Poverty Bar was estimated to be between $20,000 and $25,000,[273] which would be valued at $600,000 to $750,000 today.

Above: Miners at Poverty Bar pose for a picture. Robert McIntosh is the tall man in the black suit on the right side of the photo. The Farwell Ditch supplied the water blasting from the water cannons. Photo credit to the Hahns Peak Area Historical Society.

Following the 1881 mining season, Cody ceased operations with McIntosh and would later go into partnership with Frank

---

[272] Morgan, Helen. (1970). *Snake River Profiles, Volume 1*, Page 44.

[273] Robert McIntosh, Pioneer Miner, Merchant and Rancher, is Dead. (December 24, 1924). *The Steamboat Pilot*, Page 5. https://nrrbook.com/SP-1924-12-24

Hinman. McIntosh, determined to find the source of Poverty Bar gold, continued prospecting and mining whenever possible, despite his many commitments that limited his time. *"The heart-breaking thing was that all the rich deposits seemed to be in pockets and the question was from where did the gold come? Father's (McIntosh's) great ambition was to find the main vein. He would start out with a pick and shovel over his shoulder, a few biscuits tied in a bandana suspended on the shovel handle, and he would be gone for two or three days prospecting. A lot of his time had to be spent in administration of civic duties. I find an old letterhead of 1880 which reads: 'Robert McIntosh, Practical Hydraulic Miner. Mining Surveyor of Waters Rights, Ditches, Dams, Reservoirs; Machinist of Hydraulic Pipe Giants, Resisting Pressure, etc.; Prospector of Placer Mines, Grade Flumes. Gold-saving Riffles and Dumps.'"*[274]

McIntosh's production in 1883, while still solid, began to decline. *"Judge McIntosh has been working Poverty Bar under lease. This is the property of the Hon. James France, of Rawlins. The judge has taken out $16,500. He will take the bar another year, and feels confident of taking out a larger sum. For the past month he has been working three eight-hour shifts instead of two twelve-hour shifts as heretofore. He finds the three shifts to work well and intends to work this way through the coming season. This is a new departure for this camp and is hailed with joy by the men."*[275]

Elsewhere at Poverty Bar, the gold rush was in full swing.

"Carruthers & Hinman have taken out more money than ever before. Their property lies at the upper end of Poverty Bar and is very rich. Your correspondent has often gotten from twenty-five to fifty cents to the pan from this claim. They can work only about six weeks in the spring on account of the scarcity of water. They keep pushing their ditches in all directions to get more

---

[274] Morgan, Helen. (1970). *Snake River Profiles, Volume 1*, Page 44.

[275] Points on Placers. (November 15, 1883). *The Weekly Boomerang*, Page 3.
https://nrrbook.com/WB-1883-11-15

water, and have made satisfactory arrangements with Mr. France to run the McIntosh flume the coming season. This gives them an outlet that they needed badly, and will enable them to work some of their richest ground. They will take out a great deal of money next season.

Miller & Cody, after running six weeks, shut down on account of scarcity of water, since which they have been digging a new ditch which will give them a better and longer supply of water. They have some sixty acres of good ground. With this and a good supply of water your correspondent sees nothing to prevent them from making a big stake.

Charlie Wood, while prospecting and representing String Ridge, the property of Mr. France, discovered some rich ground. String Ridge is a heavy wash, similar to Poverty Bar. There are about 200 acres with an average depth of gravel of 35 feet, that prospects from 30 to 50 cents to the yard. It is immense hydraulic ground. It is the intention of the owner to extend the ditch and pick up another fork of Elk River and work this property at an early day.

A.S. Hutchinson has been and is still working the Purdy ground. From the looks of his buckskin sack we should say he had done well."[276]

Following the 1883 mining season, James France and J.B. Donaldson sold their property to Cody and Hinman for $20,000. Robert McIntosh, who had planned to lease this land again in 1884, was now off the ground. Cody and Hinman's investment quickly paid off. *"An immensely rich streak was encountered and the production in 1884 was $45,000, and the following year it jumped to $65,000. At times in Nugget Cut when the water was turned off nuggets could be picked up from the bedrock by the bucket full. There were some boom times in the old camp in*

---

[276] Points on Placers. (November 15, 1883). *The Weekly Boomerang*, Page 3.
https://nrrbook.com/WB-1883-11-15

those years and both Cody and Hinman set a pace that was hard to follow."[277]

Note that Nugget Cut was effectively the northern portion of Poverty Bar. We know this from the testimony William Flick provided in his court case against the Hahns Peak & Elk River Canal & Placer Mining Company in 1899. Flick provided the following information about Nugget Cut:

- Nugget Cut was located approximately 1,000-1,200 feet north of Hahn's Peak (town, not mountain).[278]
- On the east side of Nugget Cut, the waters of Willow Creek Ditch and Farwell Ditch came together.[279]
- Nugget Cut was excavated to a depth of approximately 10-15 feet and extended roughly a quarter mile.[280]

The gold boom attracted many others seeking to strike it rich, and in the winter of 1885, new investors arrived.

"That winter A.J. Macky of Boulder and Perry A. Burgess of Steamboat bought a half interest in the property. Cody & Hinman, shortly afterwards, mortgaged their half interest to Mr. Macky, for $30,000 and in 1886 he took it under mortgage. From 1892 to 1897 the property was worked under lease by Milner, Metcalf and Leahy with fair success. In the latter year it was purchased by the Hahn's Peak and Elk River Placer Mining

---

[277] Leahy, W. (March 31, 1915). Tales of Early Days. *The Steamboat Pilot*, Page 7. https://nrrbook.com/SP-1915-03-31

[278] William Flick vs. The Hahns Peak & Elk River Canal & Placer Mining Company, Colorado Court of Appeals Number 2024. (1899). Page 136. https://nrrbook.com/FlickCase

[279] William Flick vs. The Hahns Peak & Elk River Canal & Placer Mining Company, Colorado Court of Appeals Number 2024. (1899). Page 136. https://nrrbook.com/FlickCase

[280] William Flick vs. The Hahns Peak & Elk River Canal & Placer Mining Company, Colorado Court of Appeals Number 2024. (1899). Page 241. https://nrrbook.com/FlickCase

Company and George B. McFadden had charge of operations for several years."[281]

The Hahns Peak and Elk River Canal and Placer Mining Company was established on December 19, 1893. This company and its involvement with the Farwell Ditch, as well as the lawsuit with William Flick, will be discussed in detail in the following chapter.

After losing his lease on Poverty Bar, McIntosh quickly established a new way of life. *"During the days of his mining prosperity, Robert McIntosh had a dream of founding a town which should become the big city of Northwestern Colorado and the county seat. According to the plan it was to be a model town on the mesa near the present town of Hayden. It was planned to build a saw mill which would supply all necessary material even to doors and window sash. A pumping plant was to be installed and reservoirs on the higher ground were to supply the necessary pressure an act as reserve for fire protection. Three hundred and twenty acres were to be reserved as a public park and laid out in the most approved manner in lawns, lakes, walks, drives, etc. The plans fell thru, but up to recent years Mr. McIntosh regretted that he had not gone ahead with the plan.*"[282]

Though the plans near Hayden did not come to fruition, McIntosh left an impact on the region by founding the town of Slater. *"He came to the Slater site and liked it, and it never left his mind as he went to Hahn's Peak where he worked the mines and built himself up a modest fortune. He was a main spoke in the wheel that got the ditches dug and the mines worked in Hahn's Peak, then he went back to his dream site and started to build Slater.*

---

[281] Leahy, W. (March 31, 1915). Tales of Early Days. *The Steamboat Pilot*, Page 7. https://nrrbook.com/SP-1915-03-31

[282] Robert McIntosh, Pioneer Miner, Merchant and Rancher, is Dead. (December 24, 1924). *The Steamboat Pilot*, Page 5. https://nrrbook.com/SP-1924-12-24

He built a store, blacksmith shop, harness shop, where he made and repaired saddles and harnesses. He had a boarding house, rooming house, and a livery stable and it all belonged to him."[283]

McIntosh soon got into ranching.

"When the placers began to go down, Robert McIntosh determined to become a ranchman. Alfred McCarger and family were early residents of Hahns Peak but in 1877 moved to Snake River and located the ranch at Slater which Mr. McIntosh acquired and where he lived for 50 years."[284]

Above: Robert McIntosh and his dog in front of his general goods store in Slater, Colorado. McIntosh is perhaps most remembered for this store, which likely took influence from John V. Farwell's store in International Camp. Photo Credit to Little Snake River Museum.

---

[283] Morgan, Helen. (1970). *Snake River Profiles, Volume 1*, Page 42.

[284] Robert McIntosh, Pioneer Miner, Merchant and Rancher, is Dead. (December 24, 1924). *The Steamboat Pilot*, Page 5. https://nrrbook.com/SP-1924-12-24

"In partnership with A.W. Salisbury, he had bought the first bunch of horses trailed to the river, had opened a general store at Slater, and gone into ranching. He still owned considerable property in Chicago, which he sold, using the money to buy horses and continue mining. While he was not personally active at the Peak in the late eighties and nineties, he grubstaked numerous miners who were always looking for the main vein."[285]

The term "grubstake" means to supply another person with supplies or funds to start a business (in this case, a prospector searching for gold) in exchange for a portion of future profits. Location Certificates were filed for the following claims:

- Hiram of Tyre Lode (filed on July 22, 1896)[286]
  - Richard Paulson ⅜ share
  - A.J. Smith ⅜ share
  - Robert McIntosh ¼ share

- Admiral Lode (filed on September 21, 1896)[287]
  - Charles Irwin
  - Clayton Waterman
  - Robert McIntosh
  - Richard Paulson

  Share amounts were not provided on this certificate, so they presumably shared equally.

---

[285] Morgan, Helen. (1970). *Snake River Profiles, Volume 1*, Page 44.

[286] Hiram of Tyre Lode Location Certificate. (July 22, 1896). The Robert Mcintosh collection: Tread of Pioneers Museum. Steamboat Springs, Colorado. https://nrrbook.com/HiramofTyre

This claim was named after Hiram, who reigned as King of Tyre during the time of Kings David and Solomon. Hiram supplied Solomon with material, laborers, and artists to be used in the construction of a temple. Tyre developed into a critical port city in the Mediterranean under Hiram.

[287] Admiral Lode Location Certificate. (September 21, 1896). The Robert Mcintosh collection: Tread of Pioneers Museum, Steamboat Springs, Colorado. https://nrrbook.com/Admiral

- Quo Vadis Domine Lode (filed on April 26, 1899)[288]
  - Richard Paulson
  - Robert McIntosh

Once again, share amounts were not noted on the location certificate, so it is assumed that Mcintosh and Paulson split these profits 50/50.

On December 23, 1890, McIntosh, along with partners William and Robert Greig, incorporated the North Western Colorado Irrigation Company.[289] This company was formed to hold the water rights and rights-of-way for irrigation and manufacturing purposes (not mining). The following claims were made under this entity:

1. A ditch commencing at the head gate thereof and situated and being on the North bank of the Elk River in the Cañon of the same River below the Mouth of Willow Creek and on unsurveyed land and continuing thence on a grade of 3 ½ feet to the mile a distance from the point of departure of twenty miles or thereabouts.

2. A canal commencing at the head gate thereof situated on the right or East bank of the Yampa River.

3. A canal commencing at the head gate thereof situated on the West bank of the Elk River.

Meanwhile, McIntosh expanded his ranch into a substantial operation, reaching a peak of 1,600 horses. On January 30, 1903, he penned a letter to President Theodore Roosevelt,

---

[288] Quo Vadis Domine Lode Location Certificate. (April 26, 1899). The Robert Mcintosh collection: Tread of Pioneers Museum, Steamboat Springs, Colorado. https://nrrbook.com/QuoVadisDomine

Quo Vadis Domine is a Latin phrase meaning "Lord, where are you going?"

[289] North Western Colorado Irrigation Canal Company Articles of Incorporation. (December 23, 1890). The Robert Mcintosh collection: Tread of Pioneers Museum, Steamboat Springs, Colorado. https://nrrbook.com/NWCOIrrigation

proposing that the United States establish a preserve in northern Routt County to raise horses for military use. Having hunted there before, Roosevelt was familiar with the region.

"Honorable President Roosevelt and Cavalry Officers, and men who have the 'say so' who love and admire a cavalry or saddle horse that is worthy of appreciation:

Gentlemen-

The way to get this horse at no direct or great cost to the Government is as follows. It takes no great amount of experience nor expert knowledge, but an honest, level headed officer about fifty (50) years old as the head, and some of the heads of the proper department to mark out the lines. No private, thieving contractors, nor private citizens wanted, except two or three known and tried, trustworthy cowboys to ride the pasture, late range.

The writer has been growing horses on this proposed location for upwards of twenty-five (25) years with considerable success having had some 1600 head under good control, and now selling down and out. The writer, if he (at least myself) were an army officer, would be being retired now on account of age.

I have no 'axe to grind' either in sight or hidden, and want no favors of any kind. Naturally, though, if the following scheme should materialize, I would like to have the name of being one of the originators of the same.

I am willing, for no remuneration to myself, to show this thing up to Officer of Horse of the Army of our Uncle Sam. In the northwestern part of Colorado, in Routt Co. on the Wyoming State line from a point about 3 to 5 miles west of the Continental Divide to the Savery flats, a distance of 34 to 36 miles, the Little Snake River forms the boundary line between Colorado and Wyoming. Now, beginning at the Savory flats, a line due south a distance of 12 miles to the divide between Snake and Bear Rivers; thence east along said divide about 36 miles or 6 townships to a point that amply takes Big Red Park; thence north to the

Wyoming line and one mile still north into Wyoming; thence west to, and below the Savery flats to the place of beginning, a distance of 36 miles. Notice this takes 36 square miles in Wyoming and in Colorado some 12 by 36 miles or 432 square miles, a total of 468 square miles. The Government still owns most of this land, that is all with the exception of some 40 ranches of 160 acres each worth from $10 to $20 per acre. The river bottom is hay land. Part of these ranches are on the hill above the bottom. There are 4 to 5 good houses on this land, the balance are cabins.

On this land there are possibly 3,000 tons of hay cut now. In 1878 there were cut some 50 tons.

The proposition is for Congress and the Senate to declare this tract a horse preserve, condemn the patented land and pay for it to the ranchmen, then fence the whole thing with a six wire cable woven smooth wire fence.

To commence, buy 2,000 or more mares through the States having the qualities of a cavalry horse. Take the mare as she looks - let breed go. Get one good, honest, experienced ret. surgeon, level-headed, not extravagant, sharp as old- but harmless as a dove, then buy some 50 head of 3 year old stallion colts to grow up on the range with those mares. The facts are better colts, better horses, hardy and clean, sound and trim can be raised this way than any other. I know this. The upper ½ or snowy part is the cool summer range, the lower part is winter range. Some hay should be cut and stacked, the balance the horses can cut and bale and get fat on.

One cross fence between the winter and summer ranges is sufficient, and a chunk fenced off to put horse colts when 1 ½ years old during winter to castrate the 15th of May next. Other fencing might be done taking care that some contracted man does not overdo the matter and make a hog of himself.

The crop of horses when 3 years old past, mares and all, during the summer must be broken. Keep the best young mares to breed. To do this you will have to establish cavalry barracks on *the Savery, keep men, pick them out, all the fine young athletic, energetic, kind well bred fellows, about say 200 or less, give them their regular hay and then extra hay. They can handle and train, each one, 3 head for say 15 days, drill toot the horns, drum, shoot, maneuver around and beat 'Willie' of Prussia[290] first rattle. Then they turn those out in the pasture referred to and get another batch.*

Handle the mares first so that those which are to be kept can be turned with the stallions to breed. Then this stuff that is broken for the cavalry can be sent to be finished and matured and be the finest horses in the world. Developments will show the capacity of this range. 2,000 mares are enough to start. However there can be 100 cows, more or less, and some bulls kept in this inclosure. Let them go, castrate the bull calves and use them for beef for the outfit. One key to this is a gentle breed of stallions and the same with mares.

Any draft at all is too clumsy, and trotting or running stock is too nervous and crazy. It is the <u>saddle horse</u>. They are rare, about as rare as carriage horses. However, no need of this 'blowed up' high priced stock of stallions.

It is all lost motion. At best, horsemen belong to the United Association of Prevaricators. One more point is in the enabling act. Have it enacted that any hunter or other person who would kill a deer, elk, or antelope in this reserve be given 10 years in the penitentiary and lose all his property up to $500. The officer in charge will see that the game is killed off when it gets too thick.

The U.S. ought to own a piece of this public range and own the best of it. This proposition has a Chinook wind from the desert which melts the snow early. It is grassy from end to end. It is all grass land, no desert.

At the Savery flats the bluffs have coal, fine steam coal, two veins 16 feet thick opened now by squatters selling coal at $1.00 per

---

[290] "Willie of Prussia" refers to Kaiser Wilhelm II, who served as the last German Emperor and King of Prussia from 1888 to 1918.

load. Also, there is sandstone of the finest to build a few stables. The only healthy level in Colorado is in this horse preserve. Disease is not known. Why, a bunch of U.S. cavalry mounted on the horses apparently could run away and hide from the enemy, appearing on his flanks and larboard[291] making the fur fly, i.e. the bearskin caps, and tangle them up worse than Cervera."[292,]

"Mr. Robert McIntosh,
Slater, Routt Co.,
Colorado[293]

McIntosh put a lot of thought and planning into his proposal and believed his idea for a massive horse preserve would greatly benefit the country. Unfortunately, Roosevelt never saw the letter, and McIntosh did not receive the response he had hoped for from the U.S. Government.

"Sir:

Referring to your letter addressed to the President of the United States, dated January 30, 1903, and referred by him to this office, in which you call attention to a tract of land in Colorado, and a plan of yours for using it as a stock farm for breeding good horses for use of the Government, you are informed by direction of the Quartermaster General that there is no appropriation available for carrying out the views expressed in the letter above referred to.

Respectfully,

---

[291] Larboard is an archaic nautical term used to describe the left side of a ship. It was replaced with the term "port," as larboard and starboard (right side) were easily confused.

[292] In the Battle of Santiago de Cuba in 1898, Admiral Cervera of the Spanish Navy lost his entire fleet of six ships and 600 men to the U.S. Navy, which suffered no loss of ships and only one death.

[293] Robert McIntosh Letter to President Theodore Roosevelt. (1903). The Robert Mcintosh collection: Tread of Pioneers Museum, Steamboat Springs, Colorado. https://nrrbook.com/McIntoshProposal

Clarence B [Bolling?]
Captain and Quartermaster, U.S.A."[294]

Four years later, McIntosh tried again. He sent a letter[295] on
May 22, 1907, to Gifford Pinchot, who served as the 1st Chief of
the Bureau of Forestry for the United States. McIntosh hoped
Pinchot would personally deliver the letter to Roosevelt.

*"The following letter was written 1903. The answer follows, also
a copy of the original letter. By kindness of Mr. Pinchot he may
get it to the President personally, as he, the President, is about
the only one who knows range business. At this writing, May,
1907, I have some 400 head of horses to look after that never eat
a bite of hay and can be seen, and this range. A horse grown in
the sun and wind is the horse that is not looking for a place to
die. I enclose a map. It shows about the right boundaries and
takes part of this Forest Reserve. The ranches can be bought,
also a ranch with 150 gentle elk, and when the reserve is fenced
turn the elk loose. Let mares and stallions run in bunches. Bred
at liberty beats all breeding in captivity.*

*Get 2 year old stallions in Germany, plenty of them, such as they
have for the country. They are the best in the world being part
Arabian. The asset in this is the Government owns the land. The
balance is the fence, mares and stallions. The military can do
the balance. In 10 years it would be worth 10 times its cost and
growing better. While it would cost less than a battleship, said
battleship in 10 years is N.A.*

---

[294] War Department Letter to Robert McIntosh. (1903). The Robert Mcintosh
collection: Tread of Pioneers Museum, Steamboat Springs, Colorado.
https://nrrbook.com/ResponsetoMcIntosh

[295] Robert McIntosh Letter to Gifford Pinchot. (1907). The Robert Mcintosh
collection: Tread of Pioneers Museum, Steamboat Springs, Colorado.
https://nrrbook.com/McIntoshProposal2

Again, the time will come when the rural boys will fight anarchists with a black flag with white stars from those horses (railroads for time being out of business) and save the country.

If advisable, let two or three men who know things come here in August. At no cost I will show them over the ground and show them this strip that gets the Chinook wind which makes a mild winter. And those horses."

Once again, McIntosh's proposal was denied.

"Dear sir:

Your letter of May 27, with enclosures, is received in Mr. Pinchot's absence, and has been read with interest. Unfortunately I am afraid it will be impossible for Mr. Pinchot to take it up in the way you suggest, since he will be away from Washington for a number of months. The subject of which you write is of great public interest, but the fact, indicated in the letter to you from the Quartermaster General's office, that there is no appropriation available for carrying out your plan for breeding cavalry horses seems to make it impossible to take any action in the matter. In any event such action would not, of course, fall within the province of the Forest Service.

With much regret that I must send you this unsatisfactory reply, I am,

Very truly yours,

James B Adams
Acting Forester"[296]

Even though his grand vision for a United States horse preserve in Routt County never came to fruition, McIntosh himself eventually supplied horses directly to the government.

---

[296] Forest Service Letter to Robert McIntosh. (1907). The Robert Mcintosh collection: Tread of Pioneers Museum, Steamboat Springs, Colorado. https://nrrbook.com/ResponsetoMcIntosh2

"Besides running the business he raised a lot of good horses and cattle and broke his horses and they were used in World War I."[297]

Born in 1838 in Ormstown, Quebec, to Scottish parents, Robert McIntosh was granted United States citizenship on December 28th, 1905.[298] After a remarkable life as a Chicago contractor, builder of ditches, dams & reservoirs, sawmill operator, gold miner, surveyor, machinist, postmaster, judge,[299] general goods store owner, rancher, husband, and father, he died on December 11, 1924, at the age of 86. His impact is still felt today, as Old Mac named several landmarks in Routt County. King Solomon Creek, a branch of the Little Snake River with headwaters at the northern foot of Farwell Mountain, Diamond Park, East and West Gibraltar peaks, along with Big Agnes and Little Agnes mountains that stand tall in today's Zirkel Wilderness, all owe their name to McIntosh.[300]

"One of the oldest and best known of Northwestern Colorado pioneers passed to his reward on Thursday, December 11, when Robert McIntosh died at his home at Slater at the age of 86 years. He was one of the first settlers in Routt county, coming to Hahns Peak in 1876 with J.V. Farwell of Chicago when the merchant prince spent a small fortune in an effort to wrest gold from the gravel of that early day mining camp. 'Old Mac,' as he was affectionately called, was known to every early settler and was noted for his hospitality and the kindness of his heart. His history is the history of Northwestern Colorado, in the development of which he has borne an important part. For a number of years he worked under lease the Poverty Bar placer

---

[297] Morgan, Helen. (1970). *Snake River Profiles, Volume 1*, Page 42.

[298] Robert McIntosh Certificate of Citizenship. (December 28, 1905). The Robert Mcintosh collection: Tread of Pioneers Museum, Steamboat Springs, Colorado. https://nrrbook.com/McIntoshCertificate

[299] McIntosh served as a Judge of the probate court of Routt County in the 1880s.

[300] *History of Routt National Forest 1905-1972*. (May 4, 2020). Pages 64-78. National Forest Service Library. https://nrrbook.com/HistoryofRNF

mines at Hahns Peak. When the mines began to become exhausted he moved to Slater on Snake river, where he established a store and for many years raised horses on a large scale.

Robert McIntosh was a character who had no counterpart. He was a Scotchman, large of frame and large of heart, careless in his personal appearance, but of sound judgement and sterling character. He was loyal to his friends and had no enemies. As long as the present generation lives, stories will be told of the eccentricities as well as the loyalties and the generosities of 'Old Mac.'"[301]

[301] Robert McIntosh, Pioneer Miner, Merchant and Rancher, is Dead. (December 24, 1924). *The Steamboat Pilot*, Page 5. https://nrrbook.com/SP-1924-12-24

CHAPTER 8: REVIVAL, RULINGS, & RETIREMENT

"We have only to consider in the evolution of character that the physical should be subordinate to the mental, and the mental to the moral, to reach God's idea of a perfect man. The first Adam reversed this law, and made it necessary for the second Adam, who subordinated all those powers to the will of God, to reconstruct the race on His own model."[302]

-John V. Farwell

Following the Hahns Peak Mining District boom of the 1880s, gold production declined for several years. As noted in the previous chapter, the Hahns Peak and Elk River Canal and Placer Mining Company (HPERCPMC) was established on December 19, 1893. This company acquired mining claims and water rights, including the Farwell Ditch, throughout 1894 and 1895 to the point where it controlled virtually all of the Poverty Bar and String Ridge claims that James France had once owned following John V. Farwell's exit from the mining district in late 1879. The Board of Directors for HPERCPMC included William Stevenson, Andrew Macky, Amos Giltner, Willis Kneeland, and Lucius Abbott. George McFadden served as a Civil Engineer, Architect, Superintendent, and General Manager for the company, holding full authority and control over the properties, claims, ditches, and projected improvements. Ed Cody served as a company agent.

With 3,000 acres of land under its control, HPERCPMC's focus turned to water, and two major projects were planned to

---

[302] Farwell, John V. (1906). *Corner Stones of Character: Some Ways of Making Them*, Page 17. https://nrrbook.com/CornerStonesofCharacter

expand its supply of this valuable resource. The first was a reservoir on South Willow Creek, with a claim filed in Routt County on May 5, 1894:

"We hereby give public notice that we claim the site for Reservoir to store water for mining purposes, all the land that will be overflowed by construction of a Reservoir Dam raised fifty (50) feet high between the stakes and monuments adjacent, the notices number one and two. Said Reservoir site is situated on what is known as the South Willow, about one-half mile above the McGarger flume and at the head of the old Willow Creek Ditch situated in Hahns Peak Mining District, County of Routt and State of Colorado. We claim the above-described land for Reservoir purposes by virtue of authority of Congress granting citizens the right to preempt land for Reservoirs to be used for mining purposes.

Hahns Peak Mining District – County of Routt and State of Colorado.

Dated this 5th day of May A.D. 1894.

The Hahns Peak & Elk River Canal & Placer Mining Company,

By E. R. Cody,

Agent."[303]

Thomas Roark was hired to begin construction of this reservoir. *"With teams and wagon he hauled big timbers and heavy rocks for breastwork of the dam. With horses and go-devil shovels all the earth moving was done to halt those torrents of water."*[304] After completing *"what probably was the first earthen*

---

[303] South Willow Creek Reservoir Claim. (May 5, 1894). Book E Page 213. Routt County Clerk and Recorder's Office. https://nrrbook.com/WillowReservoir

The South Willow Creek Reservoir is known as Hahns Peak Lake today.

[304] Stevenson, Thelma. (2005, 4th Printing). *Historic Hahns Peak*, Page 30.

dam in Routt County,"[305] Roark began constructing a ditch that would carry South Willow Creek Reservoir water to Poverty Bar. Note that this was a separate ditch from the one built by the Hans Peak Gold & Silver Mining Company in 1875, which was fed by the north fork of Willow Creek. Separated by approximately fifty feet in elevation, both ditches followed similar paths around Silver Queen Ridge, across Deep Creek, and towards Poverty Bar.

The second major project undertaken by HPERCPMC was to revive the Farwell Ditch, which had seen its use dwindle since the 1880s, when the gold boom ended, and to expand its capacity to carry more water than originally designed in the 1870s. A contract was awarded to Mr. Sanders[306] (first name unknown) in 1895 to commence work on the Upper Level of the ditch. The core objective of this contract was to replace sections of the ditch that had originally been constructed of wood fluming with a channel through solid rock.

"Hahn's Peak, like many other mining camps, has slumbered until the tread of capital awakened and enthused it with a vigorous, attractive, and permanent life. The capital spent this year in improvements by the Hahn's Peak and Elk River Canal and Placer Mining Company has so nearly completed a perfect system of ditches and reservoirs that but little remains to be done in the spring to enable this company to work their large placer fields of 3,000 acres. On the west of these placer fields are Main Willow creek, North Willow creek and Deep creek, each of which have one or more tributaries. A new ditch, nearly completed this year, will, in conjunction with reservoirs, control all the waters of these creeks. On the east of these placer fields are Cow creek, Way's creek, Beaver creek, and Elk creek, all of which supply an abundance of water to the Elk River ditch (Farwell Ditch), which conveys water to a common point with the

[305] Stevenson, Thelma. (2005, 4th Printing). *Historic Hahns Peak*, Page 28.

[306] William Flick vs. The Hahns Peak & Elk River Canal & Placer Mining Company, Colorado Court of Appeals Number 2024. (1899). Page 345. https://nrrbook.com/FlickCase

new ditch. Extensive improvements were made in the Elk River ditch this season in the way of cutting the ditch through solid rock to take place of fluming. Although snow falls to quite a depth here during the winter, this company will prosecute work all winter, tending towards the completion of its hydraulic system.

Led here by the fame of the placer fields and a desire to prospect for the source of gold, this summer has been one of great activity and interest to the prospector. An area of over seven miles square has been fairly well prospected and some big paying silver properties discovered. Between Hahn's Peak and the new mining camp, Columbine, there rises a rough mountainous divide,[307] extending northeast and southwest, and it is on the north side of this divide that Columbine is located, and where the rich silver deposits have been discovered. Four different properties will be worked all winter and are more than paying their way in the new camp. On the south side of the divide it is generally predicted that gold will predominate in all discoveries and the greater part of the south slope is already located. On account of the long winter season many have gone out to return again in the spring. But all who have been here are unanimous in their praise of the merits of the camp, and predict a population of 5,000 by July 1, 1896."[308]

George McFadden was busy during this time formally surveying the Town of Hahn's Peak, with a map[309] being produced on July 29, 1896. The Town of Hahn's Peak, as plotted, contained 28 blocks, each measuring 250 feet wide by

---

[307] This mountainous divide was labeled Silver Queen Ridge on the 1896 Hahn's Peak Mining District Map drawn by J.J. Argo and A.C. Ostrom.

[308] Hahn's Peak District. (December 21, 1895). *The New Castle News*, Page 4. https://nrrbook.com/NCN-1895-12-21

[309] Plan of the Town of Hahn's Peak. (July 29, 1896). Routt County Clerk & Recorder's Office. https://nrrbook.com/HahnsPeakPlan

The blocks plotted in this map largely line up with private property boundary lines in the Town of Hahns Peak today.

300 feet deep. Each block was divided into 24 lots measuring 25 feet wide and 118 feet deep. Streets were 80 feet wide, and alleys were 14 feet wide.

Unfortunately for HPERCPMC, neither Roark nor Sanders were able to complete their projects. William Flick, a skilled and experienced ditch builder, was contracted on June 8, 1897, to complete the work and undertake some additional items. *"His reputation as a ditch builder and a substantial, reliable contractor was, in our opinion, better than that of any other contractor with whom we had any negotiations to that time."*[310]

Flick's contract called for several major projects:[311]

1. Complete the construction of the Willow Creek Ditch (started by Roark) and all the flumes required thereon, on or before July 1, 1897, in accordance with the specifications furnished by George B. McFadden.

2. Construct a dam at the head of the Willow Creek Ditch across the west branch of said Willow Creek of sufficient size and strength to cause the waters from said creek to flow into and fill said Willow Creek Ditch.

3. Clean out and enlarge the the Elk River Ditch (Farwell Ditch), so that the same and every point and portion thereof shall be six feet wide on the top, three and one half feet wide on the bottom and three and one half feet deep, and to construct the new portions or said ditch of the dimensions and size aforesaid at all places where flumes have heretofore been constructed, except the flumes at Sand Rock Point and across Ways Gulch, so that the said ditch shall be continuous with its present

---

[310] William Flick vs. The Hahns Peak & Elk River Canal & Placer Mining Company, Colorado Court of Appeals Number 2024. (1899). Page 342. https://nrrbook.com/FlickCase

[311] William Flick vs. The Hahns Peak & Elk River Canal & Placer Mining Company, Colorado Court of Appeals Number 2024. (1899). Pages 34-35. https://nrrbook.com/FlickCase

grade and of the dimensions aforesaid from its head gate to the lower end thereof.

4. The lower level of said ditch shall be extended and constructed so that it will receive the water from the upper level of the said ditch immediately underneath the tunnel at Tunnel Hill. Flumes of sufficient size and strength shall be constructed underneath said tunnel to permanently receive the water in its fall from said tunnel and deliver the same in the lower level of said ditch without injury to the same. Rock and masonry work may also be used to catch the water after its fall.

5. Construct nearly one linear mile of new ditch above Tunnel Hill, and said new ditch will be almost entirely in rock, and that wherever a fissure or crack appears in the said rock work, it will be filled so that there will be no waste of water.

6. A good, durable, strong flume of sufficient size to carry the waters of said ditch, as enlarged, shall be constructed around Sand Rock Point; that said flume shall be so thoroughly and strongly anchored that it will remain in its position of construction permanently.

7. The head gate of said ditch shall be constructed of substantial material, and the dam across the creek, just below the head of said ditch, shall be constructed of substantial and permanent materials.

8. The flume across Ways Gulch shall be enlarged to correspond with the enlarged size of said ditch.

All work was to be completed by August 15, 1897. At that point, Elk River (Trail Creek) water would be turned into the ditch, which had to prove capable of providing a full head of water, defined as six feet wide on top, three and a half feet on the bottom, and three feet deep, for thirty days to consider Flick's work complete.

Initially, there was disagreement on how much Flick would be compensated. He quoted $8,675, but HPERCPMC only had $6,500 available in cash and refused to go into debt to pay the difference. A compromise was agreed upon where Flick would be granted stock in the company at 12 ½ cents per share (17,400 shares in total) if HPERCPMC was unable to pay the $2,175 difference within eighteen months.[312] The $6,500 in cash was scheduled to be paid in three increments:

- $2,500 on July 15, 1897
- $2,500 on August 15, 1897, or upon completion of all work
- $1,500 on October 1, 1897, contingent upon the ditch providing a full head of water for thirty consecutive days

Sixteen days after signing the contract, Flick and his team arrived to begin work. *"William Flick arrived here today from Denver. He comes with machinery and sixty men. He has secured the contract for building the ditches to carry water to the Hahn's peak placers...The Elk river ditch will be gone over and in place of flumes the canal will be built in solid rock...the flumes have fallen into decay many years. The Willow creek ditch will also be completed and next year the company will run from twelve to twenty giants, instead of two as at present. The work will be pushed with all possible speed."[313]*

Starting at the Willow Creek Reservoir, Flick's team began by reinforcing the dam that Roark originally built. *"I put some heavier logs than he had used across it, put some brush in and*

---

[312] William Flick vs. The Hahns Peak & Elk River Canal & Placer Mining Company, Colorado Court of Appeals Number 2024. (1899). Pages 346-347. https://nrrbook.com/FlickCase

[313] Rich Placers Near The Peak. (June 25, 1897). *The Rocky Mountain News*, Page 7. https://nrrbook.com/RMN-1897-06-25

filled it back with earth; and that did not satisfy him, and I hauled manure from Hahn's Peak up there, to base it."[314]

Flick and his men then got to work on completing the Willow Creek ditch, which ran from the newly reinforced dam at Willow Creek Reservoir to Poverty Bar. Beginning work at a location called "Station 35," they followed the plans of George McFadden, who had staked the line the ditch would follow. *"The ditch was to be four feet wide at the bottom, and the dirt from the ditch was to be throwed on the lower side, by the bank. There was cut stakes right along on each side of the ditch, one side run about six feet of a cut, and the other side run from six to twelve."*[315]

Portions of the Willow Creek ditch contained sections of boxed-in fluming constructed from nearly 7,000 feet of two-inch-thick lumber, and the framing was constructed from logs cut on site. *"The first was benches put up across, base put across them, then stringers put on, and then there was a frame mortised and the box was built in that...The boxes were four feet wide and three and a half feet high."*[316]

Near the end of the Willow Creek ditch was a caved-in tunnel that Flick's team dug out. Approximately sixty to seventy feet in length, this tunnel was initially started by Roark. *"There was an old tunnel that they had let a contract previous to this, and the men had not completed it. It had badly caved in, and they*

---

[314] William Flick vs. The Hahns Peak & Elk River Canal & Placer Mining Company, Colorado Court of Appeals Number 2024. (1899). Page 135. https://nrrbook.com/FlickCase

[315] William Flick vs. The Hahns Peak & Elk River Canal & Placer Mining Company, Colorado Court of Appeals Number 2024. (1899). Page 137. https://nrrbook.com/FlickCase

[316] William Flick vs. The Hahns Peak & Elk River Canal & Placer Mining Company, Colorado Court of Appeals Number 2024. (1899). Page 141. https://nrrbook.com/FlickCase

hired my teams to make an open cut instead of a tunnel and going through this Nugget Cut Hill."[317]

After completing work on the Willow Creek Reservoir and ditch, McFadden gave Flick his approval of a job well done. *"He said that the ditch was all right, and the flumes was the same as the Santa Fe Railroad bridge."*[318]

Willow Creek Ditch water joined up with the Farwell Ditch runoff[319] in the Nugget Cut area, where it was used for sluicing. *"Here is Nugget Cut; it lets the water from the Willow Creek ditch come into this draw, and here comes the pipeline; they both come together here...the pipeline is used for hydraulic pressure...they have extra water that comes around here...they use this body here that runs in as extra water to wash the gravel down."*[320]

Elsewhere in the mining district, Flick's men were busy cleaning out and expanding the capacity of the Farwell Ditch. When John V. Farwell filed his water claim back in 1876, it noted plans of constructing a ditch *"five feet wide on the bottom and seven feet wide at the top."*[321] Meanwhile, Flick's contract with HPERCPMC in 1897 stated he would *"clean out and enlarge the said Elk River Ditch, so that the same and every*

---

[317] William Flick vs. The Hahns Peak & Elk River Canal & Placer Mining Company, Colorado Court of Appeals Number 2024. (1899). Page 148. https://nrrbook.com/FlickCase

[318] William Flick vs. The Hahns Peak & Elk River Canal & Placer Mining Company, Colorado Court of Appeals Number 2024. (1899). Page 141. https://nrrbook.com/FlickCase

[319] After Robert Mcintosh extended the Farwell Ditch to Little Mountain in 1880, a portion of Farwell Ditch water was fed into the water cannons, and a portion was allowed to run down the face of Little Mountain to be gathered and used for sluicing in the mine below.

[320] William Flick vs. The Hahns Peak & Elk River Canal & Placer Mining Company, Colorado Court of Appeals Number 2024. (1899). Page 195. https://nrrbook.com/FlickCase

[321] Main Elk River Water Claim. (July 17, 1876). Grand County Clerk and Recorder's Office. https://nrrbook.com/FarwellDitchClaim

point and portion thereof shall by six (6) feet wide on the top, three and one half (3 ½) feet on the bottom and three and one half (3 ½) feet deep."[322]

At first glance, the numbers contradict, as the original water claim had larger dimensions than the specifications to which Flick agreed to expand the ditch. There are a couple of potential explanations for this:

1. The Farwell Ditch was not built to the exact dimensions specified in the 1876 water claim.

2. It is possible (if not likely) that sections of the original ditch had partially filled in with sediment over the years, and Flick's work would expand the capacity beyond its current state.

Flick's team went to work widening the ditch and raising its banks where necessary, although there were disagreements at times on whether the refurbished ditch met the new specifications. *"Then this was widened here where he had some trouble; he (McFadden) said my foreman's stick to measure the bottom of the ditch was too short...He carried on the work and made the stake two inches longer."*[323]

The fluming in the Ways Gulch area had to be enlarged as well, all to the specifications provided by McFadden. *"That's it; here is the flume on the way to the gulch. It had to be widened and strengthened and repaired...He (McFadden) gave me the way he wanted it done, how wide he wanted it, and set the grade-stakes at each end of every flume, and set stakes where he wanted his vents, and wrote it out on a piece of paper and gave it to the*

---

[322] William Flick vs. The Hahns Peak & Elk River Canal & Placer Mining Company, Colorado Court of Appeals Number 2024. (1899). Page 34. https://nrrbook.com/FlickCase

[323] William Flick vs. The Hahns Peak & Elk River Canal & Placer Mining Company, Colorado Court of Appeals Number 2024. (1899). Page 153. https://nrrbook.com/FlickCase

carpenters, so they would not make any mistakes."[324] The fluming was boxed in and measured four feet wide and four feet tall.

In addition, Beaver Creek Tunnel was enlarged to accommodate the planned increase in water flow. *"There is the tunnel that was widened four feet wide on the bottom."*[325]

Another major project was to reengineer the transition from the Upper Level of the ditch to the Lower Level. As noted in Chapter 5, the original transition occurred approximately one mile west of Tunnel Hill, where the Upper Level of the ditch discharged water into the Coulton Creek drainage channel. From there, water dropped down into the Lower Level of the ditch and continued towards the mining district. One challenge with this design was that this mile-long section of Upper Level ditch was high on a very steep flank of Farwell Mountain, making maintenance and repair work very difficult. To solve this problem, Flick and his team were contracted to extend the Lower Level of the ditch from Coulton Creek eastward directly to the base of Tunnel Hill. Now, upon exiting the Tunnel Hill Tunnel, water would immediately drop in a man-made, 450-foot waterfall to the Lower Level.

To catch the water and divert it into the Lower Level of the ditch, a reinforced sandbox was constructed. *"Over here is the point where the sand-box catches the water from the tunnel...That sand-box I believe was 12 by 16 or 12 by 14 with a*

---

[324] William Flick vs. The Hahns Peak & Elk River Canal & Placer Mining Company, Colorado Court of Appeals Number 2024. (1899). Pages 152-153. https://nrrbook.com/FlickCase

[325] William Flick vs. The Hahns Peak & Elk River Canal & Placer Mining Company, Colorado Court of Appeals Number 2024. (1899). Page 154. https://nrrbook.com/FlickCase

heavy frame under it, made out of two-inch lumber."[326] The sandbox itself sat on top of a base of large boulders.

This new sandbox would require ongoing maintenance. Mere weeks after the new transition was completed and water began flowing, the sandbox had filled in with sediment. Thus, all the water overflowed out of the box and drained towards Hinman Creek. From that point on, the sandbox was cleaned out frequently to prevent this issue.

Significant work was also done above Hinman Canyon near Tunnel Hill. Here, approximately one mile of the ditch had sections of fluming replaced with a channel cut and blasted through solid rock. *"He* (McFadden) *wanted rock taken out, along in here...I sent a gang of men out, shot the rock out, and everything was all satisfactory."*[327]

Left: An image of the rock channel Flick and his men built above Hinman Canyon. Here, pick and shovel gave way to drill bits and dynamite, as hundreds of yards' worth of ditch were blasted and channeled through the rock. At times, the walls of rock reach six feet high. Evidence of drill holes can still be seen today.

---

[326] William Flick vs. The Hahns Peak & Elk River Canal & Placer Mining Company, Colorado Court of Appeals Number 2024. (1899). Page 155.
https://nrrbook.com/FlickCase

[327] William Flick vs. The Hahns Peak & Elk River Canal & Placer Mining Company, Colorado Court of Appeals Number 2024. (1899). Page 179.
https://nrrbook.com/FlickCase

The new rock channel was not perfect, though, as some spots were leaky. *"There was some places where it leaked....Just above the Tunnel Hill...some places quite badly, and other places but little...as near as I recollect, there was four or five places, it was all the way from 25 to 100 feet in a place."*[328] The newly built channel was lined with boards in these sections to prevent leaks.

Elsewhere, the dam across Trail Creek was in rough shape and needed to be enlarged to divert more water into the Farwell Ditch. *"There is nothing there, but there is simply one log...the water runs through the log."*[329]

Flick's men went to work. *"The head-gate was shoveled out and widened, and a sufficient dam put across the river to turn all the river into the ditch."*[330]

A log measuring twelve to fourteen inches in diameter was placed on top of the existing dam, and large stones and dirt were packed in to fill the gaps. *"That is a good head-gate and it is a good dam...I put a big log across it so it would raise the water up to throw a good, sufficient flow in the ditch. At any low-water mark, it would throw all the water in the ditch; in high water you could regulate it with the head-gate."*[331] Flick, defending his work, stated, *"I constructed a dam there that*

---

[328] William Flick vs. The Hahns Peak & Elk River Canal & Placer Mining Company, Colorado Court of Appeals Number 2024. (1899). Page 326. https://nrrbook.com/FlickCase

[329] William Flick vs. The Hahns Peak & Elk River Canal & Placer Mining Company, Colorado Court of Appeals Number 2024. (1899). Page 328. https://nrrbook.com/FlickCase

[330] William Flick vs. The Hahns Peak & Elk River Canal & Placer Mining Company, Colorado Court of Appeals Number 2024. (1899). Page 157. https://nrrbook.com/FlickCase

[331] William Flick vs. The Hahns Peak & Elk River Canal & Placer Mining Company, Colorado Court of Appeals Number 2024. (1899). Page 158. https://nrrbook.com/FlickCase

would turn pretty near all the water out at a high-water mark...I don't think we could construct it any more permanently."[332]

Of all the renovations Flick did to revive the Farwell Ditch, perhaps the most notable was his work at Sand Rock Point. Per the contract, he was to build *"a good, durable, strong flume, of sufficient size to carry the waters of said ditch as enlarged...around Sand Rock Point...said flume shall be so thoroughly and strongly anchored that it will remain in its position of construction permanently."[333]*

As originally built by Farwell's men in the 1870s, fluming was anchored to and wrapped around the sandstone ledge known as Sand Rock Point. However, it repeatedly failed during the winter months because the soft, sandy rock could not withstand the regular freeze-thaw cycles. Flick was tasked with building a permanent flume here. Rather than anchoring it to the wall, he envisioned building a flume from the ground up. *"I would put the masonry work down ten or twelve feet in the ground."[334]* In addition to the masonry work, Flick planned to build benches that would support the fluming. He estimated the cost of this fluming to be $1.25 per linear foot.

There was a problem, though. Company engineer George McFadden disagreed with the contract's requirement to build fluming, believing it was doomed to fail. Ultimately, Flick agreed. *"Mr. McFadden said that no sane man would ever build a flume there; for it is an impossibility to make a flume stay, which I will acknowledge is the facts. No man, or no living being could make a flume stay there without an enormous expense.*

[332] William Flick vs. The Hahns Peak & Elk River Canal & Placer Mining Company, Colorado Court of Appeals Number 2024. (1899). Page 235. https://nrrbook.com/FlickCase

[333] William Flick vs. The Hahns Peak & Elk River Canal & Placer Mining Company, Colorado Court of Appeals Number 2024. (1899). Page 35. https://nrrbook.com/FlickCase

[334] William Flick vs. The Hahns Peak & Elk River Canal & Placer Mining Company, Colorado Court of Appeals Number 2024. (1899). Page 231. https://nrrbook.com/FlickCase

The whole side of the mountain is springy, sand rock, slide. The rock is generally settling again and again. They tried it again and again, and it never went through the winter."[335]

Instead of fluming, McFadden proposed a tunnel directly through Sand Rock Point and requested that Flick provide a cost estimate. *"He wanted to know what my figures would be on the tunnel, and how much credit would be for not building the flume...I gave him my figures...Seven dollars a foot for the tunnel, which we did not know the distance at that time, and forty cents a yard for the approaches."*[336]

McFadden brought fellow HPERCPMC executive Willis Kneeland to Sand Rock Point to further discuss the idea of a tunnel with Flick. *"McFadden and Kneeland...both came up there and looked at it. Then they said that they would write to Mr. Stevenson, and see what suggestions he would make about it, before there was any work done. In a couple of weeks after that they said they had heard from Mr. Stevenson, and he thought it was the best thing to do."*[337]

Thus, an amendment to the contract was agreed upon. *"A tunnel was ordered and directed to be constructed, in lieu and instead of the said flume, which, by said written agreement was provided to be constructed around Sand Rock point, and the said direction and substitution of said tunnel for said flume was agreed upon and acquiesced in by both the president of said company, William Stevenson, and the secretary and treasurer thereof W.C. Kneeland, the said parties being directors of said company, and constituting a majority of the board of directors*

---

[335] William Flick vs. The Hahns Peak & Elk River Canal & Placer Mining Company, Colorado Court of Appeals Number 2024. (1899). Page 165. https://nrrbook.com/FlickCase

[336] William Flick vs. The Hahns Peak & Elk River Canal & Placer Mining Company, Colorado Court of Appeals Number 2024. (1899). Page 166. https://nrrbook.com/FlickCase

[337] William Flick vs. The Hahns Peak & Elk River Canal & Placer Mining Company, Colorado Court of Appeals Number 2024. (1899). Page 166. https://nrrbook.com/FlickCase

thereof, and the said company by its said officers thereafter fully ratified and confirmed the said acts."[338]

Flick immediately started work at Sand Rock Point, taking employees who had been working on the Willow Creek ditch. *"I...went to Willow Creek camp, I moved them up there, put the boys to work at this tunnel."*[339] First, the approaches to the proposed tunnel were built. *"The approaches are making an open cut into a depth where you might start a tunnel under cover...started four feet deep and ended seventeen."*[340]

On July 28, 1897, with the approaches complete, fourteen men began construction of the tunnel. This group consisted of eight drillers, four muckers, a nipper, and a blacksmith. On average, drillers earned $2.50 per day, while muckers made $2.25. The nipper, who carried steel back and forth from the tunnel site to the blacksmith and also transported water, made $2.00, and the blacksmith was paid a daily wage of $3.00.[341]

Working from each end of the tunnel, teams of three men worked ten-hour shifts, with two shifts per day. Lights, most likely either candles or oil lamps, were strung along the roof of the tunnel to allow for the twenty-hour workdays. Each team had two men drilling and one man clearing (mucking) debris. Nine holes were drilled one to three feet deep in a 3x3 grid, packed with sticks of gunpowder, and blasted. *"We put in three*

[338] William Flick vs. The Hahns Peak & Elk River Canal & Placer Mining Company, Colorado Court of Appeals Number 2024. (1899). Page 164. https://nrrbook.com/FlickCase

[339] William Flick vs. The Hahns Peak & Elk River Canal & Placer Mining Company, Colorado Court of Appeals Number 2024. (1899). Page 167. https://nrrbook.com/FlickCase

[340] William Flick vs. The Hahns Peak & Elk River Canal & Placer Mining Company, Colorado Court of Appeals Number 2024. (1899). Page 168. https://nrrbook.com/FlickCase

[341] William Flick vs. The Hahns Peak & Elk River Canal & Placer Mining Company, Colorado Court of Appeals Number 2024. (1899). Page 226. https://nrrbook.com/FlickCase

holes in a row on each side of the center, and three holes in the center, and then we shoot out the hole...usually put about four to five sticks, - sometimes we put as high as eight sticks."[342]

Right: The approach to the entrance of the Sand Rock Point Tunnel. Flick charged $.40 per cubic yard of dirt and rock to build this approach.

Flick's men, trying to make quick progress, dangerously tamped the powder, risking an errant explosion, to tightly pack it into the holes. *"That many sticks of powder, there is half an inch, 5/8ths, along there, you cut them in two, and it all mashes down into the hole...It does its work twice as well if it is tamped, as if you lay the stick in there loose."*[343]

Going through an average of twenty drill bits and twenty to thirty pounds of powder per day, the men made slow and

---

[342] William Flick vs. The Hahns Peak & Elk River Canal & Placer Mining Company, Colorado Court of Appeals Number 2024. (1899). Page 388. https://nrrbook.com/FlickCase

[343] William Flick vs. The Hahns Peak & Elk River Canal & Placer Mining Company, Colorado Court of Appeals Number 2024. (1899). Page 389. https://nrrbook.com/FlickCase

steady progress of one to four feet from each end. *"A great deal of difference in a day; some days they would not go only a foot...One day I believe they went four feet."*[344]

Each end of the tunnel was braced with lumber that was hewn on site. *"I had the timbering on each end...I think there was about three branches on the east end, and one on the West end...I hewed them out."*[345]

Except for four days off due to a lack of powder, work continued nearly around the clock for twenty-six days until the Sand Rock Point Tunnel was completed on August 22, 1897. *"The tunnel was four feet wide at the bottom, and six feet high, with a little rounding roof, square at the bottom."*[346] At a cost of $7 per foot, the 170-foot-long tunnel totaled $1,190. The approaches were calculated at 227.4 cubic yards at a rate of $.40 per yard, totaling $90.90. Combined, the tunnel and approaches cost $1,280.90.[347] Had the original plan of "more permanent" fluming gone through, Flick estimated the cost would have been $350. *"About a thousand dollars is the difference between the whole cost, the approaches and the tunnel."*[348]

---

[344] William Flick vs. The Hahns Peak & Elk River Canal & Placer Mining Company, Colorado Court of Appeals Number 2024. (1899). Page 252. https://nrrbook.com/FlickCase

[345] William Flick vs. The Hahns Peak & Elk River Canal & Placer Mining Company, Colorado Court of Appeals Number 2024. (1899). Page 227. https://nrrbook.com/FlickCase

[346] William Flick vs. The Hahns Peak & Elk River Canal & Placer Mining Company, Colorado Court of Appeals Number 2024. (1899). Page 168. https://nrrbook.com/FlickCase

[347] William Flick vs. The Hahns Peak & Elk River Canal & Placer Mining Company, Colorado Court of Appeals Number 2024. (1899). Page 39. https://nrrbook.com/FlickCase

[348] William Flick vs. The Hahns Peak & Elk River Canal & Placer Mining Company, Colorado Court of Appeals Number 2024. (1899). Page 186. https://nrrbook.com/FlickCase

With the Sand Rock Point Tunnel finished, Flick had completed all the projects stipulated in the contract, and he was delighted with his team's work. *"It was done exceedingly well; I never was so particular with a job in my life as I was with that, never watched it so close."[349]* McFadden was also satisfied. *"He (McFadden) took a very deep interest in it too. It had to be just so, or there would be a row right there."[350]*

Above: The entrance (left) and exit (right) of the Sand Rock Point Tunnel.

Anticipation was high that massive amounts of gold would soon be had. *"This week the Hahn's Peak and Elk River Canal and Placer Mining company is in a position to resume work on the Hahn's Peak placer on a larger scale than has been attempted since 1890, when Hinman & Cody made a clear profit of $40,000 in one season. This is the result of the completion of the new ditch from the Elk River, which will carry 1,500 inches of water during nine months of the year. The new ditch...has been constructed along the hillsides for the entire distance, avoiding the system of flumes that brought the old ditch to grief. The*

[349] William Flick vs. The Hahns Peak & Elk River Canal & Placer Mining Company, Colorado Court of Appeals Number 2024. (1899). Page 159. https://nrrbook.com/FlickCase

[350] William Flick vs. The Hahns Peak & Elk River Canal & Placer Mining Company, Colorado Court of Appeals Number 2024. (1899). Page 160. https://nrrbook.com/FlickCase

ditch from Willow creek, four and a half miles in length, with a system of reservoirs, is also ready for business.

Chief Engineer George B. McFadden estimates that under the recent improvements, it will be possible to handle 1,200 yards of dirt every twenty-four hours at a cost not to exceed 4 cents per yard. As the gravel already sluiced has averaged between 25 and 50 cents per yard, the company seems to have a second Klondyke ready to pour gold into the lap of commerce. In the past twenty years twenty-nine acres of placer ground has produced $700,000 in gold and the company has 1,900 acres more that is just as good and perhaps better."[351]

There was just one thing left to do: test the newly revived Farwell Ditch. As stated in the contract, Flick would refurbish the ditch to supply a full head of water, defined as six feet wide at the top, three and a half feet at the bottom, and three feet deep, for a period of thirty days. When the tunnel began construction, a full head of water was flowing from the Trail Creek headgate to a wastegate just before reaching Sand Rock Point. *"At the part of the ditch from the head-gate down to the new tunnel, the water was turned in about the 28th of July, as near as I can remember, '97...It was three and one-half feet deep in the ditch, at the least, and that ditch is very wide up there."*[352]

Water was turned into the tunnel upon its completion to begin the thirty-day test. *"We turned it through the tunnel the 22nd day of August, '97...all the water there was in the Elk River was turned in, every drop...It run clear to Hahn's Peak at that time...All the water there was in the north branch of the Elk River went through the ditch for a period of thirty days."*[353]

[351] Hahn's Peak Placers. (September 6, 1897). *The Rocky Mountain News*, Page 3. https://nrrbook.com/RMN-1897-09-06

[352] William Flick vs. The Hahns Peak & Elk River Canal & Placer Mining Company, Colorado Court of Appeals Number 2024. (1899). Page 181. https://nrrbook.com/FlickCase

[353] William Flick vs. The Hahns Peak & Elk River Canal & Placer Mining Company, Colorado Court of Appeals Number 2024. (1899). Pages 181-182. https://nrrbook.com/FlickCase

Unfortunately, there was a major problem. Despite turning "every drop" of the Elk River into the ditch, it no longer supplied a full head. The Elk River water level had dropped significantly in a short period of time, as it tends to do in mid-to-late summer. Flick was frustrated, rightfully so, that the extra time it took to build the tunnel, as opposed to fluming, coincided with the drop in the river level. *"I was delayed about fifteen days...I would say that there was plenty of water in there to fill the ditch on about August 12th and 22nd there was only about one-third of that amount."*[354] The water level in the ditch was only one and a half to two feet deep, instead of the three feet stipulated in the contract. *"There was about a foot and a half or two feet of water running in it."*[355]

According to HPERCPMC, Flick had not fulfilled his end of the bargain to supply a full head of water. Meanwhile, Flick believed he had satisfied the terms of the contract by constructing a ditch that was capable of supplying the defined volume of water. *"I told him that I could not guarantee a flow of water; that I was not an insurance company; and didn't propose to insure anything against natural elements; that I would build a ditch that would carry that much water."*[356]

Up to this point, Kneeland had paid Flick $5,400:

- $2,500 on July 22, 1897
- $2,500 on August 12, 1897

---

[354] William Flick vs. The Hahns Peak & Elk River Canal & Placer Mining Company, Colorado Court of Appeals Number 2024. (1899). Pages 182-183. https://nrrbook.com/FlickCase

[355] William Flick vs. The Hahns Peak & Elk River Canal & Placer Mining Company, Colorado Court of Appeals Number 2024. (1899). Pages 183-184. https://nrrbook.com/FlickCase

[356] William Flick vs. The Hahns Peak & Elk River Canal & Placer Mining Company, Colorado Court of Appeals Number 2024. (1899). Page 378. https://nrrbook.com/FlickCase

- $400 on August 21, 1897 (the day before the tunnel was completed)

The $400 payment was intended to cover a portion of the additional expense Flick incurred in building the tunnel rather than the flume originally contracted. HPERCPMC, holding Flick responsible for the low volume of water, refused to pay more.

Two weeks later, Flick visited the Denver office of W.E. Sorelle, a lawyer for HPERCPMC, and asked for payment. Sorelle described the meeting as follows: *"He stated that he had just returned from Hahn's Peak a few days before...and asked me if we had any money for him. I said, what is the condition of the ditch? He said, first-class, in every particular. I said, has the water flowed through there thirty days, to the depth of three feet? He said it had not; but he said, he could not be responsible for that. I said, it was your statement that we depended upon in entering into the contract. We would not have entered into it, if it had not been for your statements."*[357]

Since an immediate cash payment was off the table, Flick then asked Sorelle about a promissory note using company stock as collateral, or potentially receiving company stock free and clear instead of cash. *"Mr. Flick said that if he could get an absolute note, without having any conditions in it, and the stock given merely as security, he could use it. He said he could use the stock alone, if he had a title to that, without the note. I said, Mr. Flick, the contract calls for a note secured by stock, leaving the option in the company to determine whether or not they will pay you the money, or deliver you the stock...I told him that if he felt that he must have the stock and note, that I would write to Mr. Stevenson about the matter, and leave it for him to decide*

---

[357] William Flick vs. The Hahns Peak & Elk River Canal & Placer Mining Company, Colorado Court of Appeals Number 2024. (1899). Pages 352-353. https://nrrbook.com/FlickCase

what should be done; that, in my opinion, the contract had not been complied with."[358]

Denied once again, William Flick's frustration continued to grow, and he filed a Mechanic's Lien[359] against HPERCPMC on November 1, 1897, for $10,262.61, minus $5,750 that had already been accounted for ($5,400 in cash payments + $350 credit for not building the flumes at Sand Rock Point). Flick wanted payment of $4,512.61. He received nothing.

The situation continued to escalate. Flick's attorney, F.E. Gregg, filed a criminal complaint against HPERCPMC in Arapahoe County District Court on December 21, 1897. Included in this complaint was an Impossibility of Performance statement, which cited a passage from *Chitty on Contracts (11 Am. Ed) 1076*: *"In contracts from the nature of which it is apparent that the parties contracted on the basis of the continued existence of a given person or thing, a condition is implied that if the performance becomes impossible from the perishing of the person or thing, that shall excuse such performance."*[360]

In other words, Flick tried to make a case that he could not be held responsible for not supplying water that did not exist at the time of the thirty-day trial run.

In the meantime, HPERCPMC extended an olive branch to Flick on October 4, 1898, by offering to tender 17,400 shares of stock through his attorney, F.E. Gregg. *"Mr. Sorelle walked into my office and said, Mr. Gregg, I am going to tender you, and now do*

[358] William Flick vs. The Hahns Peak & Elk River Canal & Placer Mining Company, Colorado Court of Appeals Number 2024. (1899). Page 353. https://nrrbook.com/FlickCase

[359] William Flick vs. The Hahns Peak & Elk River Canal & Placer Mining Company, Colorado Court of Appeals Number 2024. (1899). Page 144. https://nrrbook.com/FlickCase

[360] William Flick vs. The Hahns Peak & Elk River Canal & Placer Mining Company, Colorado Court of Appeals Number 2024. (1899). Page 3. https://nrrbook.com/FlickCase

tender you 17,400 shares of the stock of the Hahn's Peak Mining Company for Mr. Flick. He said, I don't suppose that Mr. Flick will accept it. But he says, I want at least to make a tender. In reply I said I didn't know whether Mr. Flick would accept it or not; I didn't know anything about that; and I thought, further, that he was too late anyhow that he came on that day; and Mr. Sorelle said No, he says, the contract says that he can tender it within the maturity of the note. And he said the note had three days of grace; and I said, no, I didn't think so, in this case. And I will have to state that he attached no conditions whatever to his tender, when he offered this stock. By the way, I wish to state further in that connection, though, that this certificate of stock which he offered me at that time for 17,400 shares bore date October 3rd, 1897, and was made to order, or the certificate was issued in the name of William Flick, - I mean this certificate, that he tendered to me."[361]

HPERCPMC had a stock certificate printed on October 3, 1897, anticipating that it would be used for some or all of its final payment to Flick (recall that the original contract allowed for this). However, when business went sideways, they did not tender these shares to Flick. Presumably, the tender offer expired exactly one year after the certificate was issued, and now, just one year and one day later, HPERCPMC was offering to tender that very certificate to Flick during a supposed three-day grace period. Flick rejected the offer due to the ongoing lawsuit.

The Arapahoe County District Court case did not go to trial until January 1899. The result? A mixed verdict. *"The Court, being now sufficiently advised in the premises, found the issues herein joined in favor of the defendant, upon the defendant's answer herein, and in favor of the plaintiff on the defendant's*

---

[361] William Flick vs. The Hahns Peak & Elk River Canal & Placer Mining Company, Colorado Court of Appeals Number 2024. (1899). Page 375. https://nrrbook.com/FlickCase

cross-complaint, and directed that a decree be prepared in accordance with such finding."[362]

Flick and his legal team believed that the Court made several errors in the case and filed a motion for a new trial. *"Now comes plaintiff by F.E. Gregg and G.L. Hodges, his Attorneys, and moves the Court for a new trial herein, and as ground for such motions states: First. - That the Court erred in admitting certain evidence...Second. - That the Court erred in excluding certain evidence...Third. - The Court erred in its findings and conclusions of law and fact...Fourth. - That the Court erred in finding and deciding for defendant and in giving judgement for costs."[363]*

Instead of granting a new trial, Arapahoe County District Court affirmed the original decree of a mixed verdict. Flick, refusing to concede, filed a longshot appeal to the Colorado Court of Appeals, which was granted. *"The plaintiff, by his counsel, then and there duly excepted, and prayed for an appeal to the Court of Appeals of the State of Colorado, which prayer for an appeal was by the Court granted."[364]*

Two years passed before the Colorado Court of Appeals issued its verdict in 1901. Among its statements are the following:

"Held that the guarantee in the contract was not that the stream would supply the amount of water, but only that the ditch should be capable of conveying a full head of water from the river to the mine if there was sufficient water in the river to supply the amount. And that plaintiff having turned into the ditch all the

---

[362] William Flick vs. The Hahns Peak & Elk River Canal & Placer Mining Company, Colorado Court of Appeals Number 2024. (1899). Page 391. https://nrrbook.com/FlickCase

[363] William Flick vs. The Hahns Peak & Elk River Canal & Placer Mining Company, Colorado Court of Appeals Number 2024. (1899). Page 392. https://nrrbook.com/FlickCase

[364] William Flick vs. The Hahns Peak & Elk River Canal & Placer Mining Company, Colorado Court of Appeals Number 2024. (1899). Page 393. https://nrrbook.com/FlickCase

water of the river and kept the same running therein for thirty days, he had sufficiently complied with that part of his contract."[365]

"The trial court seems to have taken defendant's view of the question, and finding that plaintiff had failed and omitted to cause a full head of water to flow through the said ditch in the complaint specified for a period of thirty days consecutively, it further found that by reason of such failure, plaintiff was not entitled to recover at all. In this we are clearly of opinion that the court was in error.

In our view, the contract is clear and specific, and sustains the position taken by the plaintiff as to the object, purpose and intent of the parties. The exclusive subject-matter of the contract was the enlargement, cleaning out, repairing, etc., of the ditches according to the specifications furnished by the chief engineer of the company. In no place is anything said about any obligation on the part of the plaintiff to furnish any water at all, nor can any such obligation be implied from anything said in the contract."[366]

Lastly, and most consequentially, the verdict ended with this simple, conclusive statement: *"The judgement will be reversed."*[367]

The Hahns Peak and Elk River Canal & Placer Mining Company continued to operate until 1911. *"This gigantic property, that belonging to the Hahns Peak and Elk River Canal and Placer Mining company, is idle now through the death of the former*

---

[365] Flick v. Hahns Peak & Elk River Canal & Placer Mining Co., 16 Colo. App. 485, (1901). Page 485. https://nrrbook.com/FlickAppealVerdict

[366] Flick v. Hahns Peak & Elk River Canal & Placer Mining Co., 16 Colo. App. 485, (1901). Page 489. https://nrrbook.com/FlickAppealVerdict

[367] Flick v. Hahns Peak & Elk River Canal & Placer Mining Co., 16 Colo. App. 485, (1901). Page 493. https://nrrbook.com/FlickAppealVerdict

owner. *This comprises Poverty bar, the scene of the most extensive workings, and hundreds of acres adjoining."*[368]

The company remained idle until it was sold in 1913 to William Woods of Los Angeles. *"Deeds were placed on record in the office of the county clerk this week transferring the entire property of the Hahns Peak and Elk River Canal and Placer Mining company, all its numerous patented and located claims, the townsite of Hahns Peak, ditches, pipe, equipment, etc., to William W. Woods of Los Angeles for the sum of $60,000.*

Negotiations for a sale have been pending for some time and last year experts made an inspection on the ground. That the transfer has been made indicates that the property was found satisfactory and leads to the belief that the ground will be worked next year. This company owns practically all of the ground around the Poverty Bar workings, the long canal from Elk River built by J.V. Farwell, valuable water rights and ranch equipment. L.G. Stevenson of Los Angeles is president of the company and George B. McFadden of Denver is secretary.

The property has produced much placer gold and a great deal of good ground remains. Several plans have been proposed for a more economical working and it is probable that they will now be carried out under the new owner."[369]

Also active in the area in the early 1900s was none other than Robert McIntosh, who, despite all of his endeavors and successes in Slater, never could shake the Hahns Peak gold bug. Perhaps this was caused by a sentimental or emotional attachment to the mining district that he helped industrialize. After supervising the construction of the Farwell Ditch in the 1870s, it is fitting that McIntosh, now in his early 80s, was there to witness its use come to an end in the early 1920s after roughly forty-five years of on-and-off operation.

---

[368] Mineral Districts Have Great Value. (July 26, 1911). *The Steamboat Pilot*, Page 19. https://nrrbook.com/SP-1911-07-26

[369] Hahns Peak Placers Are Sold for $60,000. (October 29, 1913). *The Steamboat Pilot*, Page 1. https://nrrbook.com/SP-1913-10-29

"The first year that Father (McIntosh) *himself went back was about 1910. He built a ditch from Way's Gulch and mined a little, but the water played out. However, he made expenses. He was then mining farther west on the Peak. Next he repaired the Farwell ditch at considerable expense and took out some gold. In mining though, he had loosened the dirt on the ditch and it slid in. In 1914, I think, he bought lumber to repair the ditch. The lumber burned in the yard before he could use it. He then used some of the pipe from the Farwell ditch to control his water, and mined for some time. The top dirt which he had to wash off was ten feet thick. Then he came into a layer of sand which appeared to be on bedrock. The sand carried a good gold deposit. Fall came before the whole pocket was washed out, and the overhead was so heavy that no money was made. The last time he returned to the Peak was in 1922, about two years before he died."*[370]

Details are scarce, but at some point, the McIntosh extension of the Farwell Ditch was itself extended approximately a quarter mile to the west side of Little Mountain, where it is believed downhill piping was used to feed water cannons for hydraulic mining near Deep Creek. The above quote contains a couple of clues (*mining farther west on the Peak...He then used some of the pipe from the Farwell ditch*) that suggest Robert McIntosh could be credited with doing this, though that is mostly speculation. It is entirely possible someone else was responsible for making that happen.

Even though John V. Farwell's time in North Routt County was brief, his impact on the Hahns Peak Mining District was immense. More than a million dollars' worth of gold was produced over the years, and without the water supplied by the big ditch, production would have been drastically less.

"The rich placer mines at Hahns Peak were discovered by Joseph Hahn, a prospector from Empire. This was in 1862, when the

---

[370] Morgan, Helen. (1970). *Snake River Profiles, Volume 1*, Page 44.

world was thrilling with the golden story of Georgetown, Central City and Pike's Peak. That was the first discovery of gold in what is now Routt County. The story of Hahns operations, the fabulous wealth which he was first to discover, the subsequent excitement and the tragic death of Hahn from hunger and exposure, makes a fascinating narrative, but this article is to detail with the present and future and not with the past. The mineral districts of Routt county are looking forward and not backward.

Down through the subsequent operations of J.V. Farwell to the present time the placer mines of Hahns Peak have maintained their reputation for richness. A conservative estimate of the wealth produced from the placers of the district put it in excess of $1,000,000, and the placer gold remaining there is many, many times greater than that which has been recovered.

There are several thousand acres of placer ground in the Hahns Peak basin, the territory surrounding the mountain, and gold is found on every side."[371]

Historian Thelma Stevenson summed it up nicely:

"True, the Chicago financier did not make Colorado's future his life work, as did Joseph Hahn and countless unsung heroes who braved its wilderness hazards from Wyoming's borders southward, and from the Continental Divide to the fringes of Utah. But we must credit John Farwell with giving Routt County a mighty big push back in the days when Colorado's statehood was born."[372]

---

[371] Mineral Districts Have Great Value. (July 26, 1911). *The Steamboat Pilot*, Page 19. https://nrrbook.com/SP-1911-07-26

[372] Stevenson, Thelma. (2005, 4th Printing). *Historic Hahns Peak*, Page 18.

PART TWO

GONE DITCHIN'

CHAPTER 9: EUREKA

"Young man, you may not be a Columbus or a Livingstone, to discover a new world, or to open up one of the oldest lands in human history for the conquests of the cross, but in your little circle, whatever it may be, you may open up a new world to many a young man who knows not God in Christ as a personal Saviour, the same as a little bootblack did for an educated lawyer, while he was giving his boots a five-cent shine, with this question. 'Do you know God?'"[373]

-John V. Farwell

Sometimes life has a way of putting you in the right place at the right time. My life was about to change, and I had no idea. In the summer of 2014, my wife Katie and I wanted to take our first big summer vacation with our three young kids (Blake, age 7, Brenna, age 6, and Adrian, age 3). We were ready to hit the road, and the mountains of Colorado were calling. Due to our last-minute planning, finding lodging in a mountain town proved challenging, and the best option available was in Steamboat Springs, so Steamboat Springs it was!

On June 27, 2014, we packed up our Toyota Sienna and began the 14-hour overnight drive from Cedar Falls, Iowa, to Colorado. Katie and I alternated shifts driving through the night on Interstate 80 in Iowa and through Nebraska. The hours and miles ticked by, and eventually we crossed the border into Wyoming. We soon passed Cheyenne and then reached Laramie, where we exited I-80 and turned southwest onto Highway 230. At this point, excitement was building as mountains were in full view, and we knew we were only a couple of hours from our destination. The drive through Medicine Bow National Forest and south into the North Park

---

[373] Farwell, John V. (1906). *Corner Stones of Character: Some Ways of Making Them*, Page 92. https://nrrbook.com/CornerStonesofCharacter

area of Colorado gave us a glimpse of what was to come. With the front range of the Rockies to our east and the Zirkel Wilderness to our west, we continued south through Cowdrey and Walden and eventually turned west on Highway 40. We were nearly there!

Everyone driving into Steamboat Springs from the east on Highway 40 for the first time will remember the moment they see the stunning Yampa Valley below. From 8,500 feet of elevation, you can see Lake Catamount and the lush, green, picturesque valley roughly two thousand feet below. The valley floor gets closer and closer as you descend towards Steamboat Springs. To this day, I still look forward to driving around the mountain on Highway 40 to take in that view.

Upon arriving in town, we checked into our hotel, caught a nap, and then began checking off our to-do list. As first-timers, this naturally included many common Steamboat Springs tourist activities:

- Fish Creek Falls
- Tubing in the Yampa River
- Friday Night Rodeo
- Alpine Slide
- Horseback Riding

On June 30, 2014, we decided to venture "up north" to Steamboat Lake State Park to do some hiking. The drive north on County Road 129 is very scenic, and in a way, represents a reversal of time as you make the trip. Starting in Steamboat Springs, you have the famous Steamboat ski mountain and a developed commercial district along Lincoln Avenue. A few miles outside of town, the surroundings contain ranches, pastures, and hayfields, and as you close in on Hahns Peak, you reach the North Routt area, where the county was first settled many years ago. The first time Hahns Peak comes into view is similar to the first time seeing the Yampa Valley —it just leaves you speechless (for me, anyway). With Hahns Peak in our sights, we knew we were near our destination and drove the last few miles to the Park.

With young kids in tow, we chose the Willow Creek Trail because it appeared to be an easy hike. We took our time, had a picnic by the lake, and eventually ended up at the Steamboat Lake State Park Visitor Center, where things began to get interesting. Like many Visitor Centers, there was a variety of information on display regarding the local wildlife and history of the area. Along one wall were pictures and descriptions detailing the mining history on and around Hahns Peak. First, you read about Joseph Hahn's discovery of gold in Willow Creek in the early 1860s. Fast forward to the 1870s, and a story of John V. Farwell building a 27-mile-long ditch[374] to supply water for mining operations. What? Who? How had I never heard of this? Or him?

Above: My family enjoying a picnic (bottom-right corner) near Steamboat Lake. We did not realize at the time that the peak in the distance was Farwell Mountain.

---

[374] The Farwell Ditch was 17 miles long when initially constructed. It was extended to 18 miles in 1880. Many historical records and resources erroneously cite different lengths, including 14, 23, 24, 27, and 28 miles.

The Farwell name is not common, so upon reading this (and double and triple checking that it did indeed say Farwell), I naturally became very curious. My curiosity grew further as I examined the 3D topographical map displayed in the middle of the room. There, prominently displayed, was Farwell Mountain, which, at 10,824 feet of elevation, was one of the tallest peaks in the region. The map had my full attention, and questions continued to swirl in my head.

As we left Steamboat Lake State Park that day, I looked towards the east, knowing for the first time that the prominent, vast mountain just a few miles over was Farwell Mountain itself. I had to learn more. Before heading south back to Steamboat Springs, we made the short drive to Pearl Lake State Park, now knowing from the map at the Visitor Center that Pearl Lake sat at the foot of Farwell Mountain.

Above: Farwell Mountain as seen from Pearl Lake.

Pearl Lake State Park instantly became a favorite of our family. The calm, clear water was perfect for the kids to splash around in, and that day we had the lake nearly to ourselves. We walked along the shoreline of the cove out to the main body of the lake, and behold, there was Farwell Mountain to the north in all its glory. Even on the last day of June, there was still a bit of snow near the peak. A sense of awe and wonder came over me, while an inner desire to learn more about this mountain and the surrounding area was kindled. In other words, it was stunning and intriguing, and I was hooked!

My wheels were turning. In the back of my mind, I suspected there was a chance of a family connection here. To my knowledge, most of the Farwells in America today can trace their ancestry to a common ancestor: Henry Farwell. Henry was born in 1605 in England and became one of the first settlers of Concord, Massachusetts, in 1636. I knew with certainty that I was a direct descendant of Henry; is it possible that John V. Farwell was too? Were we related? After the discoveries at the Visitor Center and seeing Farwell Mountain with my own eyes, I knew I had some homework to get to the bottom of it.

Thanks to extensive family records both in paper form and online, I discovered that yes, we were related, albeit distantly. John V. Farwell and I are technically fourth cousins, four times removed. The family tree on the following page shows the relationship. My brother, Rodney Farwell, soon becomes involved in this story and is included in the tree.

Henry Farwell (Born in 1605 in England)
↓
Joseph Farwell (1641)
↓
Joseph Farwell, Jr. (1670)
↙ ↘

Daniel Farwell (1717)	Samuel Farwell (1714)
↓	↓
Daniel Farwell (1740)	Isaac Farwell (1757)
↓	↓
Simeon Farwell (1766)	Moors Farwell (1789)
↓	↓
Henry Farwell (1795)	Edward Farwell (1816)
↓	↓
John V. Farwell (1825)	Horace Farwell (1857)
	↓
	Albert Farwell (1885)
	↓
	Dean Farwell (1928)
	↓
	Terry Farwell (1954)

↙ ↘

Nolan Farwell (1983)	Rodney Farwell (1986)

CHAPTER 10: PROSPECTING

"I remember, when a boy of seven years, watching, on my way to market with my father, a dense fog, transformed by the sun into silverlined golden clouds with which to array in kingly splendor the sides and summit of a mountain, and I shall never forget the inspiration of that scene, nor my involuntary emotion of wonder and worship toward Him."[375]

-John V. Farwell

We did not realize it at the time, but our family vacation in 2014 was going to snowball into something much larger. Having thoroughly enjoyed our time in Steamboat Springs and the North Routt area, my family returned in the summer of 2015. While we enjoyed many of the same activities, we had one additional goal for this trip: reach the summit of Farwell Mountain.

When I looked at online maps of the area, I quickly learned there was a four-wheel-drive road that takes you right to the summit. It was obvious, though, that our Toyota Sienna was not the right tool for the job. Thankfully, the Hahns Peak Roadhouse (now known as Steamboat Lake Outpost) had exactly what we needed: a crew cab Polaris Ranger, large enough to haul all five of our family, along with a cooler containing lunch and drinks. I grew up on a farm in northeast Kansas and had experience driving Rangers, so this was perfect!

It was a spectacular day with clear blue skies and temperatures in the 80s. The kids hopped in the rear seat, buckled up, and off we went. With the rental, we received a map of the area containing all the four-wheel-drive roads and trails. To reach

---

[375] Farwell, John V. (1906). *Corner Stones of Character: Some Ways of Making Them*, Page 125. https://nrrbook.com/CornerStonesofCharacter

the summit of Farwell Mountain was quite simple: follow Forest Service Road 409. Near the top, we would turn south on FS 409.2B, which would take us to the summit.

The first few miles of FS 409 cross low-lying grounds that I later learned are called Ways Gulch and Beaver Basin. The scenery was stunning, with Hahns Peak and Farwell Mountain in clear view. Wildflowers were abundant, and we even came across a herd of grazing sheep. At the western base of Farwell Mountain, FS 409 turned north, and we began to climb. The trail, which had been mainly dirt up to this point, now consisted of baseball and softball-sized rocks.

We kept climbing, totally oblivious to the fact that we crossed the path of the Farwell Ditch along the way. As we proceeded, we came across a short, unmarked turnoff and decided to check it out. It was apparent that an old mine had been located there. In my mind, I wondered if this could have been one of John V. Farwell's mine locations? In later years, I would learn that the answer was no. Instead, this was the location of the Farwell Mountain Copper Company, which operated in the mid-1900s. The site is notable for the relief pipe that comes horizontally out of the ground. Crystal-clear water flows continuously from the pipe. If you hike up the mountain from here into the forest, you can find two closed-off mine shafts.

After a brief pit stop at the old copper mine site, we resumed our trek up FS 409. The trail continued north for another mile or so and then turned to the east at its intersection with FS 414. We continued, climbing for roughly three miles before coming to the FS 409.2B intersection. From there, it was less than a mile to the summit!

The view from the top is breathtaking. To the east were the jagged peaks of the Zirkel Wilderness, to the south was Pearl Lake, and in the distance was Sleeping Giant (Elk Mountain). To the southwest was Steamboat Lake and Sand Mountain, and to the west was Hahns Peak. Turning to the north, we could see into Wyoming. At 10,824 feet of elevation, and with majestic views all around, it felt like we were on top of the world.

Above, from Left to Right: Nolan, Blake, Brenna, Adrian, & Katie Farwell on the Summit of Farwell Mountain on 7/2/2015.

Above: Looking southwest from the top of Farwell Mountain. Pearl Lake is on the left, and Steamboat Lake is on the right.

The trip up Farwell Mountain in 2015 was the first of many, and in 2016 another was planned. This was the first of several "Farwell Guys' Trips" that have taken place over the years. In addition to my son, Blake, and me, my dad, Terry, brother, Rodney, and his son, Kenton, all loaded up and headed for North Routt County. Along the way, we picked up a rental ATV and UTV in Denver. The agenda for this trip was to ride the ATV trails and explore the area further. Mission accomplished! We also made our first visit to Farwell Lake, tucked away high on Farwell Mountain just east of the summit, and even camped in a tent one night in a clearing above the lake.

This trip planted a seed in all of us, and we immediately knew that we would be doing similar trips in the future. However, rather than renting machines each time and dealing with all that entails, we began building our own fleet of ATVs and UTVs, with each of us acquiring several machines over the years. Unbeknownst to us at the time, these machines would be used for more than just recreation in the years to come.

Above: Campsite in a clearing above Farwell Lake in 2016.

The next big Farwell trip to the North Routt area occurred in July 2018. This time, the group consisted of my parents (Terry & Nanette Farwell), my siblings and me, and our spouses (Nate and Erika Sapp, Dana Jones, Nolan & Katie Farwell, Rodney & Leighanne Farwell). We rented a cabin west of Hahns Peak, and once again enjoyed our time exploring new trails on ATVs and UTVs. One day, we rode up and over Farwell Mountain and took FS 409 down to Diamond Park, where we saw a massive bull moose along the way. From there, we got on the Continental Divide Trail and headed north. We didn't realize it at the time, but along this route we had crossed the Farwell Ditch, ridden alongside it, and also came within about fifty yards of the headgate on Trail Creek.

Each trip resulted in a greater love for the Hahns Peak area. Colorado is home to many spectacular locations, and I have had the opportunity to see several with my own eyes, including Rocky Mountain National Park, the Alpine Loop, Taylor Park, the Royal Gorge, and the Garden of the Gods, to name a few. While they are all incredible in their own way, North Routt County tops my list. The scenery is incredible, and the ATV Trail system is top-notch. To make things better, it is not overrun and overcrowded like some of the other places I mentioned. I hope it stays that way! My idea of a vacation is to get outdoors and away from the crowds, and the Hahns Peak area cannot be beat in those regards.

The 2018 trip came and went, and the "lull," as we've come to call it, of waiting for the next trip began. In early 2019, my brother Rod and I began discussing the need to learn more about the area's mining history. More specifically, we needed to learn more about the Farwell Ditch that we had become aware of years prior. All we knew about the ditch at the time was what we had learned in the Steamboat Lake Visitor Center. As described, John V. Farwell came to the area in the 1870s and financed the construction of a 27-mile-long ditch from the Elk River to International Camp.

To learn more, we turned to the internet. Although the information was limited, some search results yielded old newspaper articles that offered valuable insights. However, significant gaps remained.

Some of the initial facts that we learned were:

- Hahns Peak was the namesake of Joseph Hahn, who was the first to find gold in the area in the 1860s. Hahn tragically froze to death in April 1867 while he and William Doyle attempted to abandon their camp after running out of food and supplies.

219

- John V. Farwell arrived in 1876. The ditch was constructed from 1876 to 1878, and his company was known as the International Mining Company. For Rod and me, the main questions were, "Where exactly did the ditch lie, and is it still here to this day? How do we find it?"

- Construction of the ditch was managed by Farwell's trusted lieutenant, Robert McIntosh, who came with Farwell from Chicago. Some newspaper articles stated that the Ditch was originally 17 miles long, while others reported it to be 27 or 28 miles long. Which was it? We had to figure this out.

- To undertake such a massive project, it was necessary to build the required infrastructure. Farwell had a wagon road built from Laramie, Wyoming, through Hog Park near the Colorado-Wyoming border, and to the Hahns Peak area. Once complete, he had a sawmill shipped in and set up on the south side of Farwell Mountain. Where could this have been located?

- Farwell's mining operation was largely unsuccessful, and he sold it off to a banker in Rawlins, Wyoming, for $60,000 in 1879. This short time frame baffled us. Robert McIntosh then leased the operation, extended the ditch one mile to Poverty Bar, and enjoyed great success. He later moved on to run a general store and large horse ranch near Slater, Colorado.

With this limited knowledge, our curiosity grew, as did our need to conduct further research. What we would find is that this was all happening at a fairly pivotal time. Colorado became a state on August 1, 1876, with present-day Routt County originally part of Grand County, which itself had been part of Summit County in territorial Colorado. Routt County itself was established a few months later, on January 29, 1877. With all of this going on right at the same time that Farwell was setting up his operation and constructing the ditch, official record-keeping was less than robust. Also, to state the obvious, the internet was never going to be the best source of information for detailed mining history in the 1870s. To make any progress, we would need to change our approach. Perhaps a local museum or historical society could be beneficial?

Fast forward to the summer of 2019. I began to make some phone calls to see if anyone in the Steamboat Springs or Hahns Peak area had detailed information on the Farwell Ditch. After striking out with my first few calls, I dialed the Hahns Peak Area Historical Society. A friendly woman named Marge Eardley answered the phone, and I explained who I was and asked if she had access to information regarding the Farwell Ditch. Marge replied, "I do not, but I know exactly who you need to talk to. His name is David Joe Zehner and he has been researching the ditch." Marge gave me David Joe's phone number, and later that day, I gave him a call.

David Joe and I had a wonderful conversation. I described my background and distant relation to John V. Farwell, and that my brother and I were trying to learn more about the Farwell Ditch. Zehner was now retired, but in his working days, he owned and operated an excavation and earthmoving company in Hayden. In retirement, he and his wife, Judy, spent their summers in a cabin in the small village of Hahns Peak. Just a few years prior, in the summer of 2016, David Joe had been exploring the roads and trails in the area, much like he used to do in his youth. With his experience in earthmoving, a man-made grade caught his eye, and he investigated further, finding what appeared to be an irrigation ditch. David Joe had worked on many irrigation ditches in Routt and Moffat counties over the years. After consulting with others in the area, it was determined that the ditch he had discovered was the old Farwell Ditch, dating back to the 1870s.

Zehner went on to describe how he and a few others went back in September 2016 to try to follow the ditch to its headgate. They were successful, having found the headgate at Trail Creek (a branch of the Elk River), and along the way, discovered a tunnel approximately 170 feet long.

221

I was thrilled to finally be talking to someone who had knowledge of the Farwell Ditch! And then it got better- David Joe offered to take me and any other family members on a tour to see some of the ditch and the tunnel he had found. The timing was perfect because Rod, Terry, and I were already planning to be in the area that August to spend a week volunteering with Historicorps to restore the Hog Park Guard Station near the Colorado-Wyoming border. We added a couple of days at the beginning of that trip to have some time with David Joe.

After an overnight drive, we arrived in the Hahns Peak area on the morning of August 2, 2019. The plan that day was to have fun riding our ATVs on the fantastic mountain trails, and that's exactly what we did. Our tour with David Joe was scheduled for the following day, but that evening we decided to stop at their cabin in Hahns Peak to introduce ourselves. David Joe and Judy, who were celebrating their 60th anniversary that very day, warmly welcomed us into their cabin. They were prepared! Spread across their table was a series of papers with topography maps printed on them, all taped together. Across the pages, David Joe had marked his estimated line of the Farwell Ditch with a yellow highlighter. This was the first time we had seen anything showing where the ditch was located.

Above: Paper map on the Zehner table.

David Joe shared more of his story, including more details about the tunnel he found. From what he could tell, the ditch itself used to wrap around a mountainside, but for some reason, it had been dammed up, and a tunnel was bored through the mountain in its place. We did not know it at the time, but three years later, we would discover exactly when and why that tunnel was built.

Naturally, we were thrilled to meet the Zehners and learn all the information they had for us, but the real excitement was waiting for us the following day!

Terry, Rod, and I left the Zehners and headed back down to the Hahns Peak Roadhouse, where we were staying. After the long drive to Colorado the previous night, we needed to get some sleep to recharge our batteries for the big day ahead.

CHAPTER 11: STAKING A CLAIM

"My son, you will be known by the company you keep, and this Book - well read - will lead you into such companionships as will make life a blessing to yourself and others."[376]

-John V. Farwell

On the morning of August 3, 2019, David Joe Zehner arrived at the Hahns Peak Roadhouse in his Jeep Wrangler Rubicon, and Terry, Rod, and I climbed in. We were expecting to take Forest Service Road 409 up and over Farwell Mountain to see the section of ditch and tunnel that we learned about the night before. We were familiar with this road (road is a generous term), having traversed it several times on our ATVs in previous years. However, David Joe threw us a curveball. Instead, he thought it would be faster to take Seedhouse Road off of County Road 129, take FS 433 north towards Diamond Park, and then get on FS 409 from the east.

Zehner, as usual, was right. About a mile and a half west of Diamond Park, he pulled his Jeep off the road and declared that we would be walking from that point on. It was not a long hike, though we did start with a climb up and over a hill about two hundred feet tall. The three of us Midwesterners were breathing pretty heavily by the time we made it to the top. Meanwhile, eighty-year-old David Joe had no problem whatsoever. Up he climbed, and on he went. Those of you who know him personally will not be surprised by this at all.

---

[376] Farwell, John V. (1906). *Corner Stones of Character: Some Ways of Making Them*, Page 9. https://nrrbook.com/CornerStonesofCharacter

Shortly after the hill climb, we worked our way north along the southeast flank of Dome Peak, at an elevation of roughly 9,330 feet. The mountainside was wide open with no trees nearby. While walking along, David Joe declared that we were walking on top of the Farwell Ditch, which was news to us, and maybe even a bit of a letdown, because where I was standing looked nothing like a ditch. Zehner explained that nearly 150 years' worth of rain and snowmelt coming down the mountain had slowly filled it in with sediment.

Our first reaction was to wonder how he could have ever picked this out as a ditch, as our untrained eyes never would have noticed it. All we saw was tall grass on a hillside.

Our second reaction was to wonder if this was all that was left. Our goal had been to research and learn about this ditch, and our first glimpse of it made us wonder if the ditch had been almost entirely reclaimed by nature. Was there anything left to see? Thankfully, we would soon learn that was not the case.

A short distance later, we approached a rocky ledge, and David Joe said we were nearing the tunnel. Even if the condition of the ditch had left us a little unsatisfied, knowing a tunnel was ahead had us excited. It was a bit of a climb to get up towards the ledge, as the terrain got steeper and there were downed trees to climb over, but we made it nonetheless. After working back to the east along the ledge, we rounded a corner, and there it was.

The tunnel was roughly four feet wide and four feet tall at its opening. If you looked through it, you could barely make out a speck of light on the other end. Zehner explained that we were looking at the outlet end of the tunnel. There was still some lumber anchored in place that appeared to tie into what would have been fluming long ago. We were staring history in the face, and it was fascinating! All we could think about was how this was constructed so many years ago and with such precision. How did they make it so straight? How did they keep the proper elevation?

226

It is in moments like these that all you can do is appreciate the history right before you. There we were, looking at actual, hard evidence of the Farwell Ditch right in front of our eyes. It was no longer just a story we had read on paper or a Visitor Center wall. It was very real. Over one hundred years prior, men put in back-breaking work with pickaxes, shovels, and some well-placed dynamite to bore this tunnel through solid rock. We were standing in the exact spot where all of this had happened, and in that moment, it was a humbling experience. The world is a much bigger place than our own lives and experiences, and time was the only thing that separated us from the men who created the very piece of history we were admiring. Standing at the opening of the tunnel made that clear.

Above: Seeing the tunnel for the first time as we approached it.

Less than an hour before, we were a bit disappointed when David Joe first informed us we were on the ditch. And now, we were blown away.

Naturally, when you see a tunnel like this, the next thing to do is to go through it (very carefully!). David Joe told us that he did this when he first discovered the tunnel in 2016. We crouched under the wood inside the opening and entered the tunnel, one by one. It is approximately 170 feet long and reaches a height of about 6 feet at its center. The temperature inside was ten to fifteen degrees cooler than the ambient temperature outside. Using our cell phones as a source of light, we worked our way through, trying not to bump our heads (unsuccessfully) into low points in the ceiling.

The other end of the tunnel (the entrance) was similar, with an opening again roughly four feet wide by four feet tall. However, unlike the opening into a stone face at the outlet end, the entrance end of the tunnel had clearly undergone some dirt and rock work. Right outside of the tunnel, there were stone walls roughly fifteen feet tall on each side. These walls gradually got shorter as we made our way away from the tunnel. And here, the ditch was very well defined.

Above: David Joe Zehner capturing GPS coordinates of the outlet end of the tunnel.

Above: Looking into the outlet end of the tunnel. The wood has been there since the tunnel was last used over one hundred years ago.

Above, from Left to Right: Rodney Farwell, David Joe Zehner, Terry Farwell, and Nolan Farwell standing next to the tunnel entrance on August 3, 2019.

We tried to take it all in. This end of the tunnel was vastly different. For starters, the ditch itself looked very much like a ditch. It was two to three feet deep and about six feet wide at the top, with a perfect U-shape structure. The key to its maintained form over all these years was that, in this area, the ditch ran through established forest, where tree roots stabilized the ground. The only thing that made it show its age was the numerous downed trees that had fallen across and into it. This ditch was worth exploring after all!

Above: Pile of rocks extracted from the tunnel during construction, located to the east of the tunnel entrance.

Remember David Joe telling us that it appeared the ditch used to go around the mountain, rather than through the tunnel? He would show us exactly what he meant by that. If you follow the ditch out of the tunnel, you come to a Y. To the north was the "base" of the Y, or the main ditch itself, coming towards our location. Zehner said that the headgate of the ditch was approximately one or two miles to the north, and the ditch was very well defined most of the way there. At the Y, the right branch went towards the tunnel that we had just gone through, while the left branch continued to go south. Soon after the split, the ditch had clearly been dammed up. Why? We climbed up and over the dam and continued to follow the ditch to find out.

It wasn't long before we had our answer. The ditch went straight to the edge of a cliff, where over one hundred feet below us was a massive pile of stone rubble. David Joe explained his theory to us. He believed that the ditch originally wrapped around the ledge on which we were now standing. Each winter, water would seep into cracks in the rock, freeze, and expand, causing rock (and attached fluming) to break off and fall away. To deal with this, they dammed up the ditch, bored a tunnel through the ledge, and tied back into the ditch on the other side.

Above: The ditch led straight to the edge of a cliff, with a pile of stone rubble below.

His theory made complete sense. Once again, seeing the incredible history in person and knowing that very few people alive today had seen what we were looking at was a very humbling experience. What Rod and I did not know was that three years later, we would discover detailed records of the Who, What, When, Why, and How this tunnel was built. The large rock ledge we had climbed through and were now standing upon was known as Sand Rock Point, and David Joe Zehner's theory, unsurprisingly, was correct.

After taking it all in, it was time to head back "home" for the night at Hahns Peak Roadhouse. We trekked back through the tunnel and hiked down to Zehner's Jeep. I don't recall who said it, but one of the Farwells asked about taking FS 409 back, up, and over Farwell Mountain. David Joe, stating that he had done it before in his Jeep, agreed.

While the Jeep was more than capable of traversing the road, it was very slow going. The same boulders that an ATV can easily maneuver around had to be carefully accounted for in a much wider vehicle. We had not gone far before we encountered a broken-down UTV and four people trying to determine what the machine's problem was. It appeared to have an electrical issue preventing it from starting. Amid the nearby peaks, cell coverage is nonexistent, so their only options were to hike out on foot or pile into the Jeep with us, which they did. It took us three to four hours to crawl along FS 409 all the way back to Hahns Peak Village. Along the way, one of the people we picked up sheepishly admitted to being the head of the local search-and-rescue team. We all had a good laugh at the irony of his situation, but it served as a crucial reminder to always be well prepared in these mountains.

Seeing the Farwell Ditch and the tunnel that day planted the seed for Rod and me to pursue this history further. Even though our time was limited, we would spend as much time "ditchin" as we could make available, and our desire to preserve this history only continues to grow.

The following day, Terry, Rod, and I made our way from Hahns Peak up to the Hog Park Guard Station near the Colorado-Wyoming border. We had not seen this structure before, but were aware of its existence since it was marked on the ATV Trail maps we used. A non-profit group called Historicorps was devoting time to restoring this structure, and the three of us had volunteered to spend several days there and help with the project. Our main job was to install cedar shingles on the eastern half of the roof.

Above: Rodney (Left) and Nolan (Right) on the roof of the Hog Park Guard Station.

Our time volunteering on the project passed quickly. Once again, we did not yet realize it, but John V. Farwell had a connection to the area. In later years, we would learn that the wagon road Farwell built from Laramie, Wyoming, to his mining operation near Hahns Peak passed through the Hog Park area, roughly 15 miles, as the crow flies, from the mining district.

The entity responsible for building this road was the Hans Peak Wagon Road Company, as detailed in Chapter 4. Established on July 5, 1876, the company officers were Andrew J. Bell, Daniel C. Stover, John W. Bell, and James H. Stover. The road itself was completed in 1877.

The 2019 trip would prove to be pivotal. Not only did we meet David Joe Zehner, who was an immensely valuable source of knowledge and experience, but we also stepped foot on the Farwell Ditch for the first time.

Small pieces of the puzzle were beginning to come together.

CHAPTER 12: GOLD FEVER

"No young man can build character without innate force to embody in acts the courage of his convictions. This trait creates enthusiasm, before which mountains of difficulty become a plain."[377]

-John V. Farwell

As the lull began once again, there were a couple of things that kept Rod and me busy planning for 2020. Naturally, we wanted to learn more, see more, and research more about the ditch and John V. Farwell's mining enterprise, but we were still dealing with a shortage of facts.

The first thing we did was to study Zehner's hand-drawn map in detail. Although it wasn't perfect, it was the best tool we had for determining the general path of the ditch, and we quickly realized we needed to plot the line David Joe had drawn on a digital map. There were several good mapping options available, but the app we used most at the time was Avenza, as it could be used even when off the grid, which definitely came in handy in the mountains. One evening, I took the time to carefully plot points in Avenza, creating a line that matched Zehner's yellow-highlighted line. While far from perfect, we now had the ditch generally plotted in digital form, which meant it could be shared with others and with mapping software such as Google Earth and CalTopo. These programs, if you have not used them before, are very powerful.

With the Farwell Ditch line uploaded to multiple tools, we could view the path of the ditch overlaid on various base maps, including 3D satellite imagery. This made us realize even more

---

[377] Farwell, John V. (1906). *Corner Stones of Character: Some Ways of Making Them*, Page 68. https://nrrbook.com/CornerStonesofCharacter

how extraordinary this piece of history truly was. Before our eyes was a flat line, perfectly tracking the topography of the mountainous terrain. Zooming in, we found a handful of spots where lines in the ground matched the line of the ditch we had plotted. We were looking at sections of the Farwell Ditch in modern-day satellite imagery! After nearly 150 years, some sections were still visible from above. Incredible!

The second thing we did after the 2019 trip was to turn back to the internet. Specifically, I typed "Farwell Ditch Tunnel" into Google, and surprisingly got a hit. On my screen was an old PDF document from 1972 titled *"General Geology of the Hahns Peak and Farwell Mountain Quadrangles, Routt County, Colorado. Geological Survey Bulletin 1349."*[378]

Why would an old geology report pop up? Thankfully, the PDF was searchable, and my search for "tunnel" provided two hits. First:

"A body of muscovite schist, too small to be mapped at the 1:24,000 scale, crops out near a tunnel 1.13 miles east-southeast of Farwell Lake."[379]

At first glance, not too much to glean from that one. Second:

"Artificial stream diversions were made at several places for placer mining operations during 1880-1910. Before two diversion channels were cut into the sandstone of the Browns Park by placer miners, Ways Gulch joined Beaver Creek near the SE. cor. sec. 27, T. 10 N., R. 85 W.; now, Ways Gulch drains into a formerly dry gulch that enters Willow Creek just below the Steamboat Lake dam. Upper Trail Creek was tapped by a canal

---

[378] *General Geology of the Hahns Peak and Farwell Mountain Quadrangles, Routt County, Colorado, Geological Survey Bulletin 1349.* (1972). https://nrrbook.com/HahnsFarwellGeology

[379] *General Geology of the Hahns Peak and Farwell Mountain Quadrangles, Routt County, Colorado, Geological Survey Bulletin 1349.* (1972). Page 13. https://nrrbook.com/HahnsFarwellGeology

which channeled the water through a Dakota Sandstone ledge (via a tunnel 200 ft long) to Hinman Creek. From Hinman Creek the water was conveyed by ditch around the southeast flank of Farwell Mountain, through another tunnel, and, thence, across the upper valley of Beaver Creek and its tributaries to the old placer diggings of Ways Gulch and Hahns Peak village."[380]

Now we were talking! With references to Trail Creek, a tunnel through a sandstone ledge, and placer diggings of Ways Gulch and Hahns Peak village, this was most certainly referring to the Farwell Ditch! Three words jumped off the page: *"through another tunnel."* Another tunnel! But where?

There were a couple of clues. The sentence in full stated *"the water was conveyed by ditch around the southeast flank of Farwell Mountain, through another tunnel..."* Okay - it was near the southeast flank of Farwell Mountain.

The first tunnel reference was now more interesting, as it referenced a tunnel exactly 1.13 miles east-southeast of Farwell Lake. That is a very precise statement. Back to the map I went. With Farwell Lake as a reference point, I drew a line exactly 1.13 miles in the east-southeast direction.

This point on the map was intriguing for two reasons. First, the line we plotted for the Farwell Ditch went right through this location. Second, the terrain, which was quite steep around a hill on the southeast flank of Farwell Mountain, seemed like a spot where a tunnel could be beneficial.

Nothing we had read up to this point had ever mentioned a second tunnel, so this was all very exciting. We reached out to David Joe to see if he knew anything about it. While he had never hiked to that area, he did recall hearing rumors from some old-timers that there was a tunnel in that area and that the water fell into a pond after it passed through.

---

[380] *General Geology of the Hahns Peak and Farwell Mountain Quadrangles, Routt County, Colorado, Geological Survey Bulletin 1349.* (1972). Page 54. https://nrrbook.com/HahnsFarwellGeology

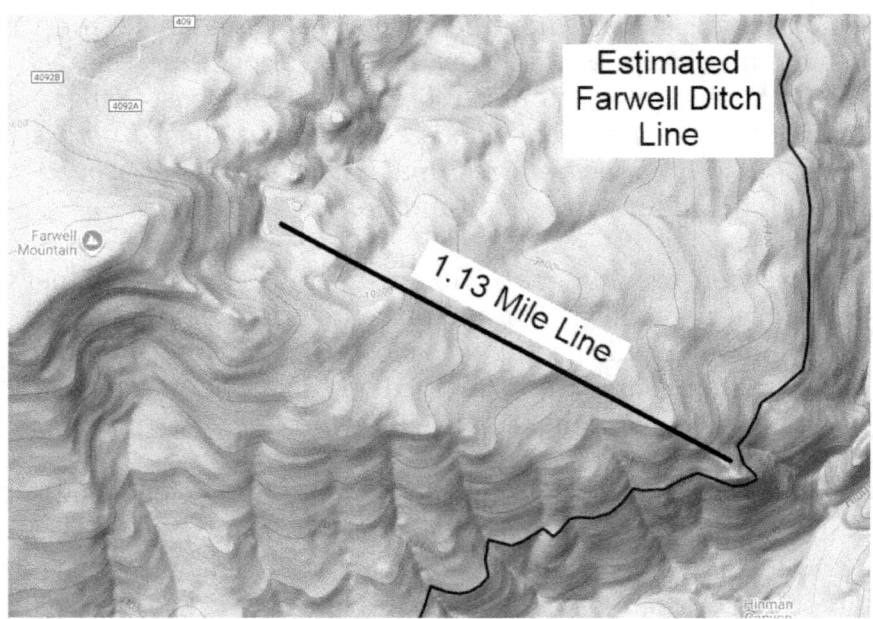

Above: Line drawn 1.13 miles East-Southeast of Farwell Lake

We could not wait to make our trip back out there in 2020. This potential tunnel had to be investigated!

That year, four of us made the trip over Labor Day weekend. Rod, his wife Leighanne, my wife Katie, and I loaded up our ATVs and headed west on I-80. We were getting pretty familiar with the drive at this point. Across Nebraska, into Wyoming, exit at Laramie, through Walden, onto Highway 40, and when the Yampa Valley came into view, we knew we were getting close. Through Steamboat Springs we drove, and once again we pulled into the Hahns Peak Roadhouse. As always, it felt great to be back in the Hahns Peak area, and it was starting to feel like a second home.

September 5, 2020, was the big day. To kick it off, we awoke early to watch the sunrise from the summit of Farwell Mountain, which meant an alarm at 5:00 AM and a chilly ride in the dark up FS 409 on our ATVs to the peak. Once at the top, we grabbed blankets and walked to the east so we had a clear view of the Zirkel Wilderness in the dim morning light. It wasn't long before the horizon began to change, displaying pink, orange, red, and every possible combination of these colors. In an instant, at 6:45 AM, a beam of light appeared as the sun started to emerge from behind the rugged wilderness peaks in the distance. Mornings like that are good for the soul.

We would have stayed longer, but there was work to do. Back on the ATVs, we headed north and east on FS 409. The plan that day was to park where we estimated that the ditch crossed FS 409, and then follow it to where we suspected the second tunnel could be located on the southeast flank of Farwell Mountain. The challenge was that we didn't know exactly where our starting point was. We had a general idea, thanks to David Joe's map of the ditch, but a hand-drawn yellow highlighter line on a paper map plotted onto a digital map was far from an exact science.

Nonetheless, we pulled off when we felt we were close, and off we went, hiking up and across Hinman Creek before turning south and following the terrain towards the western slope of Hinman Canyon. At this point, we had seen no signs of the ditch. We figured if we were lucky, we would be within 100 vertical feet of it in either direction. Using Avenza and our plotted line as a guide, we kept walking, knowing that our main target was where we suspected a second tunnel might exist on the southeast flank of Farwell Mountain. Eventually, we came to a large, washed-out area. As we were climbing up and out of it, Rod pointed out what looked like a ditch along the rim of the washout. Bullseye! This was a critical moment because it was the first time we located the ditch ourselves.

Having located the ditch, navigating became much easier. If we were going to find a tunnel, all we had to do now was follow the ditch, so that's what we did. We continued south, and the forest became thicker and thicker, with hundreds of dead, fallen pine trees that we had to climb on, around, and over. The hike was turning into hard work! We knew that when we crossed Farwell Creek, we would be roughly halfway to our destination.

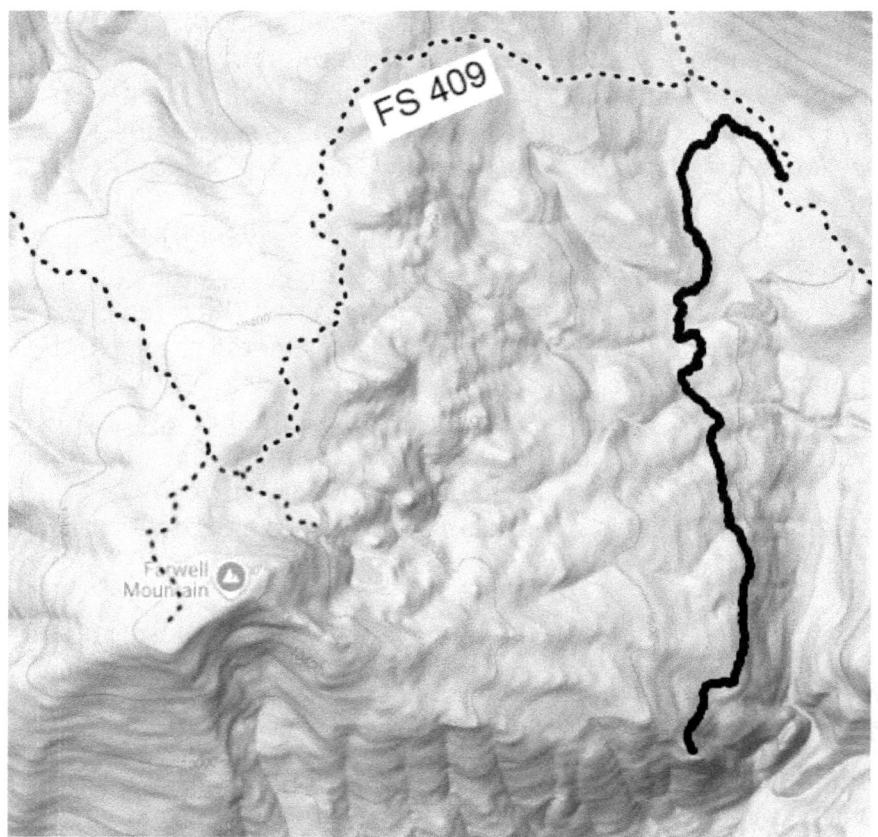

Above: GPS tracks of our hike on September 5, 2020.

What we did not know is that shortly after crossing Farwell Creek, our minds would be blown. The ditch transformed from a well-preserved U-shape dug in the forest floor into a channel blasted through solid rock. The west (upper) wall of the ditch was generally solid, with the east (lower) wall of the ditch a pile of blasted rock.

Once again, it was humbling to stand there and take it all in, knowing that many men put in back-breaking work over one hundred years ago to build this channel and make it functional. Every single one of the thousands of boulders making up the lower wall of the ditch had to have been moved by hand. We tried to envision the sights and sounds of drilling, blasting, and

240

moving all of those rocks, all in the pursuit of gold, but in the end, all we could do was marvel at the thought of it all.

Above: Rock channel just south of where the ditch crossed Farwell Creek

We kept moving south through the channel, and before long, we were back in thick forest. Again, hiking became very difficult due to the countless downed trees, as the effects of the dreaded pine beetle were evident everywhere. To our amazement, we came across another rock channel, this time with the upper wall being six feet tall.

We continued, and soon enough, a third rock channel appeared. From here, the forest once again got very thick, and we resumed our "combat hiking." Instead of a hike, it was more like an obstacle course. At times, the ditch itself was clear enough that we could walk directly in it. Usually, though, it was a constant criss-crossing of the ditch to try to find the path of least resistance moving forward.

Above: Rod Farwell walking through the second rock channel. While these channels had a few loose rocks lying in them, they were largely still in perfect condition after more than 100 years.

Above: Fairly clear, well-preserved section of the ditch today.

Eventually, we reached a point where the ditch turned to the west. The vantage point here was stunning, as Hinman Canyon was below us to the east. Just as exciting for us, though, was that the hill where we suspected a tunnel to be located was now in view to our southwest. Knowing we were nearing our destination gave us a much-needed boost of energy, and the combat hiking continued.

Three hours and three miles after starting the hike, Rod, who was out in front, loudly declared, "WE HAVE OURSELVES A TUNNEL!" We were obviously thrilled with the discovery. The old geology report was right, and our planning had paid off. As our Grandpa Meyer used to say, "Plan your work and work your plan." Mission accomplished! The tunnel was precisely where we had speculated it would be, 1.13 miles east-southeast of Farwell Lake.

Left to Right: Katie, Leighanne, Rod, and Nolan Farwell standing in front of the entrance to the tunnel discovered on September 5, 2020.

In general, the tunnel was similar to the first tunnel David Joe Zehner showed us in 2019. It was approximately four feet wide and ranged in height from four to six feet. We carefully climbed inside and walked towards the other end, estimating it at roughly 120 feet long. Unlike the first tunnel we had seen, the far end of this tunnel had unfortunately collapsed. There would be no exit from the tunnel on the west end.

We climbed back out of the tunnel. The terrain was very steep in the area, but I wanted to see if there was any evidence of the tunnel exit or ditch on the other side of the hill. I climbed up and over, and the terrain got even steeper. If I wasn't careful, I could slip and fall, and probably not stop for a long time. This prevented me from exploring very far on the other side, and during my limited time looking around, I couldn't see anything that resembled a ditch. It was frustrating, but it was what it was. Trying to explore further would have been foolish.

Left: Looking into the tunnel at Tunnel Hill. The far end has collapsed.

We took a few minutes to eat lunch and rest our legs, and then began the long hike back. That evening, we had plans to join the Zehners for supper on their deck. David Joe and Judy would be thrilled to see our pictures and hear the story of our day, and we could not wait to share the good news!

The hike back to our ATVs was challenging, as expected, since we followed the ditch back to the north. Combat hiking resumed. Back through the rock channels we went. As we progressed, the combination of high altitude and a shortage of bottled water had me feeling rotten. After another three-hour journey, the ATVs were a sight for sore eyes...and legs!

Once on our machines, we followed FS 409 up and over Farwell Mountain, all the way back to Hahns Peak Village, and then made our way to the Hahns Peak Roadhouse. After a quick shower, we drove back to the Zehner cabin for supper and fellowship with the Zehners, as well as some of their family and friends who were visiting.

David Joe and Judy loved hearing the story of our day and were excited to see the pictures we had taken of the rock channels and the tunnel. David Joe had not hiked this section of the ditch, so he was particularly interested in our findings. Despite now being 81 years old, he told Rod and me that if we ever planned to go back to that tunnel, he would love to tag along. And just like that, we had the start of our plans for 2021. Plan your work, and work your plan!

For Rod and me, the discovery of this section of the Farwell ditch, the rock channels, and, of course, another tunnel, only increased our desire to keep researching this remarkable history. What had started two years prior as a simple desire to ask a few questions and learn about the Farwell Ditch was growing rapidly into a feeling of responsibility to do all we could to capture the history, share it with others, and preserve it.

CHAPTER 13: BETTER THAN GOLD

"Corner stones must be well chosen and well laid in character building, before the capstone can have a sure and safe position on a finished record of life's best results from human efforts."[381]

-John V. Farwell

For 2021, the plan was straightforward. After all that David Joe Zehner had done to help us with our research, it was our turn to return the favor and do all we could to honor his request to see the newly discovered tunnel. The Farwell group that headed west that year was similar to the 2018 group, but a bit smaller: Terry & Nanette, Erika, Dana, Rod, and me.

We hit the road on the evening of August 31st, drove through the night, and arrived at the Hahns Peak Roadhouse on September 1st. The first couple of days, as usual, were spent enjoying the ATV trails and acclimating ourselves to the higher elevation. We even made a trip up to the Hog Park Guard Station so Nanette, Erika, and Dana could see the work that we had done on the roof of that building two years earlier. It was fun to revisit the site and see that our cedar shingles still looked great.

The main item on the agenda was scheduled for September 3rd. We planned to recreate the hike from the previous year so that David Joe could see the ditch, rock channels, and tunnel along the east side of Farwell Mountain. At 6:00 that morning, Terry, Rod, Dana, and I departed the Roadhouse on our ATVs and

---

[381] Farwell, John V. (1906). *Corner Stones of Character: Some Ways of Making Them*, Page 110. https://nrrbook.com/CornerStonesofCharacter

made our way to Zehner's cabin in Hahns Peak Village. Waiting for us were David Joe and his neighbor, Josh.

Our caravan began the familiar trek out of the village on FS 409. As the sun rose to the east, we ventured across Beaver Basin and started the climb up and over Farwell Mountain. It was about 8:00 when we pulled our machines off the trail, having reached our destination near FS 409's intersection with FS 1203.

Above, from Left to Right: Rod, Dana, David Joe, and Josh preparing for the hike.

Similar to 2020, the journey from that point forward would be on foot. We had the advantage of knowing exactly where the ditch was this time, which was to our benefit; however, with a larger group, we had to maintain a more measured pace. With all the fallen trees, this hike becomes difficult, and we also needed to ensure David Joe had an extra hand when necessary to help navigate the obstacles. He was now 82 years old, but could still outwork most people fifty years younger. His "do what you say you will do" mentality and his ability to accomplish whatever task he sets out to do are legendary, perhaps making him a little like John V. Farwell or Robert McIntosh. That said, we still wanted to be extra cautious and make sure he went home to Judy in one piece!

To the south we went, initially through open terrain, then into thick forest. Before we knew it, we were traversing the onslaught of downed logs. For Zehner, failure was not an option, and regardless of the obstacle, forward progress was the only acceptable movement.

Progress was slow but steady. As we crossed Farwell Creek, Rod and I knew the rock channels were near, and we were excited for the rest of the group to see that spectacular history. It was especially neat to share that with David Joe. He knows this area and the surrounding mountains as well as anyone, so showing him something new was just wonderful.

We continued south, with Hinman Canyon narrowing and getting steeper beneath us. Around noon, the hill containing the tunnel came into view, and our destination was near. About thirty minutes later, I was the first to arrive at the tunnel, followed shortly after by the rest of the group. Dana, Rod, and Josh were checking out the inside of the tunnel when David Joe arrived, put his eyes on the tunnel, and declared, "I'll be damned!"

While there, Rod and Josh went up and over the hill to see if they could find any evidence of the ditch on the other side. Like me a year earlier, they came up empty. It is so steep in that spot that exploring on foot is virtually impossible, and there were no obvious visual signs of the ditch. The difficulty of the terrain makes the construction of this tunnel all the more impressive. If it was hard for us to find a stable footing, how in the world were men able to stand their ground and blast a tunnel through the rock? It is mind-boggling.

We took a quick break to recharge our batteries and began the long trek retracing our tracks to the north. Along the way, the weather changed. As is common, a light afternoon storm flared up. The temperature dropped, gray clouds filled the skies, and before we knew it, there was light rolling thunder, rain, and even some very small hail. The good news is that we had all packed rain gear. While this did a fine job of keeping our upper bodies dry, the water running off our jackets and down our pant legs dripped right into our boots. The rush we felt at the tunnel had worn off, and now we were all getting tired, cold, and wet. There was no choice but to keep going, and around 5:30 PM, we finally made it back to our ATVs, breathing a sigh of relief.

Above: David Joe Zehner arrives at the tunnel entrance.

With the hard part behind us, we took the machines back to the Zehner cabin in Hahns Peak Village. Judy was relieved to see David Joe back, scraped up arms and all. Truthfully, we were relieved that we had all made it back in good shape. There is most certainly risk involved when venturing far off the beaten path in these mountains, especially when cell signal is nonexistent.

It was a very long, yet satisfying day. While Rod and I were still far from being experts, we had come a long way. Our knowledge of the Farwell Ditch was growing, including rock channels and a tunnel that we had discovered on our own and were now sharing with others. That was a new milestone for us.

The following night was another group gathering on the Zehners' deck, which was quickly becoming one of my favorite traditions. Cold beverages, steaks on the grill, and good fellowship are a perfect way to end a long day of ditchin'. David Joe, Judy, and Marge were becoming close friends, and any time we got to spend with them was priceless. What a blessing it was to get to know them!

Above, from Left to Right: Nolan, Terry, Rod, and David Joe together on the Zehner deck.

CHAPTER 14: PAY DIRT

"The man who does the most, individually, is the one who inspires the doing of things by others, and thus multiplies himself a thousand-fold by starting influences upon other characters, the continuity of which never ends."[382]

-John V. Farwell

2022 would turn out to be a pivotal year.

Rod and I began work on the ditch in February with a research trip to Denver and Steamboat Springs, aiming to locate official records about the Farwell Ditch and its affiliated entities.

The first stop on this trip was at the Colorado State Archives in Denver. We had been in contact with the Archives in advance, and they had pulled all records pertaining to John V. Farwell, Hahns Peak, and other keywords related to the mining history we were researching. Upon our arrival, we were greeted by a large cart filled with boxes, ledgers, papers, and other old records. As Judy Zehner would say, "The best way to start is to start!" So, we each grabbed a few items and dug in.

It was fascinating to open these documents and examine original records dating back to some of Colorado's earliest days. Seeing the actual historical records felt similar to setting foot on the Farwell Ditch for the first time. History definitely feels more real when you can see it with your own eyes. The smell of the old paper and the fragility of the pages we flipped through only reinforced the historic nature of these records.

---

[382] Farwell, John V. (1906). *Corner Stones of Character: Some Ways of Making Them*, Page 40. https://nrrbook.com/CornerStonesofCharacter

Above: Cart containing the records we reviewed at the Colorado State Archives.

Of all the records we went through, two stood out the most:

1. Hans Peak Wagon Road Company Articles of Association - John V. Farwell established this entity to construct wagon roads from the Hahns Peak Mining District to the outside world. In our hands, we held the nearly 150-year-old entry in Colorado's official ledgers recording the establishment of this company. As noted previously in the book, Hahns and Hans were used interchangeably in those days.

2. William Flick vs. The Hahns Peak and Elk River Canal and Placer Mining Company. This was a legal case decided in Arapahoe County District Court in 1899 and then appealed to the Colorado Court of Appeals. The Archives had this case in two forms: 1) the actual typed, original court documents, and 2) the entire case printed in book form.

This court case was a significant and unexpected discovery for us. To summarize, the Hahns Peak and Elk River Canal and Placer Mining Company (HPERCPMC) acquired a vast amount of mining claims and also took ownership of the Farwell Ditch in the 1890s (John V. Farwell had been out of the area since late 1879).

HPERCPMC hired a contractor named William Flick to renovate the ditch and increase its capacity to flow more water. Unfortunately, the two parties ended up in court because they disagreed over whether Flick had satisfied the contract's terms. While the legal battle dragged on for years and was undoubtedly difficult for the parties involved, it was a huge benefit for Rod and me, as the information we learned from reading this document truly blew our minds. Had there not been a legal dispute, all the detailed information we learned from the testimony of Flick and others, provided under oath while being questioned on the stand, would not have existed.

The case provides extensive detail about the Farwell Ditch, from the headgate at Trail Creek to the sandbox on Little Mountain, where water flowed into large pipes that descended the mountain. We were mesmerized as we flipped through the court documents, page by page. So much history was contained on those pages, and we couldn't help but wonder when the last time anyone had looked at them. Some of the major bullet points include:

- The first tunnel we saw with David Joe Zehner in 2019 was referred to as the Sand Rock Point Tunnel. Appropriately named, this tunnel was built through a sandstone ledge by Flick's crew in 1897 as a solution to the constant failure of fluming in the area. The sandstone proved to be a poor material for anchoring fluming, and it failed repeatedly. In an instant, we knew Zehner's theory was correct. Fluming originally wrapped around the ledge, but the ditch had been dammed up and rerouted through the tunnel. We had seen this with our own eyes, and now a 123-year-old court case told the story in vivid detail. This tunnel was built roughly twenty years after the ditch itself was initially constructed, so it was not an original feature of the ditch.

- The second tunnel we found was called the Tunnel Hill Tunnel. This is the tunnel we discovered in 2020 and revisited in 2021. Given the area's topography, Tunnel Hill is a fitting name. This tunnel was an original feature of the Farwell Ditch.

- After exiting the tunnel at Tunnel Hill, water fell over 300 feet (per the court case; we believe it is actually closer to 450 feet) into a man-made sandbox, which then redirected the water into the ditch. This explained why we could not see any evidence of the ditch when searching around the collapsed outlet end of this tunnel- it was far below us! The ditch from the headgate to Tunnel Hill was referred to as the Upper Level, and the section from the Tunnel Hill sandbox to the end was referred to as the Lower Level. Further examination of the court case taught us that the transition from Upper Level to Lower Level was re-engineered and rebuilt by HPERCPMC and Flick.

When originally constructed, this transition took place roughly one mile west of Tunnel Hill.

- The rock channel work above Tunnel Hill was a renovation project undertaken by Flick.

- There was a third, smaller tunnel near Beaver Creek, which most certainly caught our eye. A third tunnel? We were not expecting this, and neither was David Joe. He had hiked most of the ditch around Beaver Basin and had not seen a tunnel. We kept this in the back of our minds, hoping to one day find it, but mostly expecting that it had probably caved in by now.

After a full day at the Colorado State Archives, Rod and I walked two blocks to the Denver Public Library. We only had an hour there before they were going to close, so we had to make it quick. The main item of interest at the library was this picture[383] of John V. Farwell.

The library closed, and Rod and I departed for Steamboat Springs, where we had two stops planned. First, we visited the Tread of Pioneers Museum. The

J. V. FARWELL, PRESIDENT OF CHICAGO ASSOCIATION.

highlight of the records we searched there was their collection on Robert McIntosh, Farwell's trusted lieutenant. This collection includes his Certificate of Citizenship (he was born in Canada in 1838 to Scottish parents), corporate documents, claims, and correspondence. One fascinating piece of history

---

[383] *Harper's Monthly V. 64.* (January 1882). Page 269. Denver Public Library Western History Collection.

was a letter dated January 30, 1903, that McIntosh wrote to President Teddy Roosevelt. By this time, McIntosh had established a large horse ranch, and he proposed that the U.S. Government should establish a 468-square-mile horse preserve in northwest Colorado for breeding, raising, and training horses for the United States military.

In what seems impossibly fast by today's standards, the War Department sent a response on February 7, 1903, stating that there were no funds available to execute McIntosh's plan. Four years later, he tried again by sending another letter to Washington, D.C., but was denied once more.

Although official records regarding John V.'s involvement with the Farwell Ditch and his mining enterprise continued to elude us, our time at the Tread of Pioneers was still beneficial. While there, Rod and I met with Arianthé Stettner, cofounder and Emeritus Director of Historic Routt County (HRC). We had previously been in touch with Arianthé and HRC regarding an application to place the Farwell Ditch on the Routt County Register of Historic Properties. She and her team had put in many hours working on the application and supporting documents. We were able to discuss the ditch, share information and photos, and also pass along some of the incredible details we had learned from the William Flick vs HPERCPMC court case the previous day. Rod and I were very encouraged by the progress HRC was making, as the application was nearly complete.

Later that day, we visited the Routt County Clerk and Recorder's Office, again hoping to find records regarding Farwell's mining endeavors. Two entries stood out:

- Record of J.V. Farwell (as written) selling his operation in 1879. Though we had read about this transaction in various historic newspaper articles, this was the first time we had seen a legal record with John V. Farwell's name regarding his mining operation.

- Mechanic's Lien filed by William Flick on October 21, 1897, as general contractor for HPERCPMC. It was fascinating to see this piece of history come full circle, as the previous day, we had discovered the court case in the Colorado State Archives resulting from the contract between Flick and HPERCPMC. Here, right before our eyes, was the original recording of the Mechanic's Lien in Routt County's official records. Nearly 125 years prior, the county recorder put a pencil to that very piece of paper in that very ledger to record that lien. It had likely been a long, long time since anyone else had laid eyes on that record. History was coming alive, once again!

Before leaving town, we made a quick stop at the U.S. Forest Service Hahns Peak/Bears Ears Ranger District office, where Rod and I met with the local archeologist for the Forest Service to discuss the project. While we were currently pursuing historic designation at the county level, our ultimate goal was to place the Farwell Ditch on the National Register of Historic Places. While archaeologist Jason Strahl agreed it deserved to be on the list, he cautioned us that it would be a long and arduous process to make it happen.

With that, our research trip came to a close, and it was time to return home and resume our day-to-day lives.

Approximately six weeks later, on March 15, 2022, Arianthé Stettner presented the application for the Farwell Ditch to the Routt County Historic Preservation Board. She did a fantastic job, and the board was very enthusiastic in their support for the nomination. One member even stated it was one of the most interesting applications she had heard in all her years of service on the board. This comment was very reassuring for Rod and me, as it meant our work in preserving this important piece of history was making a difference. The Historic Preservation Board unanimously approved the application. Two weeks later, the Routt County Board of Commissioners also unanimously approved the Farwell Ditch, officially adding it to the Routt County Register of Historic Properties.[384]

*****

In August 2022, another Farwell Guys' Trip was scheduled. It had been six years since we made our initial guys' trip to Farwell Mountain, so this was long overdue! We had a group of eight this time, consisting of Terry, Rod, his boys (Kenton, Dean, and Evan), me, and my boys (Blake and Jace). Dean, Evan, and Jace were making their inaugural guys' trip to the area.

Riding the trails, exploring the forest, and fishing in the evenings from the shore of Steamboat Lake were all highlights. One fun memory that stands out is having Blake and Kenton, both now teenagers, navigate the group back "home" after a full day of riding the trails. We shared lots of laughs and gave them a hard time by trying to confuse them, but they ultimately did a great job, and it was fun to see them think and work their way through the challenge.

At one point, we made the trek up and over Farwell Mountain to take the boys to Sand Rock Point, and it was neat to see them excited about exploring a "secret tunnel." We thoroughly enjoy exploring and learning about the ditch, and it was particularly rewarding to see the next generation of "ditchmen" experiencing its history firsthand!

At the end of the trip, we stopped at the Tread of Pioneers Museum in Steamboat Springs. The Curator, Katie Adams, had asked Rod and me to give a presentation about the Farwell Ditch as part of their summer Brown Bag series. We were happy to oblige, as the more people who know about this history, the better! Although we are not natural public speakers, we did our best to share our knowledge of the ditch at the time. In subsequent years, as we learned and discovered

---

[384] *Routt County Register of Historic Properties - Farwell Ditch.* Routt County Historic Preservation Board. https://nrrbook.com/RouttCoFarwellDitch

more about the ditch, we found that some of the details we presented were inaccurate; however, the presentation remained generally valid.

After the presentation, a local rancher, Jay Fetcher, approached from the audience to visit with us. At first, Rod and I were unsure of what to expect. Had we come across as outsiders trying to teach locals their own history? Thankfully, we had nothing to worry about. Jay was very kind and appreciative of the information we had shared, and even better, said that he had a twenty-foot section of metal pipe that came from "our" ditch. He wanted to donate the pipe to us to use as we saw fit. Rod and I were thrilled with this development! As more people learned about the project, momentum was building to preserve the history, which was exactly what we had hoped would happen when we agreed to give the presentation.

We departed for home after the presentation, but Rod and I soon planned a trip to retrieve the pipe that had been offered to us. We couldn't stand the thought of waiting another year to get our hands on it, so one last trip in 2022 was planned for late September. The timing turned out to be perfect, as the fall colors were starting to reveal themselves, and the cooler weather was more suitable for long days of exploring the ditch.

Since it would just be the two of us, we began making plans to hike more challenging sections of the ditch. Two options stood out to us. The first was to complete the Upper Level. We had already hiked from where the ditch crossed FS 409 to Tunnel Hill (twice). What remained of the Upper Level was to start at the same spot on FS 409 and head in the opposite direction towards the Head Gate at Trail Creek. This route would take us to and through the Sand Rock Point Tunnel.

The other option was much more ambitious: the start of the Lower Level, from the sandbox at the base of Tunnel Hill, all the way around Farwell Mountain to the lone piece of private property that the ditch crosses. This section of ditch alone was estimated to be about seven miles long, and we expected it to be through very thick forest. Adding to the challenge, there is no easy way to reach the starting point at the sandbox. The nearest ATV trails are FS 409.2B, which ends at the summit of Farwell Mountain, and FS 409 itself. Neither was a great option. FS 409.2B was roughly 2,000 feet higher in elevation than the ditch itself, and also over two miles' worth of hiking down Farwell Mountain just to get to the sandbox at Tunnel Hill. Meanwhile, FS 409 would require three miles of combat hiking to reach the top side of Tunnel Hill. Once there, we would have to figure out how to descend 500 feet of very steep terrain and then hike to the sandbox. The cherry on top is that we wouldn't be starting and ending our hike at the same location, so how would we even handle the logistics of that?

Rod and I debated what to do. My original thought was to complete the Upper Level, which seemed more manageable and would give us the satisfaction of having hiked and mapped the entire level. Meanwhile, Rod leaned towards the bigger challenge of starting the Lower Level, as he saw no better opportunity than this trip. Ultimately, I knew he was right. We made the decision to start the Lower Level and committed to it.

Before all of that would happen, though, there was other business to take care of. We arrived in Hahns Peak Village on the morning of September 21, 2022, with the Zehners graciously allowing us to stay at their cabin. Upon arrival, we said hello and unloaded our gear and luggage from the truck into the cabin. After a quick rest, we contacted Jay Fetcher and headed to his ranch near Steamboat Lake. There, on the ground in the middle of a pasture, was the old, twenty-foot-long pipe he had mentioned to us after our presentation at the Tread of Pioneers Museum. Considering it was nearly 150 years old, it was still in great shape!

What we had not figured out yet was what to do with it. There was no sense in taking it home with us. This piece of history needed to be on display somewhere in the local area. Our initial thought was to donate it to the Hahns Peak Museum, where other relics and artifacts from the local mining history were on display. The problem is that the museum lacked the space for it. They did, however, have space for half of it.

Thus, we needed to figure out a way to cut this pipe in half. Our best bet was to head back to the Zehner cabin and see what tools David Joe had available. It turns out he had the perfect tool —an oxygen/acetylene torch. I didn't have experience operating a torch like this, but Rod did, so we loaded it into the truck and drove back to the Fetcher Ranch. There, Rod cut the pipe into two ten-foot-long sections, and we loaded them onto our trailer.

Above: Metal pipe lying on the ground at the Fetcher Ranch. Hahns Peak and Farwell Mountain are in the background.

Back to the Zehner cabin we went. The first section of pipe was moved from our trailer onto a utility trailer that David Joe pulled with his ATV to the Hahns Peak Museum. There, we placed it next to two sections of similar-sized wooden pipe that were already on display. Perfect!

We still needed a home for the second section of pipe. For that, we reached out to the Steamboat Lake Visitor Center. Behind their building, they had a couple of old mining dredge gears on display. We thought they might be interested in having this section of pipe to lay next to the gears, and they were! It felt like things were starting to come full circle. Eight years earlier, in 2014, I first learned about Farwell Mountain and some of the local mining history inside that very building. Now, we were presenting an artifact of that very history back to the Visitor Center to be permanently displayed.

The following day was spent enjoying time on our ATVs and continuing to acclimate to the higher elevation. The cool fall weather provided spectacular riding conditions, and we covered a considerable amount of ground. One thing we wanted to try out was tracking our elevation. I had recently purchased a watch with a built-in altimeter, which we suspected could help locate and track the ditch. Additionally, Rod was using his phone, which also had an altimeter function.

We tested our devices in the general area where we knew the lower level of the ditch crossed FS 409. Three years earlier, David Joe had pointed out to us the remains of an old cabin below FS 409, next to the ditch. Rod and I parked our ATVs on the trail and hiked down to the cabin, which was roughly fifty to seventy-five feet lower in elevation. From there, we located the ditch and noted the elevation displayed on our devices. After that, we hiked back up to the ATVs and descended FS 409 until we reached the same elevation. Within seconds, we located the ditch on the other side of the trail. We had ridden past that exact spot dozens of times by this point and had no idea the Farwell Ditch had been right there this whole time. The ability to track elevation and use it to our advantage was a major development. Since the ditch was generally level, we knew we should be able to locate it anywhere along its general path by ensuring we were at the correct elevation. We would put that to the test the next day.

September 23, 2022, was the day of our big hike. Rod and I were up early and out the door at 6:00 AM. We had arranged for

James Clouse, owner of the private Warhorse Backcountry property that the ditch crossed, to lend us a hand. We planned to leave our ATVs on James's property, which would be our ending point for the day. From there, James took us in his UTV to the summit of Farwell Mountain, which would be our starting point. Rod and I had decided that this was our best option for accessing the start of the Lower Level.

A lot of planning went into the route for this hike. The biggest issue was navigating the extremely steep terrain surrounding Tunnel Hill. We couldn't hike in a direct line towards Tunnel Hill, or we would end up above the sandbox on very steep ground, which would be of no benefit to us. Thus, we made plans to initially drop off the summit of Farwell towards the southeast, and then make our way straight south along Coulton Creek. At around 9,200 feet of elevation, we would work our way southeast again until we intersected the ditch. From there, we would follow it to the east towards Tunnel Hill and the sandbox. Following that, we would reverse course and follow the ditch back to the west around Farwell Mountain until we reached our machines on Clouse's property.

At an elevation of over 10,800 feet, the air was cold and windy when we stepped out of the UTV at approximately 7:45 AM. The good news is that the forecast was perfect, with sunny skies and a high in the mid-50s expected. It doesn't get better than that for a challenging hike!

As planned, Rod and I made our way to the eastern side of the peak and began our descent. Immediately after dropping off the top, we were shielded from the wind, and the air became calm. Things were already looking up! We followed our projected route towards the southeast using the COTREX app on my phone. As we continued descending, we encountered our first fallen tree, and one of us declared that it was likely the first of thousands that we would climb over that day. I'm not sure of the exact number, but by the end of the day, that prediction sure felt like it came true.

We turned south at a point where there was a clearing along the west side of Coulton Creek. This made for easy hiking as we continued to descend. Out of nowhere, we heard the bugling of a bull elk. The rut was just beginning. The elk bugle, one of the most majestic calls in the animal kingdom, sounded fairly close, so we stayed put for a bit to see if we could spot the elk, but we had no such luck. Onward.

Above: Rod Farwell descending through a clearing on the south side of Farwell Mountain.

Our route was working out great, and at 9,200 feet, we began to work southeast again. By this time, we had dropped over 1,600 feet of elevation in a little over a mile of hiking, for an average grade of 30%. Steep, but doable! From here forward, the grade decreased slightly. As we progressed, we passed through groves of aspens and spruces. Some sections were thicker than others, but nothing at this point was very difficult to work through. We expected to locate the Farwell Ditch at approximately 8,820 feet of elevation, which was 2,000 feet below our starting point.

Watching our devices closely, we hit 9,000 feet and then 8,900 feet. If the reported elevation was accurate, we knew the ditch should be near. We kept moving forward, and as we hit the 8,850-foot mark, we looked ahead, with Rod declaring it had to be very close. Sure enough, the Farwell Ditch was located exactly where we had hoped to find it, right at the 8,820-foot mark. We felt great satisfaction in having success with our altimeters!

After a quick break, we continued moving eastward along the ditch towards Tunnel Hill. The first half mile or so went through some fairly dense forest, but nothing overly burdensome. After that, the terrain opened up, and the ditch was generally open and exposed all the way to the sandbox. Along this section, we encountered several more areas where dynamite had been used to blast a path for the ditch through solid rock.

Above: The rock wall on the left was blasted away to clear a path for the ditch. Tunnel Hill is in the distance.

As we neared Tunnel Hill, the ditch stayed level, but the surrounding terrain got steeper and steeper, as expected. This confirmed that we made the right choice by taking the route we did. We kept moving, and roughly two and a half miles into the hike, we reached the sandbox. Or should I say, what remained of the sandbox? What was left was a base of large boulders, which we believe were placed to stabilize the ground and serve as a foundation for the sandbox. The power of water falling 450 feet would easily overcome a poorly constructed sandbox, so it had to be very robust.

This became another moment to take a step back and consider where we were standing and what we were seeing. For starters, it is hard to comprehend the sheer magnitude of what had been designed and constructed in that very spot. There were no excavators or bulldozers in the late 1800s, and even if there had been, this terrain was too steep for them to be of use. Sheer determination, grit, and manpower made this happen. How an Upper Level and a Lower Level could have been thought of, planned, engineered, and constructed by shovel, pickaxe, and dynamite baffles my mind. In my mind, I tried to picture and hear all that water crashing down the mountainside. At one time, this very location was the site of a critical feature of the ditch, and would have been religiously monitored and maintained. Now, only a trained eye would recognize the remnants of its industrial past.

It was also humbling to consider that Rod and I were likely the first two people to stand at the location of the sandbox in a very, very long time. It is so remote that there is no reason anyone would ever go there. Even if someone had been there, the odds of their knowing the history were small. Thankfully, we were recording our GPS tracks and taking pictures so we could share this information with others.

Rod and I took a quick lunch break and then started back towards the west, initially backtracking on the ditch until we came across the spot where we had first descended upon it. We knew this was the spot because when we first arrived there on the descent, we had taken our sweatshirts off and tied them to an aspen tree so we wouldn't have to carry them. But now that we were back to this spot, we crammed them into our backpacks and kept moving.

From this point forward, we were back on "new" ditch again, and though we were determined to make steady progress, it did not take long for the forest to give us a mean mug and start fighting back. I cannot put into words how thick the forest was or how strenuous hiking became. Huge, dead logs from beetle-killed pines were lying everywhere, filling in the area between the trees that remained standing. We were no longer hiking, but rather enduring an obstacle course that involved climbing over, under, and through an endless onslaught of trees and logs. Sometimes we resorted to crawling on our hands and knees to get under logs lying across the ditch. Instead of steadily moving forward, we found ourselves zigzagging back and forth across the ditch, looking for the path of least resistance, but the only answer was usually to move one step at a time and then figure out the next. I carried a machete while Rod had a hatchet. Both were constantly used to clear small branches and twigs as we moved forward. The "combat hiking" we experienced in 2020 and 2021, hiking from FS 409 to the top side of Tunnel Hill, suddenly didn't seem so bad after all. This was taking things to an entirely new difficulty level! Our pace slowed to less than one mile per hour.

The trees surrounding us represented several centuries' worth of time. On the ground were huge, old trunks of trees that probably began life in the 1700s or early 1800s, grew tall, and then succumbed to old age or the dreaded Mountain Pine Beetle. Towering above us were giant trees, both dead and alive, representing a more recent past and immediate future. At eye level were the young aspens and spruces, only a few years old, which will be the towering giants decades from now. In a sense, we were looking at the past, present, and future all at once, which was fitting, as we were there in the present to research the past.

Speaking of young spruce trees, we discovered that walking through (yes, through) them, rather than around, was a viable option when they blocked our path along the ditch, which was remarkably well-preserved. The branches were still young and easily pliable, so we could push ourselves through without too much resistance. But usually, the resistance was in the form of logs, logs, and more logs. There were occasional clearings through aspens, but these were few and far between, and even when we encountered them, they seemed to pass very quickly because we could walk at a normal pace again. This stretch of combat hiking spanned a couple of miles but took several hours to traverse.

As our progress took us towards the southwest quarter of Farwell Mountain, we encountered relatively little resistance from the forest for roughly one mile. Much of this mile was wide open, with other parts featuring aspen groves and reddening ferns on the forest floor. Naturally, our pace increased, and simply walking normally, rather than working through a maze of obstacles, was much easier on our bodies. In one area with a clear view of the summit of Farwell Mountain, we took a quick break to have a snack and rehydrate. Soon after this, we came across a beautiful view of Pearl Lake to our left, below us. Views of Sand Mountain, Steamboat Lake, and Hahns Peak also came and went.

We had put in a long day by then, but we knew a challenging section to finish our hike was looming. Having planned our route meticulously in advance, we knew from looking at satellite imagery that the forest would become very dense for the final two and a half miles. In fact, we had even considered various options to start our hike from this end and work our way east towards Tunnel Hill. This would have allowed us to hike through this thick section on fresh legs, but ultimately, we could not come up with a plan that seemed feasible. If we hiked east to the sandbox (the start of the Lower Level), there was no good way to get out of there. We would still have several more miles of hiking to do, and we would also have had to figure out how to stage our machines on the far side of Farwell Mountain, away from Hahns Peak Village. The west-to-east route posed too many issues to resolve. Thus, we landed on our chosen path, knowing that the last couple of miles would be extremely challenging with exhausted bodies. We were right.

By this point, my right knee was throbbing with every step I took, caused by the 2,000-foot descent we made to start the day. Taking thousands of downhill steps puts a beating on the knees. Not to be outdone, the outside of my left foot, near the heel, had developed a blister roughly the size of a quarter. Every step brought pain in some form, but we had no choice but to embrace it and keep moving.

The ditch turned back to the north as we reached the western flank of Farwell Mountain, and this is where the obstacle course started anew. Being able to record our movement was a blessing and a curse. It mainly felt like a curse through here, though, because every time I would look at my watch, our total distance covered had barely moved. A tenth of a mile seemed like a milestone worth celebrating.

The other thing working against us was time. If we lost daylight, all progress would stop, and we would be spending the night on the mountain. Completely drained of energy, we kept fighting our way forward. The sun was gradually lowering, eventually beginning to set. As the daylight turned to dusk, our eyes adjusted, but eventually it was just flat-out getting dark. At this point, though, we knew the end was near, and with basically no daylight to spare, we turned a corner and saw a long, straight clearing where our ATVs were waiting for us. Hallelujah!

We made it. Completely and utterly exhausted and in pain, and using every minute of sunlight the day had to offer, but we had made it. Our Grandpa's statement to "plan your work and work your plan" had been fulfilled again, and Rod and I were deeply satisfied knowing that we had just completed the "most important day of ditchin'" we would have. The remaining sections of the ditch that we would need to hike in the future would be much more accessible from ATV trails, so completing this extremely challenging section was a significant accomplishment.

Some interesting stats about the hike:

- We hiked for 11 hours, 23 minutes, and 52 seconds.

- My watch estimated 6,636 calories burned, with an average heart rate of 129 beats per minute.

- Our average speed was .86 miles per hour.

Surprisingly, with GPS tracks recording, our exact distance was a bit of a mystery. We had three devices recording: my watch, my phone, and Rod's phone. It seemed the phones were more sensitive to the zigzagging and minor movements we made as we navigated our route. All three devices returned vastly different distance readings. For example:

- My watch showed a total of 9.84 miles from the summit of Farwell Mountain, down to the ditch, over to Tunnel Hill, and back around to our ending point. In other words, 9.84 miles for the entire day.

- My phone, on the other hand, showed roughly thirteen miles.

- Rod's phone showed a distance of roughly ten miles from Tunnel Hill to the endpoint.

It seemed strange that they could all be so different. Ultimately, here's what I think. My watch generally feels accurate for total distance, except for the zigzagging we had to do to traverse the ditch. When comparing the GPS tracks among the devices, the tracks from my watch did indeed seem a little smoother, supporting this viewpoint. Thus, I think we can say the ditch itself is roughly seven miles (maybe a tad over), from the Tunnel Hill sandbox over to where we ended on the Warhorse Backcountry property, with the other 2.5+ miles (give or take) being from the initial descent down to the ditch and over to Tunnel Hill.

Meanwhile, the GPS tracks from our phones seemed to be more sensitive, which added to the overall distance of our hike. The reality is that one mile of ditch could easily be closer to one and a half miles worth of hiking through the thick sections, since we were rarely walking parallel to the ditch. Thus, it's fair to say the ditch itself was about seven miles, but along those seven miles of ditch, we hiked roughly ten miles. Add on the approximately two and a half miles of descent from the Farwell Mountain summit down to the ditch and east over to Tunnel Hill, and we have a total in the thirteen-mile range. The numbers may not be exact, but they are somewhere in that ballpark.

In previous years, I have run two half marathons, which are coincidentally 13.1 miles in length. I can say without a doubt, this day of hiking the Farwell Ditch was easily the most challenging physical activity I have ever completed. Knowing this makes me have even more respect and appreciation for the men who constructed the ditch with their bare hands and basic tools. "Combat hiking" along the ditch is nothing compared to digging said ditch with a shovel and pickaxe. I wouldn't have lasted a day on a ditch-building crew back in the 1870s!

This trip was a resounding success. In just a few days, we had retrieved the old pipe from Jay Fetcher, put it on display (in two locations), and hiked the most challenging section of the entire ditch. This capped off a year of great accomplishment and momentum-building, including:

- Research trip to Denver and Steamboat Springs, with the William Flick vs HPERCPMC court case as the "mother lode" finding

- Designation of the Farwell Ditch on the Routt County Register of Historic Places

- Farwell Guys' Trip, where the next generation saw the ditch and Sand Rock Point Tunnel for the first time

- Presentation at the Tread of Pioneers Museum in Steamboat Springs

- Preservation of the old pipe from Jay Fetcher and hiking the most challenging section of the ditch

Back home we went, and plans for 2023 began to take shape. Big plans.

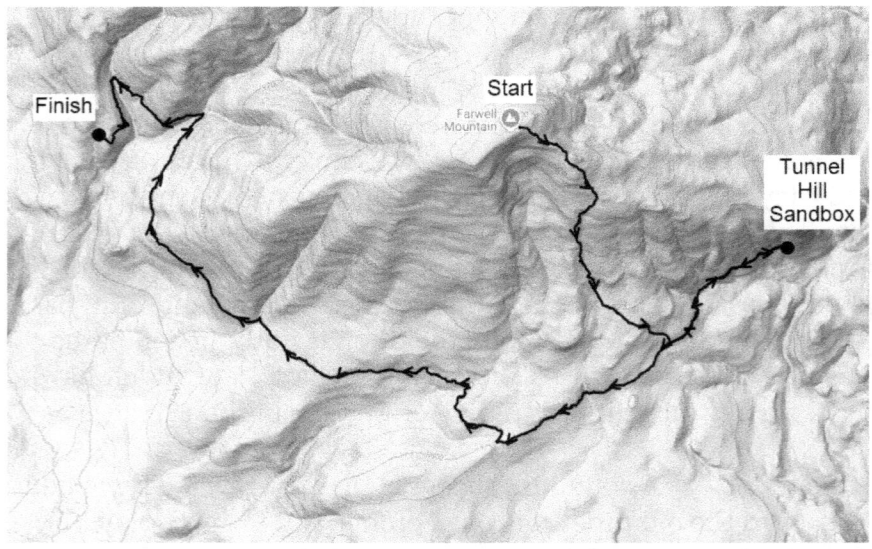

Above: GPS tracks of our hike on September 23, 2022. We started from the Farwell Mountain summit, descended to the Farwell Ditch, then worked our way east to the Tunnel Hill sandbox before hiking back west to where our ATVs were parked.

CHAPTER 15: BONANZA

"As I look back over my business life, a flood of memories comes over me, to verify the fact that 'if one's foresight was only as good as his hindsight,' how many pages, black with disappointment and regrets, might be luminous with success in every respect of the enchanting word. Yet the mistakes a man makes are often the corner-stones of that success. It is only the man who loses confidence in himself, because of them, that is obliged to make an assignment for the benefit of his creditors; but the man who trains his guns of grit, grace, and gumption upon apparently insurmountable difficulties will carry their strongholds in due time; and to begin with nothing but a sound mind in a sound body, instead of one million dollars, is the best capital a young man can have for his gun-carriages and ammunition."[385]

-John V. Farwell

Ever since we first learned about the Farwell Ditch, Rod and I had talked about eventually hiking its entire length. Early on, this seemed like an unrealistic goal. After all, we were just two average guys from the Midwest. Could we handle trekking through nearly twenty miles of rugged forest at roughly 9,000 feet of elevation? However, since we had just completed the most challenging section of the ditch, both in terms of sheer hiking difficulty and accessibility, finishing the full length of the ditch was just a matter of time.

By this point, we had officially mapped the ditch from FS 409 above Hinman Canyon around Farwell Mountain to the privately owned Warhorse Backcountry property. Three sections remained:

---

[385] Farwell, John V. (1911). *Some Recollections of John V. Farwell*, Page 65. https://nrrbook.com/RecollectionsofJVF

- Headgate on Trail Creek to FS 409 above Hinman Canyon
- Privately-owned Warhorse Backcountry parcel to String Ridge (where the original Farwell Ditch terminated)
- McIntosh Extension (String Ridge to Little Mountain Sandbox)

All three of these hikes seemed doable in 2023.

Our first trip that year was over Labor Day Weekend. David Joe and Judy Zehner, who had become dear friends, were selling their cabin in Hahns Peak Village and moving full-time to their home in Arizona. They planned to move in mid-September, and we wanted to visit them one last time before they left. The Farwells on this trip were Terry and Nanette, Rod and Leighanne, and Katie and me.

As usual, ATV riding was on the agenda, and we enjoyed time on the trails. Towards the end of one of our days riding, Terry, Rod, Leighanne, Katie, and I decided to hike the McIntosh Extension. This was only about a mile out and back and, looking at satellite imagery, did not appear to be overly thick or challenging. We left our ATVs on the edge of FS 411 atop String Ridge, knowing exactly where the ditch continued, due to its elevation, off to the west. Our group followed the ditch, and things largely went according to plan. There were a few thick spots here and there, but nothing overly strenuous, and we made good progress.

It was apparent when we reached the sandbox, as there was a literal cut of sand in the ground facing towards the south. Nearly 150 years prior, water was fed into pipes from that very spot and fell almost 500 feet, using gravity to build pressure and feed the "giants" that blasted away the earth at the legendary Poverty Bar Mine below. Some water was also allowed to fall down the face of Little Mountain, where it was collected and used for sluicing. Over many years, this water eroded a large cut into Little Mountain, which remains to this day. We could clearly see the top of this cut from where we stood in the sandbox, and it was quite a vantage point, with

Hahns Peak Village, Steamboat Lake, and the Poverty Bar mine all visible below us. We could only imagine what it would have been like to stand in that spot when the ditch was in action, watching the water come in after an eighteen-mile journey from Trail Creek and then seeing it feed down the mountain to the powerful water cannons below.

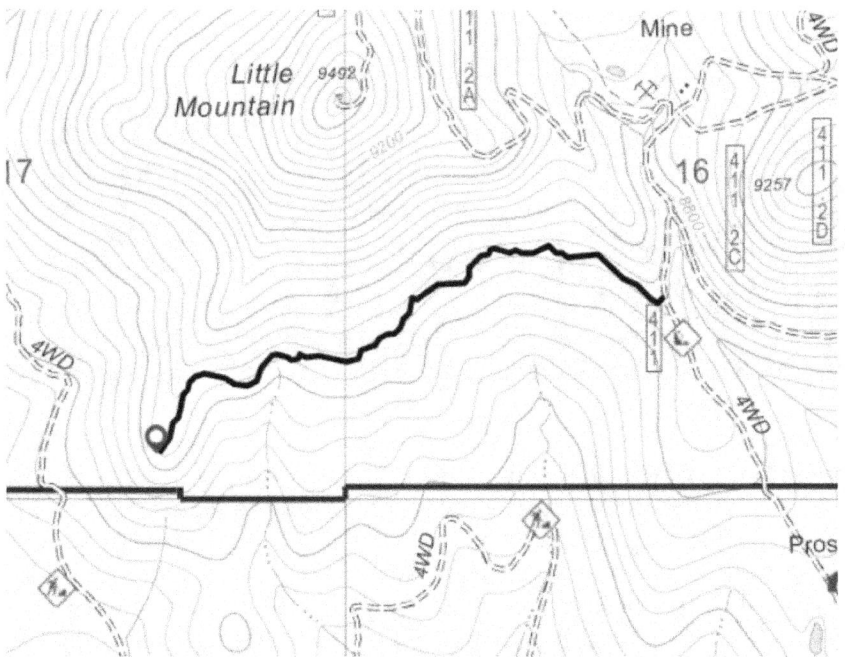

Above: Hike of the McIntosh Extension. We started on FS 411, hiked out to the sandbox on Little Mountain, and then back to FS 411.

We had an important item on the agenda that evening, so we hiked back to our machines and rode back to our rooms at the Steamboat Lake Outpost to shower and clean up. From there, we gathered back at the Zehner cabin in Hahns Peak Village for one final meal together on their deck before they moved to Arizona. It was our turn to feed them, for once, and we grilled homemade Angus burgers made from beef supplied by Farwell Farms (owned by Terry and his brother Mark. A third brother, Rex, had recently retired). The meal, including neighbor Larry's famous cornbread, was delicious, but even better were the stories the Zehners told, from taking off in a small

277

overloaded airplane while on a hunting excursion in Alaska, to attending high school class reunions. Add in Marge's sharp wit, and there was no shortage of laughter. It always felt right to be on that deck, with those people, and we will forever be grateful for the time and memories made together. How thankful I am that a phone call in 2019 to inquire about the Farwell Ditch led to moments like these!

Poverty Bar Placer
water - 27 miles from upper Elk

Above: Photo of the giants in action at Poverty Bar Mine. Note that this photo is incorrectly labeled and states the water came from 27 miles away from Upper Elk (Trail Creek). The original Farwell Ditch was 17 miles long, and Robert McIntosh extended it by 1 mile in 1880, bringing it to 18 miles. Many old newspaper articles state that the ditch was 27 miles long, but we believe this was an error that occurred many years ago and was later referenced and printed elsewhere, including in this photo. Photo credit to the Hahns Peak Area Historical Society.

Katie and I, having both turned forty that year, celebrated by taking the next day to ourselves to take on the Zirkel Circle. We had talked about doing this bucket-list hike for years, and finally had a chance to make it happen. The hike did not disappoint in the least! Stunning scenery, creek crossings, open meadows, and leg-burning climbs culminated in the hike's apex overlooking Gilpin Lake, surrounded by the jagged wilderness peaks. Katie and I had never experienced anything to this degree, and we were both in awe of the magnitude of the beauty around us. Taking the loop counterclockwise, we worked our way down to the lake, ate lunch next to the water, and then completed the second half of the hike, which was largely all downhill. Altogether, it took us about five and a half hours. I would not have minded if it had lasted longer!

Above: The view of Gilpin Lake from the apex of the Zirkel Circle Hike.

As they always do, the trip came and went, and we journeyed back home. However, Rod and I would return just a couple of weeks later for a dedicated "ditchin" trip. The goal was simple: hike the two remaining sections of the ditch.

Departure was on a Monday evening, and we road-tripped west overnight to Colorado, as had become custom. At a fuel stop in Cozad, Nebraska, we noticed one of the tires on our trailer had blown. In addition, the wheel was destroyed. Being prepared, we swapped it out for a spare wheel and tire, and completed the drive, pulling into Hahns Peak Village early Tuesday morning. Marge Eardley, who had become a close friend just like the Zehners, had graciously offered to let Rod and me stay in the recently renovated lower cabin on her property. This was very generous and helped us save on travel expenses. Thank you, Marge!

That afternoon, as we were enjoying our customary first-day ATV ride, we were cruising along on Trail 1149 (south of 500) when all of a sudden Rod's Polaris Sportsman began to sputter until it would run no more due to a dead battery. We had jumper cables and were able to jump-start it from my Can-Am Outlander, but that only got us another hundred yards down the trail before it died once again. First, we had a blown tire on the trailer. Less than twenty-four hours later, we had a dead battery on one of the ATVs. This trip was off to an ominous start!

The good news is that we had just enough time to tow Rod's Sportsman back to Marge's cabin and then head down to Steamboat Springs for a replacement battery. Once installed, the Polaris came back to life. We crashed that evening at Marge's cabin and caught up on the sleep we had missed the prior night while driving.

The next day was the first of two hikes. It was time to complete the Upper Level! Around 7:00 AM, we departed Marge's cabin on our ATVs and made the trip up and over Farwell Mountain to where the Farwell Ditch crossed FS 409. This location had become a key point along the trail during our years of research. Instead of hiking towards Tunnel Hill to the south, like we had done in previous years, we were going to hike in the opposite direction towards the Trail Creek headgate.

Soon after we began, we encountered a section through a grassy clearing lined with boulders on either side. We had seen the ditch in various forms over the years, but this was a new one. Whatever it took to get the job done!

The ditch continued to wrap around the southern flank of Dome Peak before turning towards the north. Soon after, we came upon Sand Rock Point and saw firsthand the challenge this sandstone ledge presented to the ditch builders and maintainers years ago. Right in front of the tunnel exit, a large chunk of sandstone had broken off and was partially blocking our path. This boulder had not been there before, and we could see directly above it where it had sheared off. If the sandstone could shear off on its own like that, imagine how much easier it would be when iron anchors were driven into it to support fluming for the ditch.

What we had learned about this tunnel in the William Flick vs HPERCPMC court case made total sense. For twenty years, fluming had been built here, only to fail repeatedly. The original plan to have Flick build "more permanent" fluming would have also likely been doomed to fail. The decision to build a tunnel in its place was brilliant, as evidenced by the tunnel's continued existence today, despite the nature of the surrounding sandstone.

Just beyond the tunnel, we passed an opening in the lower wall of the ditch where a wastegate had been located. The Flick court documents mentioned a wastegate near this spot, which makes sense since it would allow for water to be diverted away from the fluming (and later the tunnel), in case maintenance was needed. If the wastegate were opened, water would drain from the ditch back down to Trail Creek below, leaving the fluming or tunnel dry.

As we followed the ditch north, we passed through areas of forest and areas of open terrain. Per usual, the ditch was well defined in the sections covered by forest, and less defined in the open areas. Some spots were downright swampy, and we had to watch our steps carefully.

I don't recall if we saw it or heard it first, but we began to close in on Trail Creek and knew the headgate had to be nearby. Just as we approached the creek, however, the ditch lost its definition and the ground flattened out. It took some time, but we hiked around the area and eventually found a ditch-shaped opening that led directly into the bank of Trail Creek. This had to be it!

Except we were also confused by it. From the looks of things, this opening certainly looked like the ditch, but it looped around right back into Trail Creek. Why would it do this? At first, this did not make any sense to us, but then it dawned on Rod. The creek would have been dammed up with logs to divert water into the upper opening of the loop. Within the loop itself would have been the actual headgate of the ditch. When open, water continued into the ditch. When closed, the water was routed through the loop behind the dam and back into Trail Creek. This design was a brilliantly simple way to control the water flow into the ditch.

Feeling very satisfied at having completed the Upper Level of the Farwell Ditch, Rod and I reversed course and hiked the ditch back to our starting point on FS 409 so we could ride back to Hahns Peak Village. The scenery makes it enjoyable! Trail Creek is a picturesque mountain stream, and we also had views of the jagged peaks of the Zirkel Wilderness, as well as a clear view through Hinman Canyon. We could even see, at a distance, some of the rock outcroppings above Hinman Canyon that had been channeled through all those years ago.

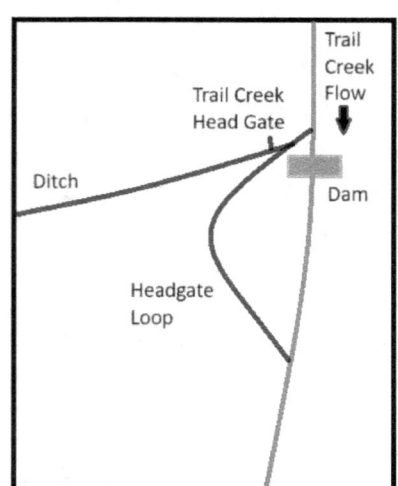

Left: Illustration of how the headgate and dam were set up. With the headgate open, water was directed into the ditch. When closed, the water looped back into Trail Creek below the dam.

One big day remained in our quest to hike and map the entire ditch. In 2022, we finished our big hike on the privately owned Warhorse Backcountry property on the western slope of Farwell Mountain. What remained was to connect the dots between this spot and the McIntosh Extension, which we had just hiked a few weeks earlier. Rod and I made plans to leave our ATVs along FS 411 atop String Ridge, where the McIntosh Extension began (and where our hike would end). From there, James Clouse was kind enough to give us a ride in his Can Am UTV to his property.

Rod and I braced ourselves for the first two miles of this hike to be very challenging, as it effectively continued from where our grueling 2022 hike had ended. Looking at satellite imagery, the forest appeared to be very dense until we crossed FS 409. To our surprise, it was not bad, and actually very enjoyable. There was enough forest to make it a hike rather than a walk, but not so thick as to be overly burdensome. There was one section that turned into combat hiking, but just enough to make for a fun challenge.

Along this section, the mountainside got fairly steep, and the amount of dirt that had to be excavated when digging the ditch became very pronounced. At some points, the upper wall of the ditch was effectively a ten-foot-tall wall of dirt dug out of the mountainside. As usual, fallen trees were lying across the ditch, but these sections made it easier to go under because the top side was so high off the ground.

Progress continued to the north, and soon the ground on the lower side of the ditch began to widen and level out to the point of appearing unnatural or man-made. Rod and I speculated that an old wagon road might have followed the ditch here. We have seen on some old maps that there used to be a road or trail off of FS 409 that led in this direction, and perhaps it ultimately ended at the location where we were standing.

The ditch turned to the northeast, and in a few hundred yards, we crossed a small tributary of Beaver Creek, at which point the ditch turned sharply to the west. It was here that we came across the remains of the old cabin that David Joe Zehner had shown to us back in 2019. We took a break for lunch before continuing west, soon crossing FS 409.

It quickly became apparent that at some point through here, the ditch had been bulldozed into a road. While that made for easy walking, losing that history is unfortunate. It went on like this for maybe half to three-quarters of a mile when we saw the ditch reappear and break off from the road. We followed it, soon passing through a small area where some rock on the upper wall of the ditch had to be blasted away.

Less than thirty seconds later, we looked up and saw the ditch track directly into the flat face of solid rock nearly ten feet tall. With our excitement building, we walked toward the rock and discovered the opening of a tunnel partially blocked by rock and sediment that had accumulated over the years. We had just located the "small third tunnel" mentioned by William Flick in the old court case! Once again, history was revealing itself right before our eyes. It took some maneuvering, but we managed to squeeze into the tunnel and make our way through. At approximately 60 feet long, it was shorter than the other tunnels along the ditch, but it still held incredible historical significance. The tunnel exit remained in perfect condition.

Rod and I discussed what this tunnel should be called. We knew the others had been referred to as the Sand Rock Point and Tunnel Hill Tunnels from the William Flick vs HPERCPMC court case. Rod recalled that Flick mentioned this third tunnel was near Beaver Creek, so we decided that Beaver Creek Tunnel was the perfect name. Beaver Creek itself consists of several small branches, and this tunnel sits right in the middle of them.

Just beyond Beaver Creek Tunnel, the terrain opened up, offering a beautiful view overlooking Beaver Basin and extending across to Beryl Mountain and Anderson Mountain, which we would be hiking around later in the day. It never gets old to see new vantage points of the North Routt area.

Following the ditch to the northwest, we came up to another small tributary of Beaver Creek. In this location, the ditch turned very clearly towards the creek, and we could see on the other bank exactly where it picked up again and made a sharp left turn towards the southwest. When functioning, there would have been fluming built here to carry water across the creek. We believe the creek itself would have been tapped into just above the fluming and also fed into the ditch.

We were not done making discoveries that day. As we kept moving southwest along the ditch, we entered a very steep clearing about 200 feet across. In areas like this, all signs of the ditch are long gone, as years of water runoff and snowmelt have eroded it away. However, we knew that if we maintained our elevation, we would find the ditch again on the other side of the clearing. But not just the ditch. There, before us, were the remains of an old metal pipe twenty-four inches in diameter. This was the first time we had discovered an actual artifact from the ditch on our own! Looking down the steep clearing, we discovered more. In all, there were five or six sections, each about twenty feet long. It was clear that, instead of digging a ditch across that steep clearing, metal piping had been used, and after all this time, most of it had succumbed to gravity and was falling down the mountainside.

We took some time to explore the area, getting pictures and videos, and then continued onward. Less than a mile later, our bonanza of discoveries continued. Arriving at another steep clearing, we paused and looked around. Our instincts proved correct as Rod yelled, "Pipe!" Another discovery! Interestingly, instead of a single 24" pipe like we had just found, this pipe was a double-barrel setup with what appeared to be 16" diameter pipes. Once again, multiple sections were found succumbing to gravity on the mountainside. We are unsure of why the pipe here differed from the previous location, but it could have simply been a case of using what was available at the time.

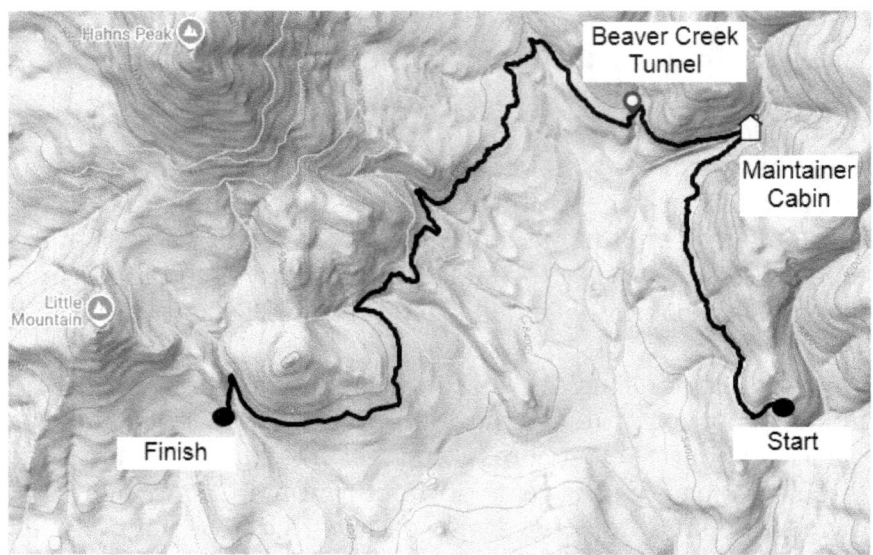

Above: Map of the hike from Warhorse Backcountry to String Ridge. In general, this section of the ditch wraps around Beaver Basin. Several key features of the ditch are located along this section.

Shortly after this spot, the ditch merges with FS 417. Unfortunately, there is not much of an actual ditch left from this spot all the way to String Ridge. At some point, the ditch was once again bulldozed to clear the way for a road. Being on a level grade, it was the path of least resistance to build a road, and unfortunately, the ditch is gone in these sections. Even so, we followed FS 417 around Anderson Mountain, and there are a few short stretches where the ditch is visible just below the edge of the road.

On the western side of Anderson Mountain, FS 417 meets FS 411, and from there, it was a short walk back to our ATVs. Not only was our day complete, but the entire Farwell Ditch, including the McIntosh Extension, had now been hiked and tracked with GPS. This was a major piece of the puzzle in our efforts to preserve the history of the ditch. While Rod and I still view our challenging 2022 hike as the "most important" day of ditchin' we've had, the hike that day in September 2023, following the ditch around Beaver Basin, was our "best" day of ditchin' due to the significant discoveries we had made. The Beaver Creek Tunnel was no longer just a reference in an old court case. It was real, and we had the proof. We had also located two types of pipe in two different sections.

It was a bittersweet ride back to Marge's cabin on the ATVs. We were thrilled to have the ditch fully mapped, but we also didn't want the discoveries to stop. Thankfully, they wouldn't.

CHAPTER 16: MOTHER LODE

"Work, Work, Work, in Christ's Yoke and ye shall find rest, blessed paradox of divine truth."[386]

-John V. Farwell

With the entirety of the Farwell Ditch now mapped, Rod and I used the lull from late 2023 into 2024 to search for additional historical records in an effort to piece together the entire story. By this point, we knew the general "what" story of the Farwell Ditch and Bugtown, but we still lacked official records that directly tied it all back to John V. Farwell. In previous years, we had visited the Colorado State Archives, the Denver Public Library, the Routt County Clerk and Recorder's Office, and the Tread of Pioneers Museum, where we gathered a wealth of information. However, very little of it was formally linked directly to Farwell.

On a hunch, we began searching online newspaper archives and immediately found hit after hit from newspapers across Wyoming and Colorado. Articles detailing the planning and construction of the wagon roads brought the story described in Chapter 4 to life. These records reinforced how vital that infrastructure was, and that several roads in use today likely began life as one of John V.'s wagon roads. We also learned of the expectation that the Hahns Peak Mining District would become a major economic hub, potentially exceeding Deadwood, South Dakota, and the surrounding Black Hills in gold production. With expectations like that, it is not surprising that John V. Farwell was willing to invest a substantial sum.

---

[386] Farwell, John V. (1907). *Early Recollections of Dwight L. Moody,* Page 148. https://nrrbook.com/RecollectionsofMoody

Other articles discussed correspondent visits to International Camp and how unique and orderly it was compared to nearly all other gold mining camps of the day. We even found a record of Routt County's first Independence Day celebration, which took place at Farwell's International Camp on July 4, 1877, featuring a large meal, blasting gunpowder, and outdoor games. Sound familiar? It was all incredibly fascinating and satisfying to see the overall picture start to come into focus.

One article in particular that jumped off the page was published in the March 28, 1878, edition of the *Laramie Daily Sentinel*, which referenced a lawsuit titled Thomas W. Brooks vs. John V. Farwell & Co. The article briefly described an agreement for Farwell to purchase land and water rights from Brooks for $100,000, but after an initial $1,500 payment, the deal went sideways. This reference had huge potential for us. In 2022, we gained significant insights into the Farwell Ditch through the William Flick vs. The Hahns Peak and Elk River Canal and Placer Mining Company case, located in the Colorado State Archives. Could this new Brooks vs. Farwell case also contain a treasure trove of information? Could it provide details on John V.'s decision to invest in a gold mining enterprise? There was only one way to find out. We had to see these court documents.

Immediately, I sent an email to the Colorado State Archives requesting all records they had regarding the Brooks vs. Farwell case. A few days later, a PDF file landed in my inbox. Giddy with excitement, I opened it up, but was quickly overwhelmed. In front of me was a 176-page document, and I knew it had to be filled to the brim with valuable information. There was a problem, though. Unlike the typed Flick court case from the late 1890s, every page of this document was handwritten. While much of it was legible, a significant portion of it was nearly impossible to decipher due to poor penmanship.

Thankfully, we had modern technology to help solve this problem. Page by page, Rod uploaded the document to ChatGPT and instructed it to read and convert the handwritten document, word-for-word, into typed text. While it was less accurate with some of the poorest handwriting, it was remarkably successful overall. After that was completed, we compared the ChatGPT output, word-for-word (as accurately as possible), with the handwritten version to manually correct any errors. Although it took many hours and wasn't perfect, we now had a document that we believed closely resembled the original verbiage.

History came alive once again. John V. was interrogated, along with Benjamin F. Jacobs, who we learned was his partner in the mining venture, Charles B. Farwell, A.J. Bell, J.W. Bell, Jerome Stillson, and James Dunn, among others. All of their testimony was very consistent and rock solid against Brooks. The story of Brooks's attempt to defraud and intimidate Farwell, Jacobs, and their team (described in Chapter 1) became clear, providing the exact kind of detail and context we hoped to find. Importantly, this document was the first record we had seen of John V. personally providing information about his gold mining venture, and the tension and drama gave the historic narrative a much more "wild west" feel.

With momentum from the Brooks vs. Farwell case, Rod and I began digging into another potential source of records: Grand County. Because Farwell's mining venture began in 1876, before Routt County was established on January 29, 1877, we suspected that the Grand County Clerk and Recorder's Office might hold some key records. From their website, we were able to search the historic Grantor and Grantee Indexes manually for various keywords, such as Farwell, Purdy, and Brooks. Once again, we had several promising hits, and we requested the detailed log entries corresponding to the items found in the Grantor and Grantee Indexes. Of the many items we received, these stood out:

- Purdy Mining Company placer claims

  These were detailed descriptions of the Purdy Mining Company's mining claim filings. Farwell's company would later acquire them.

- A record of the agreement between Brooks, Farwell, and Jacobs, dated May 11, 1876[387]

  This was very fascinating, as it was this very agreement that led to the legal dispute we had just learned about. It was always satisfying to see pieces of the historic puzzle start to fit together.

- A record naming A.J. Bell as Power of Attorney for J.V. Farwell and B.F. Jacobs dated June 10, 1876[388]

  This was directly related to the Brooks agreement above, as A.J. Bell was tasked with inspecting the claims outlined in the contract. Farwell and Jacobs clearly trusted Bell's judgment if they were comfortable naming him their Power of Attorney.

- A copy of the agreement between Purdy Mining Co., Farwell, and Jacobs, dated July 4, 1876 (our nation's centennial!)[389]

  This was notable because it recorded the transaction that ultimately led to Farwell's mining venture.

- Elk River Water Claim by Farwell, Jacobs, & A.J. Bell dated July 17, 1876[390]

---

[387] J.V. Farwell & B.F. Jacobs agreement with T.W. Brooks. (May 11, 1876). Grand County Clerk and Recorder's Office. https://nrrbook.com/FarwellBrooks

[388] A.J. Bell Power of Attorney for John V. Farwell & B.F. Jacobs. (June 10, 1876). Grand County Clerk and Recorder's Office. https://nrrbook.com/AJBellPOA

[389] Purdy Mining Co. agreement with J.V. Farwell & B.F. Jacobs. (July 4 1876). Grand County Clerk and Recorder's Office. https://nrrbook.com/FarwellPurdy

[390] Main Elk River Water Claim. (July 17, 1876). Grand County Clerk and Recorder's Office. https://nrrbook.com/FarwellDitchClaim

Jackpot! This was the very water claim that led to the construction of the seventeen-mile ditch from a fork of the Elk River (Trail Creek) to String Ridge, between 1876 and 1878. We had been looking for years for records on the ditch itself, and here was the record of its establishment!

- Ways Gulch Water Right-of-Way filed by Farwell, Jacobs & Bell on July 20, 1876[391]

  While the Elk River Water Claim was intended to provide a source of water, Farwell needed a way to release the water after it had run through his water cannons and sluice boxes. This Right-of-Way provided details on exactly the route this water would take back into the Elk River.

- Receipt filed by James Dunn for labor provided to build the ditch dated August 11, 1876[392]

  This receipt documented the labor of James Dunn, who assisted in building the dam and the beginnings of the Farwell Ditch from August 8 to 11, 1876.

All of these records helped us fill in the gaps. We now had details on Farwell's acquisition agreements, water claims from the moment water was diverted out of the Elk River all the way to and through the mining district and returned to the same river, and even a labor receipt from the very ditch that we had been researching for years.

When we initially began trying to learn about the Farwell Ditch in 2019, most resources we could find had nothing more than a few sentences to say about John V.'s involvement. It was common to read something along these lines: "In 1876, John V.

---

[391] Ways Gulch Water Right-of-Way. (July 20, 1876). Grand County Clerk and Recorder's Office. https://nrrbook.com/WaysGulchWaterRight

[392] James Dunn Labor Receipt. (August 11, 1876). Grand County Clerk and Recorder's Office. https://nrrbook.com/DunnReceipt

Farwell, a wealthy businessman from Chicago, financed the construction of a seventeen-mile ditch from the Elk River to String Ridge to provide water for hydraulic mining purposes. Mining results were poor, and he cut his losses and sold his operation to James France of Rawlins, Wyoming, in 1879." The multitude of records we had found, combined with the time we had spent hiking and mapping the ditch, really began to help us see the big picture and piece the history together. The story that had previously been summarized in two or three sentences now had deep, fascinating details that intertwined with other critical events of America's history. Our sense of responsibility to document everything we had learned only grew larger. This history needed to be shared with others and preserved for future generations.

As we continued researching, a thought occurred to us. Was it possible that there were direct descendants of John V. Farwell alive today who knew of his mining history? Perhaps someone still had old family records with helpful information? Back to the internet I went, going through genealogical records and Google searches until I was pretty sure I had the name and email address of a great-great-granddaughter of John V. At this point in our project, I had learned that making the extra phone call or sending the extra email was always worth it, as it could help make a connection or gain access to valuable information. After all, the worst thing that could happen is to be ignored or told "no." More commonly, proactively reaching out had been incredibly beneficial. Hoping for the best, I sent an email to a stranger named Edie, although this time it was a little different, as I believed Edie was my distant cousin.

A few days later, I received a response, not from Edie, but from her cousin, James (Jim) Phelps. Jim, who served on the Board of the History Center of Lake Forest, Illinois, where Farwell lived for most of his adult life, confirmed that he and Edie were direct descendants of John V. He and his close cousins had an extensive knowledge of their prominent ancestor; however, none of them were aware of the mining history in Colorado. It was exciting to share what we had been learning and

294

researching with them, and Rod and I began discussing the need to visit Lake Forest someday.

In the meantime, we knew that an application to nominate the Farwell Ditch for the National Register of Historic Places was on the horizon, and it became apparent that a tour of the Farwell Ditch for those involved in the process could be beneficial. Informally, Rod and I began discussing what that would look like and how we could organize a group to visit various points along the ditch. The sense of urgency for the tour increased significantly when Arianthé Stettner of Historic Routt County shared some great news. She was able to arrange for two individuals from History Colorado to attend a tour. The first, Damion Pechota, served as a National and State Historian. The other individual, Jacob McDonald, served as a Historic Resource Specialist. Damion and Jacob were both highly qualified and willing to visit the Farwell Ditch to learn more about what we had been researching. Opportunities like this do not come around very often, so the idea of a tour changed from "if" to "when."

Rod and I scrambled to put plans together, sent out invitations, and arranged for ATVs and UTVs for transportation. In the process, what was intended to be a one-day event in late August of 2024 turned into two, with each day involving a separate group of attendees. In addition to Damion and Jacob, we hosted representatives from the Hahns Peak Area Historical Society and Historic Routt County, as well as a handful of personal acquaintances, including David Joe Zehner, Jim Phelps, and his son, Jacob. The tours were a great success, as we were able to visit the Sand Rock Point Tunnel, Beaver Creek Tunnel, and other spots along the way where the ditch crossed the Forest Service roads we traveled. Damion and Jacob provided us with great insight and valuable tips regarding the historic preservation process and offered to help in any way they could. Rod and I were thrilled to hear this, and momentum for the National Register continued to build.

While the primary purpose of the tours was to promote the preservation of this history, it was also rewarding to take Jim and Jacob to the summit of the mountain and the small lake named after their ancestor. While taking a short break above Farwell Lake, I casually mentioned to Jim that John V.'s 200th birthday was approaching in 2025, and his mind immediately went into planning mode.

Following the tours, one last "ditchin" trip was planned before winter. We targeted mid-October, hoping to arrive in the prime of the fall foliage season. However, I contracted COVID a few days before departure, and we had to push it back a couple of weeks. This turned out to be a blessing in disguise. Even though we missed most of the fall colors, we were blessed with temperatures in the 40s and low 50s, which may seem chilly, but it is perfect for long days of hiking and exploring. We also had the new experience of riding our ATVs on trails with three to five inches of snow at higher elevations. The snow was deep enough to make it a bit challenging at times, but it made for fun riding conditions, and we thoroughly enjoyed our time. As a kid growing up in Kansas, I always thought the mountains were most enjoyable during the winter for snow skiing. After Katie, the kids, and I took our first family vacation to Routt County in 2014, I changed my mind and came to believe that the mountains are most enjoyable in the summer. But after the ditchin' trips of 2022, 2023, and 2024, I concluded that fall in the Hahns Peak area is borderline perfection, and now I look forward to it every year.

In November 2024, Rod completed a "Preliminary Property Evaluation Form" for the Farwell Ditch. This document was submitted to Damion Pechota's team at History Colorado, who used it to evaluate whether they believed the Farwell Ditch would be worthy of nomination to the National Register of Historic Places. We received a letter back in early December with an emphatic "Yes!" As a result, discussions began on formally nominating the Farwell Ditch to the National Register. Historic Routt County signed an agreement with the Routt National Forest to contract a writer to draft the nomination. Following some back-and-forth discussion, it was agreed upon that Rod and I would take this on. By this point, we felt capable of doing the job, despite having no prior experience writing these applications. Our lack of experience was offset by a sense of personal responsibility and our ever-growing knowledge base, which included files of historic records regarding the Farwell Ditch, the mining company and camp, as well as John V. Farwell's history of entering and exiting the gold mining business in Routt County.

Consulting with Damion Pechota of History Colorado was immensely helpful. He was always kind, professional, and willing to go the extra mile in helping us when needed. After two weeks of working many late hours on the nomination template, we shared our work with Historic Routt County and Routt National Forest officials. A few items were cleaned up, and then the nomination was sent to Damion for a courtesy review. Going above and beyond, he took our work and transferred it onto the official National Register of Historic Places Registration form. From there, it returned to the Routt National Forest for signatures. The document was then forwarded to the US Forest Service Federal Preservation Officer, who approved it and submitted it to the Keeper of the National Register for a final review in July 2025.

In the meantime, Jim Phelps was hard at work planning "Farwell Fest," and his vision for the grand celebration of John V. Farwell's 200th birthday was coming together. As part of the festivities, he invited Rod and me to attend and do a short presentation about the Farwell Ditch to a group of John V.'s descendants. Without hesitation, we said yes. The big event was held in May 2025 in Lake Forest, Illinois, which John V. helped establish alongside his brother, Charles. In addition to our presentation about the mining history, we learned about the present-day XIT Ranch, which had been resurrected on a section of original XIT Ranch land by Farwell's great-great-great-grandson, Drew Knowles. We were also treated to a very detailed look at the Farwell family's genealogy, which included many generations of British Royalty going back nearly one thousand years.

A highlight of the celebration was a visit to the very home John V. Farwell built in 1869 and lived in until his death in 1908. This was no ordinary home, as it is credited as being the first house in the United States constructed from poured concrete. All exterior and interior walls are solid concrete, approximately twelve inches thick. George Edbrooke was the architect, and Farwell hired Leonard Double from England to supervise construction. It was a bit surreal to walk through the front door, just as John V. himself had done thousands of times many years ago.

We were able to tour two more homes. One of them began life as a barn on the eastern edge of John V.'s property. In 1917, it was converted into a home by famed architect David Adler. Recent renovations, combined with meticulous landscaping, have made it a stunning property today. The last home we toured was once Charles B. Farwell's carriage house, located at the back of his Fairlawn estate. After a fire destroyed the main home, the carriage house was converted into a home in 1920, while the main home was reconstructed. This home has undergone a beautiful renovation in recent years.

After the home tours, we visited the Lake Forest cemetery, where John V.'s grave is marked with an obelisk towering over thirty feet tall. Many of his family members and descendants are buried nearby. The 200th birthday celebration was a huge success, and we were honored to be a small part of it.

On August 29, 2025, the National Register of Historic Places posted its weekly list of actions taken on pending nominations during the prior week. Of the twelve items on the list,[393] the third one contained the following info:

> COLORADO, ROUTT COUNTY,
> Farwell Ditch,
> Routt National Forest,
> Hahn's Peak, SG100012148,
> LISTED, 8/22/2025

---

[393] Weekly List. (August 29, 2025). National Register of Historic Places. https://nrrbook.com/NRList-2025-08-29

Upon seeing this, I sat back in my chair, struggling to comprehend the reality of those five simple lines of text. Six years earlier, I had called the Hahns Peak Area Historical Society, hoping to learn basic information about the Farwell Ditch. How could I have known this phone call with Marge Eardley would effectively snowball into a years-long treasure hunt, ending with a listing on the National Register of Historic Places? How could I have known that some of the people we would meet along the way would become treasured friends? How could I have known we would meet distant cousins and share this remarkable story about their ancestor with them? How could I have known that I would spend over 1,000 hours writing a book about it all? The simple answer is that I couldn't. But life had a funny way of putting us in the right place at the right time. Was it fate? Destiny? Divine intervention? No amount of research or digging through records will ever provide that answer, and that's okay. I don't need to know. I'll just be thankful and content that it happened at all, because it has been the adventure of a lifetime. Perhaps the biggest lesson to be learned in all of this is that when opportunity presents itself, seize it, plan your work, work your plan, and enjoy the ride along the way.

After years of hiking through the forest, recording GPS tracks, taking photos and videos, searching for, sifting through, and piecing together countless historic records, and writing an application for the National Register of Historic Places, we had our treasure. Surveyed by the Purdy Mining Company exactly 150 years earlier, and 149 years after John V. Farwell's men first put shovels and pickaxes to work, the Farwell Ditch, which was nearly lost to history, would now be preserved for generations to come.

AFTERWORD

Looking back, I cannot help but feel grateful, yet humbled by the chance encounter my family had with Farwell Mountain in 2014. I never could have fathomed that it would lead down this path of historic research and preservation, and I certainly never envisioned myself writing a book to document it all. However, once we began to learn the breadth and depth of the fascinating, yet nearly lost, true story, it became apparent that a written record was necessary.

Yet at the same time, John V. Farwell did not consider his gold mining ventures to be a significant part of his life. In all of his writings, he never mentioned it. Instead, he chose to tell the stories of his childhood, his dry goods business endeavors, the XIT Ranch, and, perhaps most notably, his partnership with Dwight Moody to spread the Good News. The only potential reference I have found from his writings regarding his Colorado mining enterprise comes from a letter he wrote to Moody on June 22, 1877, when construction of the Farwell Ditch would have been in full swing. *"...I am going West and expect to be there on my return. I cannot go to the dedication of the Bliss monument on the 9th, as requested by Whittle. I would be glad to do so, but it is a long hot journey and there will not be any real need of my being there."*[394] Where he was going in "the West" is unknown, but it is reasonable to assume he was referring to his year-old gold mining enterprise.

Many unique pieces fell precisely into place, allowing this research project to develop into a lifelong passion. Among them:

- Who gets to discover a mountain that shares their last name, and then learn it is tied to distant family history? And also find that there is an ATV-friendly trail that

---

[394] Farwell, John V. (1907). *Early Recollections of Dwight L. Moody*, Page 180. https://nrrbook.com/RecollectionsofMoody

goes directly up to the summit? It is pretty easy to become hooked on a project like this when you feel a personal connection to it.

- Our first encounter with Farwell Mountain, and our subsequent interest in learning about its mining history occurred within a relatively short window of time, when David Joe Zehner had also discovered the Farwell Ditch and was actively trying to preserve it. We would have been lost without his input and guidance, especially in the early stages of our research. Additionally, David Joe and his wife, Judy, have become dear friends.

- Nearly all of the ditch falls on public forest service land today, which allowed us to explore it freely. The one parcel of private property that the ditch crosses is owned by an individual who was very supportive of our research efforts and generously allowed us to hike on his land, provided us with rides to facilitate long hikes, and more.

- The history was nearly lost, but we had just barely enough nuggets of information to get us started down one rabbit hole after another. Timely discoveries helped us connect the historic dots one at a time, and eventually, the entire picture came into focus. What a fascinating story it was! We felt privileged to be able to gather and share this information with others. On the other hand, had a detailed and accessible account of this story been available, we would have never pursued this research endeavor ourselves.

- Much of the history we learned came from two old lawsuits, as testimony provided under oath. Unless those being questioned were committing perjury, we can assume this information was "the truth, the whole truth, and nothing but the truth." Thus, these court documents are invaluable sources of factual information. I assume many historians do not have the luxury of finding rock-solid sources of information like this.

- What we were able to do with modern technology would have been impossible not that many years ago. These tools, among others, were all critical in our research:

    - GPS - Our hikes along the ditch could be recorded and uploaded to various mapping services, such as:

    - CalTopo - Enabled us to plot our GPS tracks, combine them with other points of interest, and view them all on numerous base maps (satellite imagery, historic maps, terrain maps, etc.).

    - ChatGPT - Made it possible to decipher illegible handwritten court documents and glean incredible information directly from John V. Farwell and his affiliates.

    - LIDAR Imagery - Allowed us to see the ditch in a detailed 3D Image of the Earth's surface. After we had hiked the entire length of the ditch and plotted it into CalTopo, LIDAR confirmed that our tracks were accurate. At the same time, we were glad not to have discovered LIDAR until after we had hiked the entire ditch, because that would have taken away the thrill of discovery.

- We were able to combine our hobby of riding ATVs with a newfound passion for exploring the forest. Before this, we rode ATVs recreationally. Now, we were using them as tools, too.

- The scenery and terrain where all of this happened is absolutely stunning, featuring mountains, rivers, creeks, lakes, a national forest, and diverse wildlife. We have experienced hot, cold, wet, dry, rain, snow, and hail, and loved every minute of it.

- The nearly lost history was not only significant enough to land on the National Register of Historic Places, but also entirely unknown to John V. Farwell's direct descendants. We were blessed to be able to add a rich new story to the known facts about the incredibly successful and influential person their ancestor was.

In summary, all of these factors combined to provide purpose, intrigue, and satisfaction, in addition to what began as recreation. It became not only a hobby but also a passion, for which we will forever be grateful. Perhaps James G.K. McClure, President of the McCormick Theological Seminary, said it best while eulogizing his close friend John V. Farwell:

"Perhaps I dwell upon these things too emphatically. I dwell on them because they are my joy, my stimulus. Nothing so appeals to me as the history of men who have conquered difficulties, who have wrought righteousness, who have left worthy examples. Such men enrich life - not alone for their children, but also for us all. And when we tell the story of their growth and power, we stir hope, and we stir purpose for good, in every manly heart that hears us."[395]

May this book stir hope, and purpose for good, in every heart that reads it.

---

[395] Farwell, John V. (1911). *Some Recollections of John V. Farwell*, Page 218. https://nrrbook.com/RecollectionsofJVF

www.ingramcontent.com/pod-product-compliance
Lightning Source LLC
Chambersburg PA
CBHW070908130626
46555CB00001B/43

9 7 9 8 9 9 9 9 0 5 1 0 9